Mitchell
Beazley
Pocket
Guides

WINES OF
NEW ZEALAND

Michael Cooper

First published in Great Britain in 1997 by Mitchell Beazley,
an imprint of Reed Consumer Books Ltd,
Michelin House, 25 Victoria Street, London SW1H OEX;
39 Rawene Road, Birkenhead, Auckland;
and Melbourne.

A CIP catalogue record for this book is available from the British
Library.

ISBN 1 84000 0020 1

Editor: Alison Southby
Maps: Sandra Parkkali
Author photograph: Robin Morrison

Typeset in Veljovic
Printed and bound in Singapore

Contents

List of Maps

Preface

The transformation has been startling. Twenty years ago, New Zealand was a backwater of the wine world, producing strong, sweet 'sherries' and 'ports' and undistinguished table wines. Today, New Zealand ranks among the most exciting of the New World's wine countries.

In terms of the most fundamental factors – climate and soil – New Zealand has always had outstanding winemaking potential. New Zealand's key asset is its 'cool climate' in which grapes are able to ripen slowly, retaining their fresh, appetising acidity while building up intense aromas and flavours. In terms of heat during the grape's ripening season, there are distinct parallels between New Zealand's major wine regions and classic French districts like Bordeaux, Burgundy and Alsace.

Absent in the past, however, was the spur to excellence that all producers of premium wine need – a receptive, enthusiastic market. The modern era of New Zealand wine began in the 1960s, when rising affluence and a boom in overseas travel introduced more and more Kiwis – by tradition beer drinkers – to the pleasures of table wine consumption.

In New Zealand's fortress economy of the 1960s and 1970s, the industry grew swiftly, concentrating on the production of fortified wines and light, fruity, slightly sweet white wines from the heavy-cropping Müller-Thurgau variety. A crucial turning point was reached in the 1980s, when the economy was rapidly opened up. The New Zealand government largely dismantled the local industry's protection against overseas wines; import licensing (quantitative restrictions) was abandoned and tariffs were reduced or eliminated. Overseas wines, especially from Australia, flooded into the country.

The response from New Zealand's beleaguered winemakers was swiftly to upgrade their quality standards and launch a sustained export drive that in the year to June 1997 earned \$NZ75.9 million. Marlborough's explosively flavoured and zesty Sauvignon Blancs enjoy a worldwide reputation, and New Zealand's Chardonnays and bottle-fermented sparkling wines are also making an international impact. With just 0.1 percent of the world's vineyards but over 250 producers, New Zealand is now a significant force in the United Kingdom, commanding a small but valuable five percent share of the British premium (over five pounds per bottle) wine market.

Wine lovers around the world, confronted in shops and restaurants with a burgeoning array of New Zealand labels, are the readers for whom this pocket guide has been written. The first part of the book sets the scene with a collection of background essays which briefly outline the history of New Zealand wine; the influence of climate and soils; the principal grape varieties; winemaking techniques; and the regulations governing winemaking and labelling practices. My thanks to Philip Gregan, chief executive officer of the Wine Institute, for helping with the section on laws and labels; and to Neill Culley, chief winemaker for Babich Wines, for assistance with the section on making wine.

The major part of the book profiles all of the important wineries on a region-by-region basis, summarising the key facts about each company (production figures relate to the bountiful 1996 vintage) and highlighting their most notable winemaking achievements. The star ratings for quality are based on my tastings of each wine over several vintages, and often a particular vintage several times. Where brackets surround the stars, for example (***), this indicates that the rating is tentative, because I have tasted very few vintages of the wine.

The quality ratings are:

*****	**Outstanding quality**
****½	**Excellent quality, verging on outstanding**
****	**Excellent quality**
***½	**Very good quality**
***	**Good, above average quality**
**½	**Average**
**	**Plain**
*	**Poor**

Quality – not quantity – explains New Zealand's meteoric rise in the world of wine. This book tells the story of a fascinating and fast-changing new wine country in the South Pacific, and guides you to the top producers and labels.

Michael Cooper

A Brief History of New Zealand Wine

For over 150 years, vineyards have been cultivated and wine has flowed in New Zealand. *Vitis vinifera*, the great northern hemisphere species of vine for winemaking, was first carried south in the ships of the early colonists. Yet over a century passed before the New Zealand wine industry got off the ground, and only in the past decade has New Zealand emerged as an exciting new player on the international wine stage.

When Charles Darwin called at the Bay of Islands in northern New Zealand in 1835 during the global voyage of the *Beagle*, he saw well-established grapevines. Samuel Marsden, the Anglican missionary and chief chaplain to the Government of New South Wales, had decided to make a settlement at Kerikeri. In his journal for 25 September 1819 he wrote: 'We had a small spot of land cleared and broken up in which I planted about a hundred grapevines of different kinds brought from Port Jackson [Sydney]. New Zealand promises to be very favourable to the vine as far as I can judge at present of the nature of the soil and climate.'

The honour of being the first to produce wine in New Zealand belongs to James Busby, a Scot who is widely regarded as the father of Australian viticulture. Appointed in 1832 to the position of first British resident in New Zealand, in 1836 Busby planted a small vineyard at Waitangi, in the Bay of Islands.

The vines flourished, and the wine Busby made and sold to imperial troops also found favour in 1840 with the French explorer Dumont d'Urville. Touring Busby's estate, d'Urville saw 'a trellis on which several flourishing vines were growing . . . with great pleasure I agreed to taste the product of the vineyard that I had just seen. I was given a light white wine, very sparkling, and delicious to taste, which I enjoyed very much.'

French Marist missionaries soon spread grapevines more widely around the country. The first Catholic bishop of the South Pacific, Bishop Pompallier of Lyons, had arrived in 1838 with French vine cuttings on board. To supply the missionaries' need for table grapes and for sacramental and table wines, vines were planted wherever mission outposts were established. In 1851 Catholic priests established the first vineyard in Hawke's Bay and the oldest winemaking enterprise in New Zealand, the Mission Vineyards, is descended from these early ventures.

An Englishman was the first to prove the commercial possibilities for winegrowing in the colony. Charles Levet, a Cambridge coppersmith, and his son planted a 7-acre (2.8-hectare) vineyard on an arm of the Kaipara Harbour near Auckland and from 1863 to 1907 earned a living from making and selling wine.

The most successful non-British winemaker was a Spaniard, Joseph Soler, who made his first wine at Wanganui, on the west coast of the North Island, in 1869 and until his death in 1906 sold wine all over New Zealand. From grapes grown on his 2^1/$_2$ acre (1 hectare) property and other grapes purchased by the canoe-load from Wanganui River Maori, each year Soler produced around 20,000 bottles of wine.

Generally, however, there was little wine being made in New Zealand in the latter part of the century. Partly to blame was the onslaught of oidium, a powdery mildew which covered the grapes with a felt-like mould, splitting them open to the ravages of fungi and insects. Also inhibiting the development of a local industry was the pattern of wine consumption by the educated elite, who ignored antipodean wines and drank Portuguese ports and Spanish sherries. The working class preferred beer and spirits.

The fledgling wine industry was soon further undermined. The rigours of pioneering life made for hard drinking, often in squalid grog shops. The 1860s witnessed the foundation of a large number of temperance societies, which increasingly called for the total prohibition of liquor. The Licensing Act of 1881, which severely restricted the conditions under which new liquor licences could be granted, was the prohibition movement's first major success, and from 1881 to 1918 there were more and more restrictions.

At the end of the century, the future of the wine industry hung in the balance. On the one hand, pressure mounted for the prohibition of alcohol; on the other, there were many attempts to find new industries that could boost the country's economy.

New vineyards appeared as several Hawke's Bay landowning families explored the economics of winemaking. Their interest was aroused by Wairarapa winemaker William Beetham, who planted his first vines in 1883 and by 1897 was producing about 1,850 gallons (8,410 litres) of wine from Pinot Noir, Meunier and Hermitage (Syrah) grapes.

During the 1890s New Zealand wines enjoyed a decade of unprecedented popularity, when they accounted for almost a quarter of all commercial wines sold in the country. At the Te Mata Station, Bernard Chambers planted his first vines in 1892. By 1909 Te Mata was the largest vineyard in the country, making 12,000 gallons (54,552 litres) of 'claret', 'hock' and 'Madeira' from 14 hectares of Meunier, Syrah, Cabernet Sauvignon, Riesling and Verdelho vines.

Further impetus was given to the spread of winemaking when Romeo Bragato, a graduate of the Royal School of Viticulture and Oenology in Italy, came to New Zealand in 1895 on loan from the Victorian government to investigate the possibilities for viticulture and winemaking in the colony. Bragato travelled widely through the country and furnished the New Zealand government with a highly favourable report. Bragato's enthusiasm tipped the balance in favour of the industry's expansion, and a surge in vineyard plantings followed.

Bragato's other major contribution in 1895 was the identification of phylloxera, a parasitic disease of the vine that had rampaged like a prohibitionist zealot through French vineyards in the 1870s. In New Zealand it had wiped out many vineyards.

Perhaps the most important of all nineteenth-century developments in the wine industry was one of the very last. In the 1890s, Croatians digging for kauri gum in the Far North began to make wine. (The descendants of these winemaking pioneers, who came mostly from the Dalmatian coast of Croatia, were until recently known as Dalmatians, but since the collapse of Yugoslavia, most prefer to be called Croatians.)

'It is a curious fact,' observed *The Auckland Weekly News* in 1906, 'that although men of British blood were the first to prove that the vine would flourish in New Zealand, and even now have the largest and most up-to-date vineyards, the expansion of vine-growing is due at the present time largely to the efforts of foreigners.'

In 1902 Romeo Bragato was appointed government viticulturist and took personal charge of New Zealand's war on phylloxera. By 1905, the viticultural research station at Te Kauwhata, south of Auckland, possessed an 8 hectare vineyard and a small new winery. Vines from all over Europe were imported and tested for their suitability for grafting on phylloxera-resistant American rootstocks. Bragato also embarked on a programme of experimental winemaking.

Under Bragato's tutelage and with the aid of the government research station, the wine industry looked set to prosper. In 1902, the same year that the Lebanese Assid Abraham Corban purchased a 10-acre (4-hectare) block of gumland at Henderson in West Auckland, down the road, Stipan Jelich at Pleasant Valley made the first wine at what has now become the oldest surviving Croatian vineyard in New Zealand.

The influence of the prohibition movement, however, peaked in the second decade of the century – with disastrous results for the winegrowers. Prohibitionists achieved their first victories in wine districts in 1908 when Masterton (in the Wairarapa) and Eden (an Auckland electorate including part of Henderson) voted 'no-licence'. Denied the right to sell, although not to make, wine within a no-licence area, many winemakers were forced out of business.

A change also emerged in the government's attitude towards the wine industry. The vineyard area at Te Kauwhata was restricted and in 1908 Bragato lost control of the station. Disillusioned, he resigned his post in 1909 and left the country.

Then in 1919 New Zealand voted in favour of national prohibition. Only the crucial votes of returning servicemen, primarily anti-prohibition, tipped the balance and rescued the winegrowers from economic oblivion.

The 1920s and 1930s witnessed a slow but definite expansion in the wine industry. The prohibition tide had been stemmed; there then came a long period of stalemate between 1918 and 1939 during which there was no significant legislation on liquor.

With winemaking once more a feasible proposition, new vineyards were planted and wine production increased. This was the period of the main settlement of Croatians in West Auckland, bringing to the area, according to the *New Zealand Herald* in 1935, 'something of the charm of a home industry with simple apparatus and unpretentious sheds'. There were 40 licensed winemakers in 1925 (barely more than half the 70 winemakers in 1913); by 1932 there were a hundred.

Hawke's Bay lacked cheap land and close markets of the size that made Auckland attractive to European immigrants. The trend there was to fewer and larger vineyards, and specialisation in winemaking was more advanced. Friedrich Wohnsiedler, born on a tributary of the Rhine, established Gisborne's first commercial vineyard in 1921; Tom McDonald, the legendary Hawke's Bay winemaker, bought his first land in 1927; and in 1933 Robert Bird founded Glenvale Vineyards (now Esk Valley Estate) in Hawke's Bay.

Another major problem for the wine industry lay in its own vineyards. Most *vinifera* vines were in a very low state of health. Blight and viruses had left the vines so weakened that it was widely believed *vinifera* varieties could not successfully be grown in New Zealand.

Bragato's earlier decision to import native American rootstocks also backfired when many growers chose not to graft onto *vinifera* vines and simply planted the American varieties, which although hardy were very inferior for winemaking.

Another contribution to the declining standards of the national vineyard came in 1928, when Franco-American hybrid vines were imported and distributed from Te Kauwhata. Gone was the attention devoted in Bragato's time to the low-yielding *vinifera* varieties. The Department of Agriculture now encouraged the production of cheap ordinary wine from the heavy-cropping Seibel and Baco hybrid vines, a switch which left winemakers stranded when the call went out for higher-quality table wine in the 1960s.

The Labour Party's ascension to power in 1935 and long tenure in office proved of great benefit to the winegrowers. After increasing the funds for wine research, at the request of the winemakers the government raised the duty on Australian and South African wines, enabling New Zealand wines to compete on a price basis with imported wines. From 1938 the quantities of wines and spirits that could be brought in were slashed.

Sales of local wine soared during the Second World War. An influx of American servicemen in 1942 on leave and in search of liquor – any liquor – further excited the demand. With wine selling easily and at top prices, the financial position of winegrowers rapidly improved. Brick wineries supplanted tin sheds, concrete vats replaced wooden, and many part-time winemaking operations emerged as profitable small businesses.

Unfortunately, quality took a back seat in the wartime rush for easy profits. With demand for wine exceeding the supply, growers made up the difference less from grapes than from sugar and water. Huge amounts of 'plonk' were made and sold in the name of wine during the war. In 1946 the Royal Commission on Licensing was scathing in its criticism: 'The Department of Agriculture states that more than 60 percent of the wine made by the smaller winemakers is infected with bacterial disorders . . . [and] a considerable quantity . . . would be classified as unfit for human consumption in other wine-producing countries.'

A first step towards making New Zealand wine more freely available to the public was taken in 1948, when the wine reseller's licence was created. This licence opened up a whole new avenue of sale, by allowing growers and others to establish retail outlets for New Zealand wine throughout the country. However, the wartime wine boom collapsed in the late 1940s after the easing of import restrictions when a wave of Australian wines entered the local market. The market for New Zealand wines tightened and by 1949 prices had fallen markedly below wartime levels.

A new impulse was felt when George Mazuran was elected president of the Viticultural Association in 1950. One of three industry bodies in that period (until unity was achieved by the formation of the Wine Institute in 1975), the Viticultural Association represented mainly small, family-owned, Croatian vineyards. Convinced early that the future prosperity of the wine industry hinged on relaxation of the country's restrictive licensing laws, Mazuran subsequently carved out a long career for himself as one of the most successful political lobbyists that New Zealand has known.

A crucial breakthrough came in 1955 when Parliament reduced the minimum quantities of wine that could be sold by winemakers and wine resellers, from 2 gallons (9 litres) to a quart (1.14 litres) for table wines and a half-gallon for fortified wines.

Another important contribution to the resurgence of interest in the wine industry was made by the Winemaking Industry Committee, set up by the National Government in 1956 to investigate all aspects of New Zealand wine. The committee recommended that wine-reseller licences should be more freely granted; the outcome was that by 1965 the number of New Zealand wine shops had doubled.

The incoming second Labour Government rendered further assistance to the winegrowers. Imports of wine and spirits dropped in 1958 and 1959 to half their former volume. Another shot in the arm came with the high taxes slapped on beer and spirits in the 'Black Budget' of 1958. The effects of Labour's moves are well described in the 1959 Annual Report of the Department of Agriculture. The tax and licensing adjustments had 'created an immediate and unprecedented demand for New Zealand wines. The market position for New Zealand wines changed from one of difficult and competitive trading to a buoyant market capable of absorbing all the wine that producers could supply.' As *The Weekly News* declared in 1958: 'Today, New Zealanders who wend their way homeward after 6 p.m. with brown parcels under arm will often have a bottle of wine as well as the traditional nut-brown brew.'

The wine industry now entered a sustained period of rapid growth. An outstanding feature of the 1960s was the heavy investment by overseas companies. McWilliam's of Australia led the way, establishing vineyards and a winery in Hawke's Bay between 1947 and 1950. In 1961 McWilliam's joined forces with McDonald's at Taradale to form what then became the largest winemaking group in the country.

Like McWilliam's, Penfolds of Australia decided that the establishment of vineyards in New Zealand would best serve their interests in the local market. In a new company, Penfolds Wines (NZ) Ltd, founded in 1963, the parent company in Australia owned 62 percent of the capital and local brewers and merchants held the rest.

The greatest impact by foreign capital on New Zealand wine was made by Montana. Montana was established as a one-fifth hectare vineyard high in the Waitakere Ranges west of Auckland. A subsequent crash expansion programme culminated in 1973 when Seagram of New York acquired a 40 percent share in Montana. American finance and expertise subsequently enabled the company to emerge as the dominant force in the New Zealand wine industry.

The wine industry also derived great benefit from a proliferation of new forms of liquor licences. From the 1960s the trend towards liberalisation of the licensing laws, evident since 1948, grew much more decisive. Restaurants were licensed in 1960, and the creation of a permit system in 1976 gave belated legislative recognition to the BYO (bring your own) wine phenomenon by allowing the consumption of wine in unlicensed restaurants.

In the early 1960s, New Zealanders each drank an average of two bottles of wine annually – today the average is over 21 bottles. The migration of continental Europeans introduced thousands of Italian, Croatian and Greek wine drinkers into the New Zealand community. Thousands of New Zealanders stationed in European wine districts during the Second World War had had their first fumbling encounters with wine, and countless New Zealanders passing through Europe during the post-war boom in overseas travel were exposed to the traditional European enthusiasm for wine. The mushrooming restaurant trade promoted wine as an essential aspect of 'the good life'.

Wine, finally, became fashionable.

Vineyard acreages tripled between 1965 and 1970 as contract grape-growing swept the Gisborne plains. Traditionally, New Zealand winemakers had grown all their own grape requirements, but this pattern altered in the mid-to-late 1960s when several companies, seeking to avoid the heavy capital expenditure needed to establish new vineyards, persuaded farmers to plant their surplus acres in grapevines. Today independent grape growers produce two-thirds of the country's grape harvest.

The 1970s brought an overall improvement in wine quality and heavy emphasis on the production of table wines. Wine production rose between 1960 and 1983 from 4.1 million litres to 57.7 million litres, giving New Zealand one of the world's fastest expanding wine industries. The growth area was table wines, which captured 12 percent of the market in 1962. By 1983 that figure stood at 73 percent and slightly sweet, fruity white table wines dominated the market.

The predominance of these wines reflected the sweeping changes in the composition of New Zealand vineyards. In 1965, the most common grape was the white hybrid Baco 22A and less than one-third of the vines were classical *vinifera* varieties. By 1983 the German Müller-Thurgau vine was four times as extensively planted in New Zealand as any other variety.

Since then, Müller-Thurgau's importance has nosedived. At the same time as many Kiwi wine lovers began to acquire a taste for fully dry wines, the winemakers themselves realised that most New Zealand wine areas have climates more akin to French than to German wine regions. Between 1983 and 1996, New Zealand's Müller-Thurgau plantings contracted from 1,873 hectares to 711 hectares. Dominating plantings in 1996 were the classic French white-wine varieties, Chardonnay and Sauvignon Blanc, which together were approaching a 50 percent coverage of the national vineyard.

A further boost to wine quality came in the early 1980s, after it became widely known that the illegal practice of wine-watering was common in New Zealand. Many wineries had taken advantage of the continuing shortage of wine to 'stretch' their products. Confronted by a heavy barrage of adverse publicity – and an impending grape glut – the winegrowers finally agreed in 1982 to support moves to prevent watering. Since 1983, table wines have been permitted to contain up to 50 millilitres of water per litre of wine, where the water has been used as a processing aid for legal additives.

After the sustained prosperity of the 1960s and 1970s, heavy overplanting of vineyards in the early 1980s created a wine glut of record proportions. Simultaneously, demand for wine was slashed by the Labour Government's November 1984 Budget, which almost doubled the sales tax on table wines from 54 cents to 99 cents per bottle. The decision by the giant

Cooks/McWilliams group to unload its surplus stocks then set alight a ferocious price war in 1985-86.

In February 1986 the government intervened with an offer of up to $NZ10 million to fund a vine-uprooting programme. A quarter of the national vineyard – 1,517 hectares of vines – was destroyed. The heaviest vine pulls were in Hawke's Bay and Gisborne; Müller-Thurgau suffered the severest losses.

The government, although funding the vine-removal scheme, also moved in 1985 to speed up the removal of barriers against overseas wines. By mid-1990, the government had entirely abolished trans-Tasman tariffs on wine, allowing Australian wineries to contest the New Zealand market on an equal footing with local producers. In 1996, imported wines commanded one-third of the total New Zealand market and were deeply entrenched in both the bulk cask and premium bottled wine markets.

Spurred into action by their heavy loss of domestic market share, the winemakers launched a sustained export drive. The value of wine exports, based on the new breed of Sauvignon Blancs and Chardonnays, leapt from $NZ1.2 million in 1983 to $NZ18.4 million in 1990. By 1997, exports – notably to the UK – were worth $NZ75.9 million and accounted for about 25 percent of the industry's total sales.

Paralleling the removal of trade barriers has been the deregulation of the domestic market, which created new opportunities for wine sales. The most spectacular example derived from the Sale of Liquor Act 1989, which gave supermarkets and grocery stores the right to sell wine. By 1997, the grocery trade had captured over 40 percent of the total New Zealand retail wine market.

As the Wine Institute has put it, together the government's free-market measures 'forced New Zealand wineries and grapegrowers to become competitive and market oriented ... Twenty years ago, the industry was a reflection of the country – it was insular, generally uncompetitive and, with a few notable exceptions, had little vision of the future ... [Today] quality has become the watch-word of the industry.'

Samuel Marsden observed almost 180 years ago that 'New Zealand promises to be very favourable to the vine'. That distant prediction has lately been brilliantly fulfilled – leading one overseas enthusiast to suggest that New Zealand should even be planted in a sea of Sauvignon Blanc vines stretching from Stewart Island in the south to North Cape.

A decade ago, Müller-Thurgau dominated plantings in New Zealand; now Chardonnay and Sauvignon Blanc reign supreme. Other white grapes such as Riesling, sweet whites, reds and sparklings all show great promise. In view of the industry's infancy and whirlwind pace of change, who knows what will emerge as the great New Zealand wines of the future?

Climate and Soils

A cool climate is New Zealand's key viticultural asset. The world's finest table wines are grown in temperate climates, where the temperatures are warm enough to carry the bunches to optimal ripeness, but not so hot that the fruit's more subtle aromas and flavours are lost. New Zealand – like the classic wine regions of France and Germany – has a temperate climate ideal for growing high-quality grapes; this is the fundamental reason its wines are so garden-fresh, appetisingly crisp and deep-flavoured.

The influential Californian 'heat summation' index (admittedly shown to work better in California than elsewhere) evaluates New Zealand as a classic cool-climate wine-growing country. Based on research that showed that the single most important aspect of climate for viticulture is temperature, the index measures the amount of heat the vine receives during the growing season, above the minimum needed for active growth. Region One climates are characterised by moderately cool weather under which ripening proceeds slowly.

Such areas, including Burgundy, Alsace, the Loire, Champagne, the Mosel and Rheingau, Sonoma and Coonawarra, produce some of the world's finest table wines. In some vintages sugar accumulation is a problem and acidities tend to be high. However, the cool ripening weather brings to the fruit optimum development of its aroma and flavour constituents. The major wine regions of New Zealand all possess Region One climates for grape-growing.

Precise parallels cannot be drawn between the latitudes north and south of the equator that offer the best prospects for making wine. Alone in vast seas and far from the influence of continental hot-air masses, New Zealand has a temperate, maritime climate with cooler summers and milder winters than regions at comparable latitudes in the northern hemisphere. For instance, South Canterbury lies in latitudes parallel to Bordeaux, yet in climatic terms New Zealand's most Bordeaux-like region is Hawke's Bay, in the north.

Rain is the villain of New Zealand's climate, so far as wine-making is concerned. In most regions, high humidity and heavy rainfall combine in difficult years to cause problems with such wet-weather diseases as botrytis and downy mildew. Ripening is delayed and the bunches rot.

In respect of rainfall during the critical February–April ripening period, some regions are much more fortunate than others. The rains fall most frequently and heavily on the west coast, with a long, drier belt running down the east coast of both islands. By world standards the autumn rainfall in Henderson and the Waikato is excessive; Gisborne and Nelson are borderline. In

Central Otago, Canterbury, Marlborough, the Wairarapa and, to a lesser extent, Hawke's Bay, the lower autumn rainfall and reduced risk of disease enables growers to hang their fruit longer on the vines in pursuit of maximum ripeness and flavour development.

In New Zealand's cool, frequently rainy climate, the selection of a vineyard site with warm, free-draining soils is critical. In the past the tendency was to establish vineyards on high fertility, poorly drained soils which enhanced grape yields at the expense of quality. Most Auckland vineyards are planted on heavy clays that require ploughing, draining and 'grassing down' to reduce waterlogging of the soil. Gisborne's wet, highly fertile soils promote a luxuriant growth of the vines' canopies which retards fruit ripening by casting the bunches into shade.

Hawke's Bay's soils range from wet alluvial silts to lighter, stonier soils far better suited to quality grape-growing. Marlborough's soils are also variable, with the less fertile, shingly sites (which often need irrigation to alleviate water stress of the vines during dry years) the most sought-after. The recent trend in New Zealand to locate new vineyards in moderately fertile, well-drained soils has played a pivotal role in boosting wine quality.

New Zealand's wines display clearcut regional differences. A thousand kilometres separate the northernmost and southernmost wine regions – equal to the distance between Koblenz, at the confluence of the Rhine and Mosel rivers, and Rome.

The late-ripening Cabernet Sauvignon variety, for instance, performs well in Auckland's warm, often wet climate, whereas Central Otago's relatively cool, dry climate is better suited to the earlier-ripening Pinot Noir. Hawke's Bay's Chardonnays are more robust, riper and rounder than the leaner, flintier Chardonnays of Marlborough. The marked differences of climate and soil between the country's numerous and far-flung wine regions add much to the diversity and fascination of New Zealand wines.

The Key Grape Varieties

Only by revolutionising the composition of their vineyards have New Zealand's winemakers been able to make their dramatic switch from fortified wines to world-class table wines. In 1960 the most common variety was Albany Surprise (a clonal selection of Isabella, a black American *labrusca* variety), followed by two French hybrids, Baco 22A and Seibel 5455. Although popular for their hardiness and heavy yields, all three grapes produced quaffing wine, at best. By 1970 Palomino, the classic Spanish sherry variety, topped the list.

From 1975 to 1990, Müller-Thurgau, a German grape that typically yields pleasant, fruity but rather bland wines, was the most extensively planted variety, but has since swiftly lost ground. By 1999, according to the 1996 vineyard survey, Chardonnay and Sauvignon Blanc will account for almost 50 percent of the producing national vineyard area, with three other classic French grapes – Pinot Noir, Cabernet Sauvignon and Merlot – dominating the country's red-wine plantings.

The radical transformation in the raw materials with which New Zealand's winemakers are working can be seen by comparing the vineyard surveys for 1983 and 1996. Note that there is a basic difference in the two surveys: whereas the 1983 survey focused on planted vines, whether they were cropping or not, the 1996 survey projects the areas of producing vines through to 1999.

NEW ZEALAND'S TOP TEN GRAPE VARIETIES

		1996 (% of producing vineyard area by 1999)	1983 (% of planted vineyard area)
1)	Chardonnay	27.5	6.8
2)	Sauvignon Blanc	21.8	3.4
3)	Pinot Noir	8.6	5.0
4)	Cabernet Sauvignon	8.0	7.1
5)	Müller-Thurgau	6.3	31.9
6)	Merlot	6.1	0.7
7)	Riesling	5.2	2.5
8)	Sémillon	3.0	1.5
9)	Muscat	2.2	5.6
10)	Chenin Blanc	1.7	6.3

Grape varietes ranking among the 25 most widely planted but not discussed in detail below include: Blauburger, an Austrian red-wine crossing of Portugieser and Blaufrankisch; Breidecker, a crossing of Müller-Thurgau with the white hybrid Seibel 7053;

Chasselas, a heavy-cropping, low-acid blending grape; Palomino, the mainstay of New Zealand's fast declining 'sherry' output; Pinot Blanc, a non-aromatic grape well established in Alsace, Germany, Italy and California, which in New Zealand yields wines with good weight and depth of appley, earthy flavour; and Reichensteiner, a high-yielding grape whose wine is highly reminiscent of one of its parents, Müller-Thurgau.

Trials currently under way with hitherto neglected classic grapes of France (Grenache, Gamay and Viognier), Italy (Sangiovese and Nebbiolo) and Spain (Tempranillo) promise to add an exciting diversity to New Zealand's future wine output.

White Wine Varieties

CHARDONNAY

Sauvignon Blanc launched New Zealand onto the international wine scene, but on the domestic market Chardonnay is the more prestigious and popular variety. The great grape of white Burgundy is New Zealand's most extensively planted variety of all, with about 300 different labels produced.

The vine is widely spread across the country, with heaviest plantings in Marlborough (35 percent of the national total); Hawke's Bay (27 percent), where it is the number one grape; and Gisborne (21 percent), where it is now supplanting Müller-Thurgau as the principal variety.

The most common clone, Mendoza, is the foundation of almost all of New Zealand's top Chardonnays, with its relatively light crops of 'hen and chicken' (large and small) berries harbouring richly flavoured juice. Also important are the heavy-cropping clones 4 and 5; clone 6, which has a more even fruit set than Mendoza and is the foundation of many of New Zealand's mid-priced Chardonnays; and clone 15, a shyer bearer than clone 6, which has produced some highly rated wines in New Zealand.

New Zealand Chardonnays reveal clearcut regional differences. In the relative warmth of Gisborne, Chardonnay yields deliciously full-bodied and fragrant, softly structured wines, hugely drinkable in their youth. The finest Hawke's Bay Chardonnays are robust, with rich grapefruit-like flavours underpinned by firm acidity and the ability to mature well for several years. Marlborough's Chardonnays are typically leaner, with fresh, citrusy, sometimes appley flavours and a crisp, flinty finish.

New Zealand's lower priced Chardonnays are typically handled entirely in stainless steel tanks (like Nobilo Poverty Bay Chardonnay) or lightly oaked (like Montana Gisborne Chardonnay). Mid-priced wines (like Matua Eastern Bays Chardonnay) are generally fermented in tanks and then matured in oak casks. Top models (like Delegat's Proprietor's Reserve

Chardonnay) typically display flavour richness and complexity gained from barrel fermentation, aging (with regular stirring) on yeast lees, and varying proportions of new oak and malolactic fermentation.

How good are New Zealand's top Chardonnays? The finest have proven themselves on the world stage. At the 1995 International Wine and Spirit Competition in London, for instance, Oyster Bay Marlborough Chardonnay 1994 won the trophy for the champion Chardonnay. Kumeu River Chardonnay 1994 was rated sixth in *Wine Spectator*'s prestigious Top 100 for 1996.

CHENIN BLANC

Chenin Blanc until recently yielded austere, sharp wines in New Zealand, lacking ripeness and richness. The potential of this great grape of the Loire has still to be fully explored, but the latest vintages are stronger flavoured and better balanced, with much greater drinkability.

Chenin Blanc's stronghold in New Zealand is the east coast of the North Island – Hawke's Bay (where over half of the vines are concentrated) and Gisborne. However, its tight bunches are highly susceptible to botrytis rot and in the past decade plantings have contracted by 40 percent.

On the right sites, Chenin Blanc should succeed in New Zealand. Planted in devigorating soils, where its canopy can be controlled and its yields reduced, it is starting to produce softer and more approachable wines. Much of the crop disappears into cask wines or is blended with Chardonnay to produce fruity, flavoursome, modestly priced bottled dry whites. The much more characterful, vibrant, steely, tropical fruit-flavoured Chenin Blancs from Collards and the lush, slightly honeyed oak-aged wines from The Millton Vineyard point the way to the future.

GEWÜRZTRAMINER

This great Alsatian grape has recently dropped out of the group of New Zealand's ten most widely planted varieties, yet at its best yields pungent, perfumed wines packed with spiciness.

Most of the vines are concentrated in Hawke's Bay, Marlborough and Gisborne, with the latter region enjoying an especially high profile for its intensely varietal Gewürztraminers from Matawhero, Montana and Revington Vineyard. Other top examples have flowed from the Wairarapa (notably Dry River), and the variety is also showing promise in Canterbury and Otago.

However, for many growers this grape has proved too susceptible to adverse weather at flowering, which can dramatically cut yields. Since 1983, the area devoted to Gewürztraminer has contracted by almost two-thirds and its share of the national vineyard has plummeted from 4.8 percent to 1.4 percent.

On the local market, Gewürztraminer has never enjoyed the popularity of Chardonnay, Sauvignon Blanc or (latterly) Riesling. Fortunately, a number of winemakers are still committed to this temperamental variety, and the top wines rank among the finest produced outside Alsace.

MÜLLER-THURGAU

The cornerstone of the New Zealand wine industry in past years, this early-ripening, heavy cropping German variety is now in rapid decline. In 1980 it comprised 38 percent of the national vineyard; in 1995 12 percent. By 1999, its share of the producing vineyard is predicted to fall to 6.3 percent.

When New Zealanders' love affair with white wines began in the 1960s, growers flocked to Müller-Thurgau because it offered a big leap in wine quality from the old hybrid grapes, without any major disadvantages in ripening or cropping ability. Müller-Thurgau's light, fruity, mild-flavoured wine proved instantly popular and a distinct splash of sweetness broadened the appeal.

When tastes began to swing to drier wines, Müller-Thurgau's popularity waned. Over a third of the vines were uprooted during the 1986 vine-pull scheme, and since then plantings have continued to shrink. (Yet in 1997 the heavy-bearing Müller-Thurgau still produced over 16.7 percent of the total national grape crop.) Forty percent of the vines are in Gisborne, with other significant plantings in Hawke's Bay and Marlborough.

In the past popular as a bottled wine, today most Müller-Thurgau is sold in casks. However, even its future as a bulk-wine variety is in doubt. New German grapes like Arnsburger and GM312-53 are arousing interest as possible substitutes, and in recent years Montana and Corbans have imported millions of litres of bulk wine from Europe, South America and Australia to fuel their cask production lines.

Müller-Thurgau produces pleasant *vin ordinaire* in New Zealand. Typically 'backblended' to a slightly sweet style by adding a small amount of unfermented grape juice, it is fresh and lightly floral, citrusy and soft – very undemanding.

MUSCAT

Although rarely marketed as a varietal wine, Muscat grapes are quite extensively planted in New Zealand, especially Muscat Dr Hogg, an old English table variety which yields heavy crops of large, fleshy berries.

Plantings are concentrated in Gisborne (where Muscat Dr Hogg is the third most common variety), Hawke's Bay and Marlborough. However, in New Zealand's relatively cool growing temperatures, the grapes ripen late and the wine tends to lack lusciousness. Since 1983, plantings have shrunk by 50 percent.

Muscat is principally used as a blending variety in New Zealand, adding an aromatic 'lift' to the bouquet of many Müller-Thurgaus and a perfumed fruitiness to low-priced Asti Spumante-style sparklings. A few freeze-concentrated sweet Muscats are made in a vibrantly fruity, fresh, drink-young style.

PINOT GRIS

Pinot Gris could be a future star of New Zealand wine. With growers' interest mounting, the area of bearing vines will triple between 1996 and 1999 to 63 hectares, making it the country's ninth most widely planted white-wine variety.

Pinot Gris is well adapted to New Zealand's cooler regions, ripening early with fairly low acidity and high sugar levels. A third of the vines are concentrated in Marlborough, but Otago, Hawke's Bay, the Wairarapa (home of the outstanding producer Dry River) and Canterbury all have significant pockets. With its typical sturdy body and rich, spicy, stone-fruit flavours, Pinot Gris is increasingly winning favour as an ideal alternative to Chardonnay.

RIESLING

Riesling is fast emerging into the white-wine spotlight traditionally focused in New Zealand on Sauvignon Blanc and Chardonnay. Sales soared by 500 percent between 1991 and 1996 and well over 100 labels, ranging in style from bone-dry to honey-sweet, are now on the market.

New Zealand Riesling (often labelled in the past as Rhine Riesling) was confused by many consumers with Riesling-Sylvaner – the most common name in the 1960s and 1970s for Müller-Thurgau. The growing trend to dry wines also ran counter to the slight sweetness of most Rieslings. Yet plantings doubled between 1983 and 1989, and surged again by 50 percent between 1992 and 1995, establishing the great German grape as New Zealand's fourth most extensively planted white-wine variety.

Riesling's New Zealand stronghold is Marlborough, where more than half of the vines are concentrated. Over 80 percent of all plantings are in the cooler South Island, where the lower humidity reduces the risk of botrytis rot and the slower ripening coaxes out the variety's most magical scents and flavours. 'Noble rot', the beneficial form of botrytis, has produced luscious dessert Rieslings of exceptional quality in most regions, notably Hawke's Bay, the Wairarapa, Canterbury and, above all, Marlborough.

The finest New Zealand Rieslings are richly scented and racy, with a sliver of sweetness and fresh, piercing lemon/lime flavours. Fuller in body than most German Rieslings, yet lighter and more delicate than Australia's, the top wines are attractive in their youth but cellar well for at least a decade.

SAUVIGNON BLANC

Supercharged Sauvignon Blanc, overflowing with freshly acidic, herbaceous flavour, is New Zealand's biggest claim to fame in the wine world. When Ross and Bill Spence of Matua Valley imported trial vines from California and produced New Zealand's first Sauvignon Blanc in 1974, who could have foreseen what lay ahead?

Montana was sufficiently impressed to include Sauvignon Blanc in its new Marlborough vineyards and in 1979 its first Marlborough Sauvignon Blanc nosed its way into the market. By the mid-1980s, the intensely aromatic, rapier-like Marlborough Sauvignon Blancs from Montana, Hunter's and Cloudy Bay were winning international applause. Plantings leapt by 480 percent between 1986 and 1995, establishing this classic grape of France's Loire Valley and Bordeaux as New Zealand's second most extensively planted variety. Between 1996 and 1999, the bearing area of Sauvignon Blanc will rise by a further 45 percent.

Marlborough is New Zealand's – some say the world's – Sauvignon Blanc capital. Over two-thirds of all plantings are in Marlborough, where Sauvignon Blanc is the most widely planted grape. With their leap-out-of-the-glass aromas and explosion of gooseberry and capsicum-like, mouth-wateringly crisp flavour, the Sauvignon Blancs here are of breathtaking intensity. The Wairarapa, Nelson and North Canterbury regions also produce a stream of freshly acidic, vividly flavoured Sauvignon Blancs. In warmer Hawke's Bay, where 18 percent of the country's plantings are found, the relatively restrained style of Sauvignon Blanc is typically more mouthfilling, ripe and rounded.

Two basic styles of Sauvignon Blanc are produced in New Zealand. Most commonly, the wines are bottled straight out of stainless steel tanks, placing their emphasis squarely on their fresh fruit flavours, which range from the sharp, nettley characters of slightly unripe grapes through a riper, gooseberry-like fruitiness to the lower acidity and tropical-fruit overtones of very ripe grapes. These unwooded wines are normally labelled simply as Sauvignon Blanc. More complex models, fermented and/or matured in oak casks, are typically labelled as Reserve Sauvignon Blanc or Sauvignon Blanc Oak Aged.

SÉMILLON

Sémillon has a low profile in New Zealand. Much of the crop is added anonymously to wines labelled Sauvignon Blanc, to which Sémillon contributes complexity and aging potential. The great grape of white Bordeaux is also often used as a flavour-packed component of affordably priced blended dry whites, such as Babich Fumé Vert and Coopers Classic Dry.

After a steady growth in plantings over the past decade, Sémillon is now New Zealand's fifth most widely planted white-wine variety. Over half of all plantings are in Marlborough, with a further 29 percent in Gisborne.

Most New Zealand Sémillons in the past were pungently grassy – even more so than the country's verdant Sauvignon Blancs. However, it was recently discovered that the grape's uncharacteristic resistance to bunch rot in New Zealand and the cutting herbaceousness of its wine – which both raised doubts as to the variety's true identity – are the result of virus infection, which retards ripening. By planting virus-free vines, manipulating their canopies to expose the bunches to more sunshine, and importing a superior Barossa Valley clone, the winemakers have improved the ripeness levels and sheer drinkability of their most recent vintages. Sémillon looks set for a more prominent role in the future.

Red Wine Varieties

CABERNET FRANC

More often encountered as a minority ingredient in claret-style blends than as a varietal wine in its own right, Cabernet Franc is New Zealand's fourth most widely planted red-wine grape.

Between 1986 and 1996, plantings of this classic variety of Bordeaux and the Loire Valley climbed from 15 to 97 hectares (one-sixth the area devoted to Cabernet Sauvignon). Cabernet Franc has not performed well in New Zealand's cooler vineyard sites, where viticulturists have experienced greater problems with *coulure* (failure of the vine flowers to develop) and green, unripe flavours. Over half the vines are concentrated in Hawke's Bay, with most of the rest in Auckland, Gisborne and Marlborough.

The variety's ability to yield rich, deeply flavoured, firm reds with strength of character has been demonstrated by Matua Valley in West Auckland and Clearview Estate in Hawke's Bay. More often, however, New Zealand's Cabernet Francs are genial wines with raspberryish aromas and flavours and a fruity, supple, easy-drinking appeal.

In its principal blending role, as a minority partner of Cabernet Sauvignon and Merlot in many of New Zealand's top claret-style reds, Cabernet Franc provides a scentedness, vibrant fruitiness and softness that acts as the perfect foil to the tougher Cabernet Sauvignon.

CABERNET SAUVIGNON

For decades, Cabernet Sauvignon dominated New Zealand's red-wine output. Regarded in the 1970s as the variety that could transform the country's red-wine quality, by 1983 the great grape of the Médoc was New Zealand's second most common variety of all. Today, Cabernet Sauvignon still accounts for 8 percent of the national vineyard, but its ascendancy is being strongly challenged by Merlot and Pinot Noir.

As a late ripener, in New Zealand Cabernet Sauvignon has performed best in the warmer North Island. Its stronghold is Hawke's Bay, where almost 60 percent of the vines are concentrated. Cabernet Sauvignon is also well established in Auckland, the Waikato and the Wairarapa. In Marlborough, however, which has almost 20 percent of plantings, the grape often struggles to achieve full ripeness, producing light, fruity, leafy-green wines that lack warmth and richness.

New Zealand's Cabernet-based reds cover a wide spectrum of quality. Too many wines, produced from virused vines grown in overly fertile sites, lack colour depth and exhibit the green, herbaceous flavours and high acidity of unripe fruit. Yet the top wines of Hawke's Bay and Auckland (notably Waiheke Island) can be of arresting quality, with a fragrance, flavour depth and delicacy that can be distinctly reminiscent of a fine Bordeaux.

Today, in their bid to produce ripe, attractive reds with greater consistency than they have achieved with Cabernet Sauvignon, many growers are turning to the earlier-ripening Merlot and Pinot Noir varieties. Nevertheless, planted in low-fertility sites in the warmer regions, the aristocratic Cabernet Sauvignon still looks assured of a key role in New Zealand's production of premium reds. The top wines need at least three years before drinking, ideally five, and can mature well for a decade.

MALBEC

A minor but growing influence in New Zealand reds, this traditional Bordeaux variety is stirring up interest with its rich, plummy, sweet fruit flavours. Between 1989 and 1996, plantings expanded from 3 to 39 hectares (0.5 percent of the national vineyard).

Malbec, whose susceptibility to *coulure* often leads to poor fruit 'set', crops best in New Zealand's warmer sites, where it ripens readily with brilliant colour and strong, tannic flavour. Over 40 percent of the vines are in Hawke's Bay; there are also significant pockets in Marlborough and the Waikato. Malbec is invariably blended into claret-style reds, adding an extra dimension to such premium labels as Esk Valley, The Terraces, Stonyridge Larose and Providence.

MERLOT

A fast-rising star, Merlot is now challenging the long-term primacy of Cabernet Sauvignon among New Zealand's red-wine grapes. In New Zealand's cool grape-growing climate, Merlot's ability to ripen its fruit two to three weeks ahead of Cabernet Sauvignon is a crucial asset.

The variety is spreading like wildfire. Plantings expanded by 300 percent between 1986 and 1992, and during the next three years doubled again. Merlot – the most widely planted black-skinned variety in Bordeaux – is now New Zealand's sixth most common grape and third most extensively planted red-wine variety. At its current rate of expansion, within a few years its plantings could surpass those of Cabernet Sauvignon.

Over half of all New Zealand's Merlot is in Hawke's Bay, where its riper flavours, higher grape sugars and lower acids (compared to Cabernet Sauvignon) are fast winning favour. The major drawback is Merlot's erratic and sometimes low yield, due to its susceptibility to *coulure*, although new clonal releases have reduced this problem. Marlborough, Gisborne and Auckland also have sizable pockets of Merlot.

For many years, Merlot's primary role was to impart a lush, vibrantly fruity, easy-drinking charm to its blends with the predominant, more slowly evolving and tannic Cabernet Sauvignon. Now, with a stream of seductively perfumed, rich-flavoured and velvety reds, Merlot has emerged from Cabernet Sauvignon's shadow and been recognised as a premium red-wine grape in its own right.

PINOTAGE

New Zealand's soft, peppery and gamey Pinotages are rarely exported, but they add a welcome diversity to the country's limited red-wine selection.

Pinotage, a thick-skinned South African crossing of Pinot Noir and Cinsaut, was planted in New Zealand 30 years ago, during the rush to replace hybrid vines. Its ability to withstand heavy rains and generous yields proved especially popular in Auckland. Today, with 96 hectares in 1996, Pinotage is New Zealand's fifth most widely planted red-wine grape. The heaviest plantings are in Marlborough, followed by Hawke's Bay, Gisborne and Auckland.

Several wineries – notably Nobilo, Pleasant Valley, Babich, Montana, Soljans and Villa Maria – produce flavoursome, smooth, early-maturing reds from Pinotage, but none approach the concentration and complexity of South Africa's finest.

PINOT NOIR

Pinot Noir may well prove to be New Zealand's greatest red-wine gift to the world. The notoriously temperamental Burgundian variety flourishes in the cooler regions of New Zealand, where the grapes are able to ripen slowly, building up a seductive richness of perfume and flavour.

After heavy recent plantings (and the planned extraction of many Müller-Thurgau vines), by 1999 Pinot Noir's area of bearing vines will trail only Chardonnay and Sauvignon Blanc, establishing it ahead of Cabernet Sauvignon as New Zealand's most important black-skinned variety. Plantings of Pinot Noir almost doubled between 1986 and 1989, doubled again over the next three years, and then between 1992 and 1995 leapt by a further 40 percent.

Over 40 percent of the vines are concentrated in Marlborough, where the production of Pinot Noir-based red wines is only a trickle; the majority of the crop is reserved for bottle-fermented sparkling wines. Hawke's Bay, Otago (where it is the most common variety) and Canterbury also have substantial plantings, but it is the Wairarapa's Pinot Noirs that enjoy the most illustrious reputation, with Ata Rangi, Dry River and Martinborough Vineyard vying for top honours.

The dominant clones are AM 10/5, highly regarded for its good colour and soft, vibrantly fruity palate; Bachtobel, whose red wine lacks flavour depth and colour but which suits high volume sparkling wine production; and UCD5 ('Pommard'), prized for its colour richness and firm, tannic wines. In their pursuit of complexity, most leading winemakers blend their Pinot Noir from at least two different clones.

New Zealand's finest Pinot Noirs are intensely varietal, with a rich, cherryish fragrance, sweet fruit flavours and a velvety texture. The top labels typically reach their peak at between three and five years old.

SYRAH

Syrah (Shiraz) is still a rarity in New Zealand, but the signs are encouraging. The tiny Stonecroft Winery in Hawke's Bay has led the way since 1989 with a series of densely coloured, robust, plum and black pepper-flavoured wines, similar in style to a good Crozes-Hermitage.

With 43 hectares established in 1996, Syrah is New Zealand's sixth most widely planted red-wine grape. Plantings doubled between 1989 and 1992, and then from 1992 to 1995 almost tripled. Half of the vines are clustered in Hawke's Bay, especially in warm, sheltered, stony sites inland from Hastings, but there are also pockets of Syrah in Marlborough and the Wairarapa.

Syrah has not previously succeeded in New Zealand, because it needs a warm growing environment and does not have Cabernet Sauvignon's ability to withstand persistent rains. However, with careful site selection, vigour control and yield restriction, Stonecroft, Te Mata, Babich, Okahu Estate and others have started to produce satisfying, ripely flavoured wines with delicacy and intense varietal characteristics. In style, they are more reminiscent of the Rhône than of Australia.

Making Wine in New Zealand

Modern wine production is a challenging task – a fact clearly illustrated by the presence of specialist winemaking graduates at the production helm of most of New Zealand's larger wineries. Take Michelle Richardson, winemaker at Villa Maria, or Kim Crawford of Coopers Creek, or Brent Marris of Delegat's; all are high-profile oenologists trained at the famous wine school of Roseworthy Agricultural College in South Australia. Some of New Zealand's most successful winemakers – Kerry Hitchcock, chief operating officer of Nobilo and formerly chief winemaker of Corbans, Joe Babich and Bruce Collard – are nevertheless living proof that a tertiary degree is not an essential element in the training of a talented winemaker; intelligence, common sense and a preparedness to keep abreast of recent developments are more vital.

Growing Grapes

The unsung heroes of New Zealand wine are the viticulturists. Overshadowed by the 'cult of the winemaker' found throughout the New World, they operate largely in the industry's background. Yet a favourite saying of New Zealand winemakers is that 'you can't make good wine from bad grapes'. It is in the vineyards that the raw materials of wine are grown, and there that each wine's basic potential is set.

The viticulturist's annual cycle begins in late autumn, after the bunches have been gathered in. When the weather cools further, the leaves drop from the vines in a flaming shower of crimson, yellow and rust-brown.

In winter the vines rest, building their resources for the burgeoning of growth that will take place later in the year. In June, pruning begins and dominates vineyard activity through to the end of August. By trellising and pruning the vine, the viticulturist is able to control and shape its foliage growth, gaining greater ease of cultivation and finer fruit quality. In New Zealand, most vines are planted about 2 metres apart in rows 3 metres wide, and trained along trellises varying between 1 and 1.7 metres in height.

Cane pruning is the most popular system in New Zealand. Between two and four canes are chosen to carry the new season's growth, each having ten to twenty buds. A few spurs, carrying several buds, are also retained to provide the fruiting canes for the following season. After the canes are cut, the bearing arms are laid along the bottom wire and later the new season's foliage is trained above.

When spring comes, sap rises and nudges fragile buds out from the gnarled canes that have protected them through winter.

Shoots and flower-clusters emerge, and tiny leaves unfurl. In early December the flowers 'set' as small, hard green berries. From now until the vintage the vines need constant care.

Drip irrigation systems are a common sight in vineyards from Hawke's Bay south, where summer droughts can cause the vines to suffer severe water stress. On sites with light, free-draining soils, irrigation is used to assist ripening and maintain yields in dry years – a sort of viticultural insurance policy.

To arrest weed growth, the vineyards are ploughed or sprayed under the rows several times during the growing season. Cover crops such as lupins and clover, which supply the vines' nitrogen needs, are turned under. The soil is disced until the earth is well broken up and aerated. Chemical spray programmes to protect the vines against fungous diseases and insect pests commence and continue to just before the harvest.

Botrytis is the worst problem. Late in the season warm, wet weather encourages grapes to swell with moisture and split open. Botrytis, which appears as a grey, fluffy mould on the leaves and bunches, causes the grapes to rot on the vines. Fine dry autumn weather can allow botrytis-infected, 'nobly rotten' grapes to develop a luscious intensity of flavour and sweetness. In New Zealand's often wet autumns, however, botrytis can severely damage the grapes. To combat botrytis, growers rely heavily on precisely timed applications of fungicide sprays.

In summer, from December to February, the vines reach their peak period of growth. The tangled canes are trimmed back, tucked and tied. Leaf removal around the fruit zone, by hand or machine, to open up the fruit to maximum sunshine, has recently become common.

Dr Richard Smart, the eminent Australian viticultural scientist, worked in New Zealand from 1982 to 1990. His most publicised research focused on New Zealand's problem of excessive fruit shading. The conventional system of training grapevines on a restrictive vertical trellis was unsatisfactory, said Smart, because New Zealand's highly fertile soils promote exuberant foliage growth, which casts the ripening fruit into shade. Crop levels and grape quality are retarded by excessive shading.

The answer, according to Smart, was 'canopy division' – splitting the foliage into separate curtains to maintain good fruit and leaf exposure to sunshine. New trellis systems were developed which are capable of being installed in existing vineyards without too many alterations. With the addition of only two movable foliage wires, the 'Scott Henry' system recently adopted by many owners of small New Zealand vineyards creates two separate curtains of foliage, one positioned above the other. The result – riper grapes.

In New Zealand the vintage, the first, vital step in the making of the new season's wine, usually begins in late February or early March with the gathering-in of the early-ripening varieties –

Müller-Thurgau and Gewürztraminer – and lasts until mid-May. Until 25 years ago the entire harvest was picked by hand, in the traditional manner. The arrival of the first mechanical harvester in New Zealand in 1973, however, soon forced the hand-pickers into retreat. Hand-pickers now survive only in the smaller or steeper vineyards or where meticulous fruit selection is sought.

After the harvesters have lumbered away, the vineyards fall silent. It will soon be time for the cold days of winter, seemingly barren but full of promise, to set in again.

Making Wine

New Zealand winemakers returning from visits to the classic wine regions of Europe have often claimed that although the French and Germans lead New Zealand in the standard of their vineyards, New Zealand has a clear edge in the cellars. Most wineries were technically ill-prepared when public demand switched from heavy dessert to white table wines. It is a fortunate irony that New Zealand's late development of interest in wine science allowed the industry to avoid other countries' mistakes and to adopt only the established best. An outstanding example is refrigeration, a late arrival on the New Zealand wine scene, but now widely used to stabilise wine, hold back unfermented grape-juice and control fermentation.

As Corbans' production manager from 1952 to 1976, Alex Corban was the first New Zealand winemaker to adopt such modern technical wizardry as pressure fermentations, stainless steel, refrigeration and yeast starter cultures. Only the second New Zealander to gain a diploma in oenology from Roseworthy College, Adelaide, Corban was exposed during his Australian studies to winemaking equipment and techniques unknown to an older generation.

In 1949, the entire Corbans range was fermented with cultured yeasts – the first time natural, 'wild' yeasts were not used in New Zealand. Stainless steel tanks made their New Zealand wine industry debut in 1958 at Corbans. Then the company's Dry White 1962, based on hybrid Baco 22A grapes, was pressure-fermented at controlled temperatures – another first. Refrigeration, centrifuges, freeze concentration, pasteurisation, cold sterile bottling – the range of equipment and techniques Corban introduced to New Zealand is vast.

Nevertheless, when premium grapes like Chardonnay and Sauvignon Blanc first came on stream in commercial volumes in New Zealand, few winemakers had detailed knowledge about how to handle them. 'During the late 1970s and early 1980s, when more Chardonnay grapes became available, the winemaking procedures followed the pattern of white winemaking of that time,' recalls Kerry Hitchcock, Nobilo's chief operating officer, who was previously Corbans' chief winemaker for many years.

'This involved quick separation of the juice from its skins and stainless steel fermentation at low temperatures, followed by aging in oak barrels for a short period. Then, as the market became more demanding, winemakers looked at Chardonnay-making in the traditional French way, and we saw different styles being produced in New Zealand. These involved longer skin contact time to extract flavour; fermenting in oak barrels with higher solids in the juice; leaving the wine on its lees for flavour development; and a partial or complete malolactic fermentation in the traditional French way.' The fresh, uncomplicated Chardonnays of the early to mid-1980s were swiftly surpassed by a new breed of Chardonnay – mouthfilling and multi-dimensional.

WHITE WINES

To produce a fine white wine the winemaker must be meticulous, because the juices of white grapes are highly vulnerable to oxidation. If the grapes' journey from the vineyard to the crusher is long (Gisborne or Hawke's Bay to Auckland is common), sulphur dioxide is frequently added at the harvester to protect fruit quality (although a current trend is to add less or no sulphur dioxide at the harvester, in the belief that gentle oxidation of 'sensitive' phenols prior to fermentation results in improved wine colour, stability and flavour). However, wines made from machine-harvested grapes trucked long distances reflect the inevitable 'skin contact', which by increasing the extraction of polyphenols – flavour compounds including anthocyanins (colouring matter) and tannins – from the skins into the grapejuice, results in more deeply coloured, strongly flavoured wines.

A truckload of white-wine grapes arriving at the winery is usually swiftly crushed and destemmed. At this stage sulphur dioxide may be added to the crushed fruit ('must') to help guard against oxidation and to inhibit bacteria and natural ('wild') yeasts.

Separating the juice from the skins is the next major task. 'Drainer' tanks enable the winemaker to recover superior quality juice ('free-run') simply by draining the must through a slotted screen at the base of the tank. The residue of pulp, pips and skins is still saturated with juice, recovered by mechanical pressing.

In most large wineries, however, tank presses have recently superseded the combined use of drainer tanks and multi-stage continuous presses. By giving the grapes a much gentler pressing, modern tank presses are able to obtain a greater volume of juice without extracting unwanted, harsh phenolics and compounds.

White-wine juice is normally swiftly separated from its skins, especially if a light, delicate wine is sought, but if a more substantial wine is the goal, the juice may be held in contact with the skins for up to 24 hours to boost the level of phenols, and thus the colour and flavour depth, of the finished wine.

A precisely opposite approach is 'whole-bunch pressing', whereby the winemaker loads bunches of hand-harvested grapes straight into the press, bypassing the crusher. This gentle juice separation technique involves much less skin contact, and therefore yields juices harbouring less colour, solids and phenols, but greater flavour delicacy. Grapes with high levels of flavour and phenols are particularly well-suited to the whole-bunch pressing technique, whereas less flavoursome and phenolic juices often benefit from a greater degree of skin contact.

Before the fermentation gets underway, the juice is clarified to get rid of suspended particles of pulp, skin and yeast cells. It may also be necessary to adjust the juice's sugar and acid levels. In cooler vintages New Zealand's winemakers – like their colleagues in other cool-climate wine countries – may legally supplement their grapes' natural sugars ('chaptalise') to enable their wines to achieve the desired levels of alcohol.

If the grapes' natural acidity is too high, various options are available to the winemaker to de-acidify the must, including the simple addition of $CaCO_3$, known as 'chalking', and blending of high- and low-acid musts. In warmer vintages, early-season varieties can be low in natural acidity; here tartaric acid may be added to impart crispness or 'spine'.

Usually the juice is then inoculated with a selected 'pure' yeast culture (although a growing number of winemakers are endeavouring to enhance their wines' individuality by fermenting with natural yeasts) and shortly the fermentation begins to stir. The majority of New Zealand's white wines are fermented in enclosed stainless steel tanks; first-time visitors to New Zealand wineries are invariably struck by their gleaming batteries of stainless steel fermentation and storage tanks. The standard technique is to 'cold ferment' white wines at 12–15°C. By using refrigeration to slow the ferment from a few days to three weeks or more, the winemaker is able to produce markedly more fragrant and delicately flavoured white wines than can be achieved using traditional, warmer fermentation techniques.

After the fermentation has subsided, the wine is again clarified, stabilised and sweetened if necessary, prior to bottling. If the desired wine style is slightly sweet, a small portion of unfermented grapejuice can be added; this process is called 'backblending'. Another option for slightly sweet wines is 'stop fermentation', whereby a wine's fermentation is arrested by chilling before all the grape sugars have been converted into alcohol. Rich, lusciously sweet dessert wines are normally produced by stop-fermenting late-harvested, ultra-ripe, botrytis-infected fruit, or – less often and with a less magical result – by the freeze concentration method, whereby a proportion of the natural water content in the grape juice is frozen out, leaving a sweet, concentrated juice to be fermented.

Bottling of the new season's white wines usually commences in June or July, only three or four months after the harvest. The last of the whites to be bottled are those matured in casks – the majority of Chardonnays and oak-aged Sauvignon Blancs, Sémillons and Chenin Blancs.

French and American oak barriques (225 litres) are commonly used in New Zealand to mature full-bodied dry whites. Premium Chardonnays and some Sauvignon Blancs are usually also fermented in casks, and then matured in oak on their yeast lees – with regular lees stirring another option – for six months to a year. Barrel fermentation and lees-aging add a yeast-related flavour complexity to the wines and achieve a more seamless integration of wood and wine flavours.

Another technique widely practised is to put full-bodied dry whites, or at least a part of the final blend, through a secondary, bacterial malolactic fermentation. The search here is for a softer-acid style with heightened complexity.

RED WINES

The production of red wines departs from that of whites in two fundamental ways. First, fermentation takes place with the skins in contact with the juice; secondly, red wines are much more often matured in oak for long periods before bottling.

To secure the richest possible extraction of colour and tannin, New Zealand red wines are fermented at 25–32°C, markedly warmer than for whites. The cap of skins forced to the surface by the incessant rise of carbon dioxide bubbles during the ferment is re-immersed in the juice by drawing off the juice and pumping it back over the skins until the cap is broken up or, less often, by regular hand-plunging.

For drink-young styles, where fruitiness and a soft tannin structure are desired, after the fermentation the young wine is swiftly removed from the skins. However, if the goal is a more robust, complex and tannic style, following the fermentation the winemaker may continue to macerate the skins in the new wine for up to a month. The current trend among New Zealand's red-wine makers is towards longer periods of skin contact.

After their initial alcoholic fermentation, New Zealand red wines all undergo a secondary, softening malolactic fermentation, based on the bacterial conversion of malic acid to lactic acid and carbon dioxide. Since lactic acid is softer than malic acid, and there is also a decline in total acidity, the malolactic fermentation produces a rounder, more palatable wine.

For any red wine aspiring to quality and longevity, wood maturation is essential. Some of the top wines are matured exclusively in 225 litre French oak barriques, although often a combination of French and American oak is employed. The percentage of new oak varies – 30 percent for Babich Irongate Cabernet/

Merlot, 50 percent for the Vidal Reserve reds and Goldwater Estate Cabernet/Merlot.

Several types of French oak are encountered in New Zealand wineries – Nevers, Limousin, Alliers, Troncais, Vosges and centre of France. American oak, which imparts a more lifted perfume and sweeter wood flavour, but less extract and tannin, is most commonly used to mature middle-tier wines (and, with its forceful, 'obvious' nature, wine competition gold medal winners!)

Premium Cabernet Sauvignons, Merlots and Pinot Noirs are generally oak-matured for at least a year and often up to eighteen months.

SPARKLING WINES

New Zealand 'bubblies' are produced by three different methods. The lowest priced wines are simply 'carbonated' – a technique whereby carbon dioxide gas is pumped into the base wine. Since there is no secondary fermentation, the bubbles are not dissolved in the wine; once it is poured they race out of the glass and vanish.

A few wines like Corbans Diva Marlborough Cuvée are produced by the 'Charmat' or bulk fermentation method, which involves the secondary fermentation of a dry base wine in a sealed tank. After yeasts and sugar have been added, a proportion of the carbon dioxide gas generated during the resulting secondary fermentation is bound with the alcohol. Upon pouring, the bubbles linger briefly in the glass.

New Zealand's top sparklings, however, are exclusively made by the classic technique until recently known as *méthode champenoise*, but now widely called *méthode traditionnelle*. Here the secondary, bubble-creating fermentation takes place not in a tank but in the bottle itself, following which the yeast cells gradually decompose, conferring distinctive, bready, yeasty characters on the wine. The bottles are then stacked away to mature for anywhere between nine months and three years – most commonly eighteen months to two years – before being, disgorged, topped up, sweetened, corked and wired.

The 'transfer' method (employed by Montana for its hugely popular Lindauer) is a modern approach to bottle-fermentation designed to speed up the final stages. Instead of being individually riddled and disgorged, the wine in each bottle is transferred into pressurised tanks where it is cleaned up and sweetened in bulk, before being re-bottled (hence the small print on the Lindauer label: 'fermented in the bottle' rather than 'fermented in this bottle'.)

Laws and Labels

Four major pieces of legislation control the production, labelling, ex-winery sale and export of wine in New Zealand. However, the production and labelling requirements imposed on winemakers in New Zealand are generally less rigorous than in the traditional wine-producing countries of Europe.

The Food Regulations 1984, which govern the production of New Zealand wine, include general sections applying to all foods and specific provisions for grape wines. The lists of permitted additives include fining and stabilising agents, sweeteners and preservatives. Upper limits are set for such additives as sulphur dioxide (200 parts per million for dry wines, 400 parts per million for sweet wines). The regulations also prescribe a maximum alcohol content for table wines of 15 percent by volume, and 23 percent by volume for fortified wines.

The Wine Makers Levy Act 1976 gives legislative recognition to the Wine Institute, and secures its funding via a mandatory levy on all grape winemakers based on their annual level of sales. The sale of wine directly to the public from the winery is covered by the Sale of Liquor Act 1989.

Ensuring that wines shipped overseas are of sound quality falls within the jurisdiction of the Wine Makers Act 1981. To be eligible for export, all New Zealand wines must secure a Health Department certificate stating that they comply with the Food Act and its regulations and are without obvious faults. The testing is twofold: a chemical analysis by the Environmental Science Research Institute and a blind tasting by a panel of wine industry personnel. As a negative, rather than positive, test of quality, New Zealand's export certification system makes it difficult for faulty wines to be exported, but does not attempt to prevent the shipment of mediocre wines.

Wine-labelling regulations require several key facts to appear on all labels – the producer's name and address, the wine's country of origin, its alcohol strength and contents by volume. Identifying the use of sulphur dioxide has been mandatory since 1995 by use of the additive declaration 'Contains Preservative (220)'. The 'e' marks on the labels of most exported wines are a European Union requirement, whereby the producer guarantees that the 'contents by volume' figure stated is accurate. New Zealand wines sold in Australia must also carry declarations of the number of 'standard drinks' they contain.

Most New Zealand wines boldly feature the name of a specific grape variety or blend of varieties, and the rules governing their use are clearcut. A wine carrying the name of a single grape must contain at least 75 percent of the stated variety. A Sauvignon Blanc, for instance, must be made from no less than 75 percent Sauvignon Blanc juice. (This rule is designed to allow blending to improve the final product. A winemaker might decide, for instance, that a Sauvignon Blanc would be enhanced by the addition of up to 25 percent of another variety – probably Sémillon.) A wine carrying the names of two or more varieties – for instance, Cabernet Sauvignon/Merlot – must also comply with the 75 percent rule and name the principal grapes in descending order of their contribution to the blend.

Sparkling wines have their own nomenclature. Those labelled as 'bottle-fermented' must contain carbon dioxide gas generated by their own natural fermentation in a bottle no larger than five litres. Low priced, carbonated bubblies may only carry the description 'sparkling wine'. Since use of the name 'Champagne' is illegal in New Zealand, and the term *méthode champenoise* cannot be used on wines exported to the European Union, the trend in New Zealand is to identify bottle-fermented sparkling wines with the bland but EU-acceptable term *méthode traditionnelle*.

New Zealand's wine labelling regulations nevertheless have major loopholes. The labelling safeguards in the Food Regulations and the Fair Trading Act are often not specific to wine and do not guarantee the integrity of geographic claims made on New Zealand wine labels.

New Zealand's lack of wine-specific legislation guaranteeing the integrity of its regional labelling has made it 'very much the odd-man-out among quality international wine producers', admits the Wine Institute. Should a bottle labelled Hawke's Bay, for instance, contain at least 51 percent, or 100 percent, wine of Hawke's Bay origin? The regulations are silent on this crucial issue, and also on the matter of accurate vintage dating.

Tighter wine labelling regulations were proposed three years ago, specifying that at least 85 percent of any New Zealand wine carrying a registered geographic name must be from the stated area. This 85 percent minimum rule was also to apply to the wine's varietal and vintage claims. However, introduction of the proposed system has been delayed by the stalling of New Zealand's long-running negotiations to reach a wine treaty with the European Union.

The Winemaking Regions

From Northland to Central Otago, each of New Zealand's wine regions possesses its own unique blend of terrain, climates, soils, personalities and wine styles.

West Auckland and Hawke's Bay were the cradles of New Zealand wine. When demand escalated in the 1960s, Henderson wineries planted new vineyards in Kumeu/Huapai and then Gisborne, where the rich, alluvial soils yielded heavy crops of Müller-Thurgau. In the 1980s, the search for drier regions with less fertile soils, better suited to the production of premium quality grapes, led viticulturists to the long, dry belt running down the east coast of both islands from Hawke's Bay, through the Wairarapa and Marlborough to Canterbury.

Despite the widespread location of vineyards, three regions dominate the New Zealand wine scene. Only 35 percent of the wine companies are based in Marlborough, Hawke's Bay and Gisborne, but these regions boast 82 percent of the total vine plantings and in 1997 produced over 93 percent of the national grape harvest. New Zealand wine, therefore, despite the host of tiny wineries elsewhere, is still overwhelmingly of Marlborough, Hawke's Bay and Gisborne origin.

Given the marked differences in climate and soils between regions up to 1,000 kilometres apart, it is not surprising that New Zealand wines display pronounced regional variations. White wines grown in the relatively cool South Island, for instance, are typically more aromatic and crisper than the fuller-bodied, softer white wines of the north. Late-ripening red-wine varieties like Cabernet Sauvignon have performed better in the warmth of the North Island.

Analysis of the influential Air New Zealand Wine Awards between 1993 and 1996 reveals some especially happy matches of regions and grape varieties. Of Gisborne's 22 gold medals, 17 were awarded to Chardonnays. Hawke's Bay's haul of 48 golds, dominated by 24 Cabernet Sauvignon and Merlot-predominant reds, backed up by 9 Chardonnays, included not a single Sauvignon Blanc. Marlborough's bag of 50 golds included 15 for Sauvignon Blancs, 11 for sweet whites (principally Rieslings), 9 for drier Rieslings – and just 3 for reds.

Northland

AUCKLAND

Waikato/Bay of Plenty

Gisborne

Hawke's Bay

Nelson

WELLINGTON

Wairarapa

Marlborough

Canterbury

CHRISTCHURCH

Otago

DUNEDIN

N

Vintage Charts

1990–1997

7 = Outstanding, 6 = Excellent, 5 = Above average,
4 = Average, 3 = Below average, 2 = Poor, 1 = Bad

	Auckland	Gisborne	Hawke's Bay	Wairarapa	Nelson	Marlborough	Canterbury	Otago
Whites								
1997	6	3-5	4-6	6-7	6-7	6	5-6	4-5
1996	5	4-6	4-6	6-7	5	6	3-6	4-5
1995	4	4-6	3-7	5-6	2-4	2-3	6-7	5
1994	6	6	6-7	6	5-6	5-6	4	4
1993	7	4	3-4	4	4	3-4	3-4	5
1992	5	6	6	4	5	4-5	3	3
1991	6	5	6-7	6-7	6	6-7	4	4
1990	4	3-5	3-6	4	4-6	5	5	5
Reds								
1997	5-6	4	4-7	7	6-7	5	5-6	5-6
1996	4-5	3-4	4	7	5-6	4	4-6	5
1995	4-5	2-4	5-7	6	2-4	2-3	6-7	6
1994	6	6	5-6	6	5	5	4	5
1993	7	3	2	4-5	3-4	3-4	3-4	5
1992	5	4	4	4	4	3-4	3	3
1991	6	4	7	5	5-6	5	4	4
1990	5	4	6	4-5	4-6	5-6	6	6

Northland

A trickle of bold, rich-flavoured red wines has recently started to rekindle interest in New Zealand's oldest and northernmost wine region.

With just five licensed winemakers in 1997, Northland is one of New Zealand's smallest wine regions. Here Samuel Marsden planted the first vines and here, too, James Busby made New Zealand's first recorded wine. But the region's almost subtropical climate – heavy rainfall, high humidity and relatively warm winters – has not attracted many winemakers of late.

For much of the twentieth century, the quiet Northland wine scene consisted of scattered, small-scale enterprises of Croatian origin, focusing on the production of sweet, fortified wines. As demand for such wines slumped, the ranks of Northland winemakers plummeted from nineteen in 1976 to four in 1996.

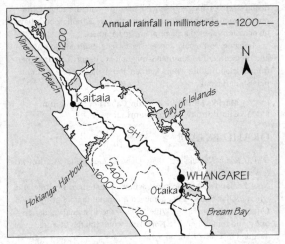

Now, encouraged by the flow of distinguished claret-style reds from the Matakana district, just north of Auckland, several winemakers are endeavouring to unravel Northland's wine potential. Continental Wines, established south of the city of Whangarei by Mate Vuletich in 1964, has changed its name to Longview Estate and since the 1993 vintage has produced several chunky, deep-flavoured Cabernet Sauvignon and Merlot-based reds. Further north, Okahu Estate is achieving success with Syrah.

You can taste Northland's warmth in the sturdiness of body and soft, rich, well-ripened flavours of its reds.

LONGVIEW ESTATE

State Highway One, Otaika, Whangarei. Est 1964. Owners: The Vuletich family. Production: 2,500 cases.

This pretty, terraced vineyard lies alongside the main highway, just south of the city of Whangarei. Of the many vineyards established over the years by Croatian settlers in Northland, only Longview (for many years called Continental Wines) has made the transition to a respected table-wine producer.

The founder, Mate Vuletich, first planted vines for his own medicinal purposes in 1964. Under the direction of his son, Mario, the original hybrid and American *labrusca* vines have been uprooted. Today, the hill-grown clay vineyard with its 'long view' over Whangarei harbour is planted in 5 hectares of Cabernet Sauvignon, Merlot, Chardonnay, Gewürztraminer and Müller-Thurgau.

The wines are all estate-grown. Longview Gewürztraminer displays rich, ripe, well-spiced flavours and the Chardonnay reveals good depth of citrusy, oaky flavour, although both have on occasions shown a slight phenolic hardness.

Longview's notable success is its reds. Both Mario's Merlot and the Scarecrow Cabernet Sauvignon are deeply coloured, perfumed, mouthfilling wines with an abundance of ripe, brambly, persistent flavour.

(****) Mario's Merlot, Scarecrow Cabernet Sauvignon
(***) Chardonnay, Gewürztraminer

OKAHU ESTATE

Okahu Road, Kaitaia. Est 1989. Owners: Monty and Bev Knight. Production: 2,250 cases.

New Zealand's northernmost winery burst into the limelight when its Kaz Shiraz 1994 achieved a unique double at the 1996 Liquorland Royal Easter Wine Show – the first gold medal anyone could remember for a Northland wine, and the first gold ever awarded to a New Zealand Syrah.

Sturdy, rich, soft reds flow from this hillside vineyard nestled between the town of Kaitaia and the sand dunes of Ninety Mile Beach. Proprietor Monty Knight, better known in the region as a successful, high profile home appliance retailer, planted his first vines in 1984 to make wine for his own consumption. Today his 2-hectare vineyard is planted in a wide array of grapes, with Cabernet Sauvignon – popular in the warmth and dampness of the north for its disease-resistant thick skins – the most important variety. Okahu Estate also purchases grapes from other Northland vineyards.

The barrel-fermented Clifton Chardonnay has been of variable, sometimes good-quality. I prefer the oak-aged Ninety Mile White, a blend of Chardonnay and Sémillon with plenty of ripe, buttery, leesy flavour. Okahu Estate's most memorable wines, however, are its generous, supple reds.

The Cabernet Sauvignon-based Ninety Mile Red is chunky, spicy and savoury, with firm tannins and some complexity. Shipwreck Bay Red, a characterful, easy-drinking blend of the French hybrid Chambourcin and Pinotage, is a robust, smooth red, at its best reminiscent of a solid southern Rhône.

Okahu Estate's finest achievement to date is its consistently impressive Syrah. Kaz Shiraz, as it is labelled in top vintages, is a lush, rich red overflowing with soft, peppery flavour. In lesser years, when it is labelled simply as Shiraz, it is still a rewarding wine, with true black pepper and spice varietal characters and a firm, lingering flavour.

(****½) **Kaz Shiraz**
(****)   **Shiraz**
***   **Ninety Mile White, Ninety Mile Red**
½   **Clifton Chardonnay, Shipwreck Bay Red

Auckland

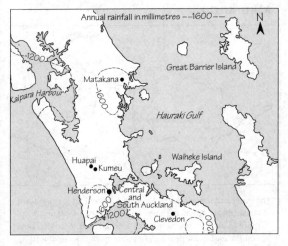

The Auckland region's wineries are concentrated in several districts – Matakana, Kumeu/Huapai, Henderson, Waiheke Island and South Auckland. A host of familiar names – Corbans, Villa Maria, Nobilo, Babich, Delegat's, Coopers Creek, Kumeu River, Matua Valley, Selaks, Collards, Lincoln, Goldwater, Stonyridge – are based here, and usually draw grapes from all over the country. Montana also has its headquarters and a giant blending, bottling and warehousing complex amidst a sea of houses in suburban Auckland.

From the turn of the century, with a cluster of Croatian wine-makers and others of English and Lebanese origin, Auckland ranked with Hawke's Bay as one of the two key centres of New Zealand wine. Today, over a quarter of the country's wine companies are still based in Auckland, but after the recent shift southwards of plantings, the region has only 3 percent of the vineyards.

After decades out of the viticultural spotlight, confidence in the region's ability to grow top class wines has lately rebounded strongly. Auckland's warmth and high sunshine hours are well-suited to red-wine production (although high rainfall, especially in West Auckland, can be a problem) and Cabernet Sauvignon is the most common variety. Consistently impressive West Auckland wines, such as Matua Reserve Sauvignon Blanc, Collards Rothesay Vineyard Chardonnay and Kumeu River Chardonnay have proven the area's white-wine potential, while the Cabernet Sauvignon and Merlot-based reds of Waiheke Island rival those of Hawke's Bay at the top of the New Zealand red-wine ladder.

Matakana

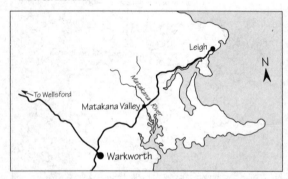

The vineyards draped across the hills surrounding the tiny town of Matakana are producing some notably classy, robust and deep-flavoured Cabernet Sauvignon and Merlot-based reds. Matakana lies on the east coast near Leigh, about an hour's drive north of Auckland city.

The Antipodean winery, now in obscurity, pioneered wine production in the district with a string of promising but ridiculously overpriced Cabernet Sauvignon-based reds from the 1985 to 1987 vintages. Heron's Flight arrived as a quality red-wine producer with its mouthfilling, brambly 1991 Cabernet Sauvignon/Merlot, and has since been joined by Providence. With eleven vineyards established in 1997, Matakana looks set to emerge as an important wine district.

HERON'S FLIGHT VINEYARD

Sharp Road, Matakana. Est 1988. Owners: David Hoskins and Mary Evans. Production: 2,250 cases.

On a north-facing clay slope overlooking the tranquil Matakana Valley, in favourable vintages David Hoskins and Mary Evans produce one of Auckland's most distinguished reds.

Hoskins (an American science and philosophy graduate who earlier worked as a teacher and community worker) and Evans planted their first vines in 1988. Today their beautiful 5-hectare vineyard is planted principally in Cabernet Sauvignon, with smaller plots of Sangiovese, the great grape of Chianti (which Heron's Flight is pioneering in New Zealand), Merlot, Cabernet Franc and Chardonnay.

Heron's Flight is one of the few New Zealand wineries to adjust its prices according to the quality of the vintage. Its 1992 Cabernet Sauvignon/Merlot, from a cool vintage, sold at $NZ20; the superior 1994 fetched $NZ27.

The first white wines were unimpressive, but the 1996 vintage whites are a big step up. La Volée, an unwooded Chardonnay, possesses good weight and depth of grapefruit and apple-like flavours in a fresh, rounded style with lots of drink-young appeal. The Barrique Fermented Chardonnay is a more complex style with strong, ripe citrus and melon characters, toasty oak and a crisp, rich finish.

Merlot-based and oak-aged, La Cerise is a supple, light-bodied red that offers buoyant, easy drinking with a touch of character. The flagship Cabernet Sauvignon/Merlot can be arrestingly good in top vintages like 1991 and 1994. Dark and sturdy, with an excellent concentration of ripe, blackcurrant-like, slightly earthy flavour, this is a bold, satisfying wine with a proven ability to flourish in the cellar.

***** ½ Cabernet Sauvignon, Merlot
(***½) Barrique Fermented Chardonnay
(***)   La Volée, La Cerise

PROVIDENCE VINEYARD

Cnr Omaha Flats Road and Takatu Road, Matakana. Est 1990. Owner: James Vuletic. Production: 1,000 cases. Winery sales by appointment.

Auckland lawyer James Vuletic is fired with a passion to produce a fine Bordeaux-style red in New Zealand. Raised at his parents' Palomino Vineyards on Auckland's North Shore, and formerly a partner in The Antipodean, in 1990 Vuletic planted a new vineyard, Providence, at Matakana.

On a north-facing clay slope, 2 hectares of Merlot (70 percent), Cabernet Franc (20 percent) and Malbec vines have been established. The wine is fermented with natural yeasts, hand plunged, given lengthy skin maceration and matured for up to two years in new French oak barriques.

The debut 1993 vintage was released at $NZ62, making it clearly New Zealand's most expensive red. 'The price is not a statement about other New Zealand reds,' says Vuletic. 'It reflects the cost of production and the wine's standard in international terms. Opus One and Dominus [from California] are no better, and any Bordeaux able to match its quality sells for more than $NZ100.'

Put to the test in a blind tasting of Auckland's most prestigious reds from the 1993 vintage, Providence performed well, matching although not outclassing the established Waiheke Island heavyweights. Perfumed, lush and concentrated, with a long, silky finish, this is a classy, beguiling red with immense charm in its youth. Vuletic also produces an impressive, mouth-filling, oak-aged dry Rosé.

(*****) Merlot, Cabernet Franc, Malbec
(****)   Rosé

THE ANTIPODEAN

Tongue Farm Road, Matakana. Est 1979. Owner: Michelle Chignell-Vuletic. Winery sales by appointment.
This tiny Matakana vineyard burst on the scene in 1988 when its first 1985 vintage red was released at a record $NZ93 per bottle, after winning high praise from several British wine writers. However, most of the New Zealand wine press was not so enthusiastic because the wine, although good, was no match for the country's finest reds, yet priced far above them.

The brainchild of brothers Petar and James Vuletic, The Antipodean was planted in 1979. The varietal mix is approximately 65 percent Cabernet Sauvignon, 30 percent Merlot and 5 percent Malbec.

After the brothers experienced a 'personal falling out' in 1988, the company was wound up. James Vuletic founded a new vineyard, Providence. Most of The Antipodean was taken over by Petar Vuletic, whose wife is now the proprietor. A trickle of high-priced, rarely seen wines is still produced, but The Antipodean is no longer a serious force.

(***½) Cabernet Sauvignon, Merlot, Malbec

Kumeu/Huapai

West Auckland's wineries are grouped in and around the Auckland suburb of Henderson and fifteen minutes' drive further to the north-west, in the gently undulating country surrounding the rural townships of Kumeu and Huapai.

Several big names of the New Zealand wine industry are based here – Coopers Creek, Kumeu River, Matua Valley, Nobilo and Selaks. Nobilo and Kumeu River pioneered winemaking in the district over half a century ago, but viticulture spread rapidly in the 1960s, when Henderson winemakers searching for cheaper land expanded to Kumeu/Huapai.

The larger companies base the vast majority of their output on grapes grown outside the district, in Gisborne, Hawke's Bay and Marlborough. Nevertheless, Kumeu River, Limeburners Bay, Harrier Rise and Bazzard Estate base their production predominantly or wholly on local fruit.

Slightly drier than Henderson, because of its distance from the bush-clad Waitakere Ranges that form Auckland's western flanks, Kumeu/Huapai is still a high rainfall area by world standards. Viticulturists have to work hard in the district's warm, humid summers and heavy clay soils, but the consistently classy Kumeu River Chardonnay, Matua Reserve Sauvignon Blanc, Collards Rothesay Vineyard Chardonnay and Coopers Creek Reserve Huapai Cabernet/Merlot show what can be achieved with painstaking vineyard management.

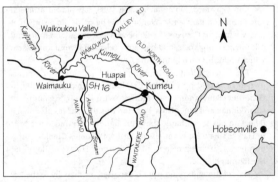

BAZZARD ESTATE

Awa Road, Huapai. Est 1982. Owners: Charles and Kay Bazzard. Production: 225 cases. Winery sales by appointment.

Passionate about Pinot Noir, Charlie Bazzard grows one of New Zealand's northernmost and rarest examples in the wooded Awa Valley, near Huapai.

Bazzard, an Englishman and former solicitor, and his Auckland-born wife, Kay, purchased their hillside vineyard, then planted in hybrids and Palomino, in 1982. After six years of replanting, the vineyard is now based principally on Pinot Noir and Chardonnay, with smaller plots of Merlot, Cabernet Sauvignon, Malbec and Cabernet Franc.

Bazzard Estate is a vineyard, not a winery – the wine is produced at a local winery to which Bazzard also sells the grapes not required for his Pinot Noir label. The initial vintages were not matured in oak, because Bazzard preferred to accentuate the wine's fresh, vibrant fruit characters. Now wood-aged, it is a chunky Pinot Noir with good depth of raspberry and dark cherry-like flavours, a touch of complexity and firm tannins.

***½ Pinot Noir

COOPERS CREEK VINEYARD

State Highway 16, Huapai. Est 1982. Owners: Andrew and Cyndy Hendry and shareholders. Production: 60,000 cases.
Of all New Zealand's small and middle-sized wineries, in recent years none has enjoyed as much success in show judgings as Coopers Creek.

Lying alongside the main road just west of Huapai township, Coopers Creek was founded in 1982 by Andrew Hendry, an accountant, and Oregonian winemaker Randy Weaver. After Weaver returned to the United States in 1988, Hendry and his wife, Cyndy, emerged as the main shareholders in Coopers Creek.

Kim Crawford, winemaker since 1988, has played a pivotal role in the company's rise. Not only has he produced a stream of classy wines for Coopers Creek; he acts as a consultant to several other wine companies, and has lately released several impressive wines under his own brand, Kim Crawford.

The estate vineyard at Huapai and adjoining properties owned or leased by Coopers Creek are planted principally in Cabernet Sauvignon and Merlot, with lesser amounts of Chardonnay and Pinot Noir. The Hendrys themselves also own a 6-hectare block of Chardonnay (predominantly) and Pinot Noir in Hawke's Bay. However, the majority of Coopers Creek's fruit is purchased from growers in Gisborne, Hawke's Bay and Marlborough.

Half of the winery's output is exported, principally to the UK but also to other parts of Europe, North America and Australia. The intensely aromatic, incisively flavoured Riesling is the finest in Hawke's Bay. The Marlborough Sauvignon Blancs (produced in unwooded and oak-aged versions) are packed with fresh, tangy, ripely herbaceous flavour. Above all, Coopers Creek is renowned for its Chardonnays.

The briefly oak-aged Gisborne Chardonnay and tank-fermented, American oak-matured Hawke's Bay Chardonnay are both rich-flavoured, vibrantly fruity wines, delicious in their youth. They are overshadowed, however, by the lush, barrel-fermented Swamp Reserve Chardonnay, a delectably rich Hawke's Bay wine with concentrated stone-fruit flavours wrapped in strong, nutty oak.

The reds, in the past less impressive than the whites, have made huge advances in recent vintages. The mid-priced Cabernet Sauvignon and Merlot from Hawke's Bay are supple, exuberantly fruity wines, highly appealing in their youth. The top claret-style wine is the powerful, complex, American oak-aged Reserve Huapai Cabernet/Merlot, one of Auckland's leading reds.

*****	Hawke's Bay Riesling, Reserve Sauvignon Blanc Oak Aged, Swamp Reserve Chardonnay
****½	Late Harvest Riesling, Marlborough Sauvignon Blanc, Reserve Huapai Cabernet/Merlot
(****½)	Reserve Pinot Noir
****	Gisborne Fumé Blanc, Hawke's Bay Chardonnay
(****)	Reserve Hawke's Bay Cabernet Sauvignon, Reserve Hawke's Bay Merlot
***½	Gisborne Chardonnay
(***½)	Hawke's Bay Cabernet Sauvignon, Hawke's Bay Merlot

HARRIER RISE

Waitakere Road, Kumeu. Est 1986. Owners: Tim and Alix Harris. Production: 4,350 cases. Winery sales weekends only.

Tim Harris, a lawyer and wine columnist for Auckland's *Metro* magazine, produces some of New Zealand's most satisfying, finely balanced and subtle reds at his small Kumeu vineyard.

The venture, until recently called Waitakere Road Vineyard, began in 1986 when Harris and several partners bought a 6-hectare block. Over the next four years, they close-planted it in Cabernet Franc, Merlot and Cabernet Sauvignon. After the syndicate disbanded in 1996, Harris and his wife, Alix, emerged as the sole owners.

Harris produces harmonious, complex, not overtly fruity reds, and readily acknowledges a debt to European winemakers. 'If you read French winemaking books,' he says, 'it's striking how for generations they've thought about their wine's structure and how best to extract colour and tannins from the skins.' Searching for 'structure and depth of fine tannins,' after the fermentation he holds his wines in contact with the skins for a long period – up to seven weeks.

Harris' reds do not enjoy a very high profile, but are well worth discovering. Harrier Rise Cabernet Franc is a supple yet powerful red, mouthfilling and deeply flavoured, with positive tannins. As a drink-young style, it's hard to beat the fleshy, meaty, slightly earthy Uppercase Merlot.

(****½)	Harrier Rise Cabernet Franc
***½	Uppercase Merlot

KERR FARM VINEYARD

48 Dysart Lane, Kumeu. Est 1989. Owners: Wendy and Jaison Kerr. Production: 900 cases. Winery sales by appointment.

Wendy and Jaison Kerr own an old Corbans vineyard in Kumeu,

near the defunct Abel and Co. winery. After buying the property in 1989, the Kerrs uprooted the hybrid vines, replaced them with Sauvignon Blanc, Cabernet Sauvignon and Merlot, and expanded the existing plantings of Sémillon, Chardonnay and Pinotage.

The wines, first produced in 1995, are made on the Kerrs' behalf at Pleasant Valley. The range includes a weighty, ripely herbal, easy-drinking Sauvignon Blanc; a lightly oaked, slightly grassy and nutty Sémillon; a savoury, creamy Chardonnay with good body and flavour depth; a berryish, supple Pinotage of variable quality; and a decent, ripe, flavoursome although not concentrated Cabernet Sauvignon.

***½ Chardonnay
***   Cabernet Sauvignon, Sauvignon Blanc, Sémillon
**½   Pinotage

KUMEU RIVER WINES

State Highway 16, Kumeu. Est 1944. Owners: The Brajkovich family. Production: 20,000 cases.

Famous for its powerful, mealy, softly seductive Chardonnay, the Kumeu River winery lies alongside the state highway, just south of Kumeu. The Brajkovich family purchased the property in 1944. With Mate Brajkovich at the helm, San Marino (as it was then called) enjoyed a strong reputation during the 1950s and 1960s for its hospitality and hybrid Kumeu Dry Red.

Since the charismatic Mate died in 1992, Kumeu River has been run by his widow, Melba, and their three sons – Michael, the winemaker, who in 1989 became New Zealand's first Master of Wine; Milan, who manages the vineyards; and Paul, who is immersed in marketing.

The Brajkovichs work solely with Kumeu fruit. The sloping 8-hectare vineyard across the highway from the winery is planted in Chardonnay, Cabernet Franc and Sauvignon Blanc. The original vineyard – now called Mate's Vineyard – is planted entirely in Chardonnay. The Brajkovichs also own a nearby 5-hectare block of Merlot vines, planted by Corbans in the 1970s, and purchase grapes from growers in the Kumeu district.

The top wines are labelled Kumeu River, with a second-tier range sold as Brajkovich. Of the three Chardonnays, the finest and most expensive is Kumeu River Mate's Vineyard, launched from the 1993 vintage, a single-vineyard wine that in some years can be clearly superior to its famous stablemate, Kumeu River Kumeu Chardonnay, which is a blend of several local vineyards. Michael Brajkovich likens the Kumeu Chardonnay to 'a village wine, with Mate's Vineyard a *premier cru* of the same village.'

Kumeu River Chardonnay, launched from the 1985 vintage, stirred controversy because it underwent a full malolactic fermentation at a time when this was rare in New Zealand. Judges rejected the wine and Kumeu River subsequently withdrew from competitions. The wine still excites a divided response. In the U.S., the 1994 vintage placed sixth in the *Wine Spectator*'s Top 100 for 1996, but in the U.K., the 1995 vintage came fourth to last in a *Wine* magazine tasting of 66 New Zealand Chardonnays in 1997.

At its best, this is a memorable wine – robust, with very rich, ripe fruit flavours and a nutty, butterscotch-like complexity. Whole bunch-pressed, fermented (with natural yeasts) and lees-aged in French oak barriques (20 to 25 percent new each year), it is an intensely flavoured, deliciously creamy wine that drinks splendidly at around three years old.

Kumeu River Sauvignon/Sémillon is a distinctive, weighty wine with lush, tropical and stone-fruit flavours and oak/lees-aging complexity. Kumeu River Merlot/Cabernet is an attractive red, savoury and spicy, but it lacks the flavour concentration of Auckland's greatest reds.

Brajkovich Chardonnay is an unwooded wine, fresh and simple. The vibrantly fruity, supple Brajkovich Cabernet Franc and deeper, firmer Brajkovich Merlot are both satisfying, everyday-drinking reds.

***** **Kumeu Chardonnay, Mate's Vineyard Chardonnay,
     Kumeu Sauvignon/Sémillon**
*** ½ **Merlot/Cabernet**
*** **Brajkovich Cabernet Franc, Brajkovich Chardonnay,
     Brajkovich Sauvignon, Brajkovich Merlot**

LIMEBURNERS BAY VINEYARDS

112 Hobsonville Road, Hobsonville. Est 1987. Owners: Alan and Jetta Laurenson. Production: 5,000 cases.

Cabernet Sauvignon, produced both as a traditional dry red and as a fortified, creamy-sweet after-dinner wine, is the chief delight at this low profile winery at Hobsonville, several kilometres to the east of Kumeu and Huapai.

Alan Laurenson and his wife, Jetta, processed their first vintage in 1987. The 2-hectare, loam-clay estate vineyard is planted principally in Cabernet Sauvignon (80 percent), with smaller plots of Merlot and Cabernet Franc. The Laurensons are also developing another, larger vineyard nearby, mainly in red grapes, including Sangiovese. White grapes are purchased from growers, usually in West Auckland.

Estate-grown and matured for fifteen months in French oak barriques (half new), the Cabernet Sauvignon is typically a strapping, densely coloured wine with concentrated blackcurrant and spice flavours and taut tannins. In lesser years, a lighter, lower-priced Cabernet/Merlot is marketed instead.

The Sauvignon Blanc is soft, full-bodied and moderately herbal; the Sémillon/Chardonnay fresh and crisp, with fullness and a touch of complexity derived from the barrel-fermented Chardonnay. Modelled on the *vins doux naturel* (fortified dessert wines) of southern France, the dark, mouthfilling (17 percent alcohol) Dessert Cabernet Sauvignon offers a delicious depth of raisiny, pruney, chocolatey flavour.

**** **Cabernet Sauvignon**
*** **Cabernet/Merlot, Dessert Cabernet Sauvignon**
½ **Sauvignon Blanc, Sémillon/Chardonnay

MATUA VALLEY WINES

Waikoukou Valley Road, Waimauku. Est 1974. Owners: The Spence and Margan families. Production: 120,000 cases.

Matua Valley – or Matua, as the winery is increasingly known – is one of the great modern success stories of New Zealand wine. From humble beginnings in a leased tin shed near Henderson in 1974, the company has expanded swiftly and carved out an international reputation for the quality and value of its wines.

The winery lies in the peaceful Waikoukou Valley, near the village of Waimauku, west of Huapai. Ross and Bill Spence, the founders, are brothers whose father, Rod, established the now-defunct Spence's Wines at Henderson in the 1940s.

The Spences are popular, high profile personalities. Ross, who describes himself as 'the thinker, the one who does the background work' is the current chairman of the Wine Institute; Bill, 'the frontman, the up-front gregarious one,' is the marketing manager. Members of the Margan family also have a sizeable stake in the company and sit on the board.

The principal grape varieties in the 22-hectare estate vineyard, planted in sandy-loam soils, are Cabernet Sauvignon, Pinot Noir, Sauvignon Blanc and Chardonnay. Matua Valley also owns vineyards in Hawke's Bay and Marlborough and since 1995 a quarter share in Rapaura Vintners, previously the contract winemaking facility known as Vintech. The company also has an interest in several joint venture vineyards. About 40 percent of the annual fruit intake is bought from growers in Gisborne, Hawke's Bay and Marlborough.

Winemaker Mark Robertson's North Island wines are marketed under the Matua label, while the Marlborough wines are branded Shingle Peak. At the pinnacle of the winery's output are the pair of Ararimu wines – the fat, lush, excitingly full-flavoured and smooth Ararimu Chardonnay (usually but not always grown in Gisborne) and the dark-hued, flavour-packed, highly concentrated Ararimu Merlot/Cabernet (most often from Hawke's Bay).

Three Sauvignon Blancs are produced. Matua Hawke's Bay Sauvignon Blanc is a full, rounded, easy-drinking style; Shingle Peak Sauvignon Blanc is aromatic, lively and incisively flavoured; Matua Reserve Sauvignon Blanc is an estate-grown, partly barrel-fermented wine with notable depth, complexity and finesse.

Apart from Ararimu, the pick of the Chardonnays is the fragrant, vibrantly fruity, gently oaked Judd Estate, a soft, elegant, finely balanced Gisborne wine that can be irresistible in its youth. The Hawke's Bay Gewürztraminer, Shingle Peak Riesling and Shingle Peak Chardonnay can also be rewarding.

Both the Smith-Dartmoor Cabernet Sauvignon and Smith-Dartmoor Merlot are Hawke's Bay wines with plenty of colour, body and flavour, although the Merlot typically shows slightly greater ripeness.

***** Ararimu Chardonnay, Ararimu Merlot/Cabernet, Reserve Sauvignon Blanc
**** Judd Estate Chardonnay, Smith-Dartmoor Cabernet Sauvignon, Smith-Dartmoor Merlot
***½ Gewürztraminer, Shingle Peak Chardonnay, Shingle Peak Riesling, Shingle Peak Sauvignon Blanc
*** Eastern Bays Chardonnay, Hawke's Bay Sauvignon Blanc, Smith-Dartmoor Cabernet/Merlot
**½ Shingle Peak Cabernet Sauvignon

HOUSE OF NOBILO

Station Road, Huapai. Est 1943. Owners: The Nobilo family and Direct Capital Limited. Production: 5,000 tonnes (equivalent to 375,000 cases but includes some bulk sales).

Of all New Zealand's wineries, Nobilo is the most export-orientated. The country's fourth largest producer, it ships vast amounts of its slightly sweet White Cloud in bulk to northern Europe, and has also established a strong presence for its premium bottled wines in the UK. Seventy percent of its output is sold offshore.

Nikola Nobilo, a Croatian immigrant now in his eighties, planted his first vines on the outskirts of Huapai in 1943. With financial assistance from a series of investors, Nobilo expanded rapidly during the 1960s and 1970s, winning a strong reputation for its stylish Huapai-grown reds and hugely popular, slightly sweet Müller-Thurgau. After a decade of being once again wholly family-owned, in 1995 the Nobilos sold a 49 percent stake to Direct Capital Limited, a publicly listed investment firm, to provide the funds for a further expansion programme designed to double its production by 1998.

Three brothers run the company. Nick Nobilo, the entrepreneurial executive chairman, has an 'overview and strategic planning' role; Steve concentrates on sales; Mark oversees the vineyards. Kerry Hitchcock, for many years chief winemaker at Corbans, joined Nobilo as chief operating officer in 1995.

The 8-hectare estate vineyard at Huapai is planted primarily in Pinotage. Nobilo also has large joint venture vineyards with Maori trusts on the east coast of the North Island, and another joint venture vineyard in Marlborough.

The company's top wine has been its exceptionally concentrated Reserve Dixon Vineyard Hand Picked Chardonnay, a single-vineyard, barrel-fermented Gisborne wine with a wealth of grapefruit-like, nutty, creamy-rich flavour; this is a striking mouthful. The Marlborough Sauvignon Blanc is a regional classic, offering very high quality at a sharp price.

The Reserve Marlborough Chardonnay and Reserve Tietjen Vineyard Chardonnay are both full-flavoured, toasty and complex, with the Marlborough wine harbouring more steely acidity. The long-popular, floral, slightly sweet Müller-Thurgau, grown at Gisborne, and the buoyantly fruity and supple Pinotage, estate-grown at Huapai, are both of consistently high quality. The unwooded Poverty Bay Chardonnay, served on British Airways, is a fresh, uncomplicated wine but can be surprisingly good, with some depth and richness.

White Cloud, designed as a generic wine to represent New Zealand, is Müller-Thurgau based, with a splash of Sauvignon Blanc, Chenin Blanc and Muscat to boost its flavour. This distinctively packaged, light, fresh, gently sweet wine has been a hit in Scandinavia, the UK and New Zealand.

The recently released range under the Fall Harvest label includes three fresh, flavourful white wines and a smooth, berry-ish, distinctly green-edged Marlborough Cabernet Sauvignon. In mid-1997, Nobilo announced it was replacing its top single-vineyard wines, such as the Dixon and Tietjen Chardonnays, with a new premium range labelled Grand Reserve and a middle-tier Icon series. The debut Grand Reserve Sauvignon Blanc 1996 is a striking wine with a powerful attack of herbaceous, steely flavour.

*****	Reserve Dixon Vineyard Hand Picked Chardonnay
(*****)	Grand Reserve Sauvignon Blanc
****½	Marlborough Sauvignon Blanc
****	Reserve Marlborough Chardonnay, Reserve Tietjen Vineyard Chardonnay Grande Reserve Chardonnay, Icon Chardonnay
***½	Müller-Thurgau, Pinotage
***	Marlborough Cabernet Sauvignon, White Cloud
(***)	Fall Harvest Chardonnay, Fall Harvest Riesling-Sylvaner, Fall Harvest Sauvignon Blanc
**½	Gisborne Chardonnay, Hawke's Bay Cabernet Sauvignon, Poverty Bay Chardonnay
(**½)	Fall Harvest Cabernet Sauvignon

SELAKS WINES

Corner Highway 16 and Old North Road, Kumeu. Est 1934. Owners: The Selak family. Production: 80,000 cases.

Selaks specialises largely in white wines, with some exceptional Sauvignon Blancs to its credit. A long-established West Auckland company, it has recently invested heavily in Marlborough, establishing its own vineyards and a gleaming new winery in the region.

Marino Selak, a Croatian immigrant, planted his first vines at

Te Atatu, near Henderson, in 1934. Six years later he was joined by his nephew, Mate Selak, who devoted his life to building up the company. In the 1960s, urban expansion forced the company to shift to Kumeu.

Since Mate's death in 1991, the winery has been run by his sons, Ivan, who handles the administration, and Michael, who concentrates on marketing. The third key figure is Australian Darryl Woolley, winemaker since 1985.

Selaks' 16-hectare Drylands Vineyard in Marlborough is planted in Sauvignon Blanc, Sémillon and Chardonnay. White-wine grapes are purchased from growers in Gisborne and Marlborough, and red-wine grapes from Hawke's Bay.

Selaks' top Marlborough Sauvignon Blancs rank among the finest of all. My favourite is the explosively flavoured Sauvignon Blanc/Sémillon, a 60/40 blend fermented and lees-aged for three to four months in French oak barriques. This is a mouth-water-ingly crisp and lively wine, bursting with fresh, subtly oaked, gooseberry and green capsicum-like flavour. The slightly higher priced, single vineyard, unwooded Drylands Estate Sauvignon Blanc and oak-matured Founders Reserve Sauvignon Blanc can be equally thrilling.

The widely available, sharply priced Marlborough Sauvignon Blanc is fresh, flavourful and zesty, with plenty of varietal char-acter; this wine accounts for over a third of Selaks' total output.

The citrusy, partly barrel-fermented Marlborough Char-donnay and more complex, more new oak-influenced, bolder and richer Founders Reserve Chardonnay are both stylish wines. The Marlborough Rieslings are scented, limey and zesty, and respond well to bottle-aging.

Selaks' reds are not distinguished, typically lacking body and flavour richness. However, the non-vintage bottle-fermented sparkling wines, Brut and Extra Dry, are bargain priced and classy, with tight, delicate, subtle, lingering flavours. The flag-ship, Chardonnay-based Mate I Selak Blanc de Blancs is notably rich, yeasty and toasty.

*****	Founders Reserve Sauvignon Blanc, Sauvignon Blanc/Sémillon
(*****)	Drylands Estate Sauvignon Blanc
****½	Founders Reserve Chardonnay, Mate I Selak Blanc de Blancs
****	Méthode Traditionnelle Brut, Méthode Traditionnelle Extra Dry
***½	Marlborough Chardonnay, Marlborough Sauvignon Blanc, Riesling, Riesling Dry
***	Ice Wine
**½	Gisborne Fumé
**	Cabernet Sauvignon

Henderson

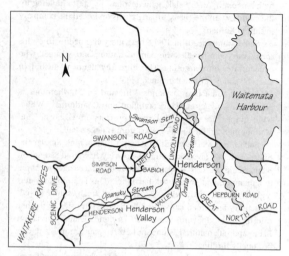

The West Auckland wine trail is unique. Most of the producers are heavily reliant on grapes grown further south. Nowhere else but in the cellars of Henderson, Kumeu and Huapai can you commonly taste wines grown in Auckland, Gisborne, Hawke's Bay and Marlborough.

Henderson's wineries lie twenty kilometres from the centre of Auckland, strung out along Lincoln Road and in the folds of the Waitakere Ranges. All are small or medium-sized (Corbans retains its headquarters but no winery here) and three – Babich, Collards and Delegat's – are of international repute. The oldest company, Pleasant Valley, first produced wine in 1902.

For several decades, the large Croatian winemaking community made Henderson one of the centres of New Zealand wine. Croatian names abound – Babich, Erceg (Pacific), Fredatovich (Lincoln), Ivicevich (West Brook), Mazuran, Ozich (St Jerome), Soljan, Yelas (Pleasant Valley). Nevertheless, the district's high rainfall, high humidity and heavy clay soils pose problems for viticulturists, and since the 1960s urban sprawl has also led the winery owners to reduce or eliminate their vineyards. In the past decade, the large Penfolds and Corbans wineries in the area have also closed.

Henderson still has about 25 producers, giving it one of the largest cluster of wineries in the country. Almost all the wines are grown elsewhere, but a few successful estate-grown labels, such as Collards Barrique Fermented Sémillon, Pleasant Valley Signature Selection Pinotage and St Jerome Cabernet Sauvignon/Merlot, show what can be done.

BABICH WINES

Babich Road, Henderson. Est 1916. Owners: The Babich family.
Production: 82,500 cases.

Nestled in beautiful rolling country on the edge of Henderson, Babich is a classic example of the long-established, middle-sized, family-owned wineries of Croatian origin that play a crucial role in the New Zealand wine industry. For decades Babich had a reputation for good, sharply priced wines, but a policy of heavy investment in premium Hawke's Bay vineyards has recently produced a stream of white and red wines of exceptional quality.

Six years after arriving in New Zealand, in 1916 Josip ('Joe') Babich produced his first wine in the gumfields of the Far North. After shifting to Henderson in 1919, he established a small mixed farm with fruit trees, vegetables – and classical Meunier vines. During the Second World War winemaking emerged as the key element in the family business.

Today Babich is controlled by Josip's two sons, Peter (chairman of the board) and Joe, the rangy, modest general manager who is also chairman of judges at the Air New Zealand Wine Awards; their sister, Maureen, is also actively involved in the company. Neill Culley, a versatile graduate of Roseworthy College and master of business administration who previously worked as assistant winemaker under Joe Babich and then as marketing manager, now holds the production reins.

Planted principally in Chardonnay, Pinotage and Pinot Noir, the 20-hectare estate vineyard is the largest in Henderson. Babich, in partnership with investors, also owns substantial vineyards at Fernhill and Gimblett Road in Hawke's Bay, has an exclusive supply contract with the owners of Irongate Vineyard, and buys grapes from growers in Gisborne, Hawke's Bay and Marlborough.

The Babich wine style is distinctive. Sledgehammer, high impact, heavily oaked styles are avoided. Instead, the accent is on delicacy, balance and finesse, which always gives the wines great drinkability.

The two Irongate wines, from an arid, stony vineyard in Gimblett Road, are both classics; the Chardonnay lean, steely and notably long-lived; the Cabernet/Merlot dark, cedary, brambly, complex and firm. Yet to achieve the same recognition in shows, but equally fine, is the richly flavoured, barrel-fermented Mara Estate Sauvignon.

The Mara Estate range (named in honour of the company matriarch, Mara Babich, Josip's wife, who died in 1994) also includes a citrusy, slightly buttery Chardonnay and a trio of impressively weighty and ripely flavoured (even in cooler vintages) reds – Syrah, Merlot and Cabernet Sauvignon. Positioned in the mid-price range, the Mara Estate reds even offer good value compared to imported wines – an achievement matched by only a few other New Zealand reds.

The Babich selection also includes a bargain priced, fresh-scented, ripely flavoured and racy Marlborough Sauvignon Blanc; two enjoyable, citrusy, gently oaked Chardonnays, East Coast and Hawke's Bay; zingy, full-flavoured, slightly herbaceous wines under the Fumé Vert and Sémillon/Chardonnay labels; a ripe, rounded Hawke's Bay Sauvignon Blanc and a supple, buoyantly fruity Pinotage/Cabernet.

Lately added to the range are flagship wines under The Patriarch label. Defined as 'the most outstanding white or red wine from any given vintage', the initial releases were a strapping, mealy, rich Hawke's Bay Chardonnay and perfumed, robust, very intense Hawke's Bay Cabernet Sauvignon.

***** **Irongate Chardonnay, Irongate Cabernet/Merlot, Mara Estate Sauvignon, The Patriarch Cabernet Sauvignon, The Patriarch Chardonnay**
**** **Mara Estate Cabernet Sauvignon, Mara Estate Merlot, Mara Estate Syrah, Marlborough Sauvignon Blanc**
***½ **Mara Estate Chardonnay**
*** **East Coast Chardonnay, Fumé Vert, Hawke's Bay Chardonnay, Hawke's Bay Sauvignon Blanc, Pinotage/Cabernet, Sémillon/Chardonnay**

COLLARD BROTHERS

303 Lincoln Road, Henderson. Est 1946. Owners: The Collard family. Production: 22,500 cases.

The Collard family does not promote its wines aggressively, but its Chardonnays, Chenin Blancs and Rieslings rank among the finest in the land.

This small to medium-sized producer in traffic-clogged Lincoln Road is one of the few Henderson wineries not of Croatian background. John Collard, an English berry-fruit expert, purchased the property in 1910 and five years later married Dorothy Averill, whose brothers in 1928 established the Averill Winery just along the road. In 1946 John and Dorothy Collard's sons, Lionel and Brian, started making their own wines.

Lionel Collard, a fiercely independent perfectionist, celebrated his fiftieth vintage in 1996. 'My greatest thrill,' he recalls, 'was when we were awarded the first gold medal in New Zealand for a Riesling [Collards 1978].' He still oversees the company's administration and sales, with one son, Bruce, as winemaker, and another, Geoffrey, running the vineyards.

Bruce Collard works with fruit drawn from Auckland, the Waikato, Hawke's Bay and Marlborough. The estate vineyard, under severe urban pressure, has contracted to only 2 hectares, but the company also owns the 15-hectare Rothesay Vineyard in the Waikoukou Valley, near Matua Valley.

Chardonnay is the focal point of the range. The flagship Rothesay Vineyard Chardonnay is a powerful, robust Auckland wine with a wealth of ripe, tropical fruit and citrus flavours and deftly judged oak. The mid-priced Hawke's Bay and Marlborough Chardonnays are both elegant wines with a touch of complexity. Blakes Mill Chardonnay, based partly on Auckland fruit, is a fresh, vibrant, fruit-driven style designed for early consumption.

The off-dry Marlborough Riesling and medium Rhine Riesling (typically a three-way regional blend of Auckland, Hawke's Bay and Marlborough fruit) are both perfumed, penetrating, immaculately balanced wines, notably fresh, delicate and lively. The Hawke's Bay Chenin Blanc, which includes a small proportion of Waikato fruit and is matured briefly in seasoned French oak casks, is richly scented, with excellent depth of ripe, pineappley flavour; this competes with The Millton Vineyard's as New Zealand's champion Chenin Blanc.

The Marlborough Sauvignon Blanc is typically fresh, crisp and verdant, but often outshone by the Rothesay Vineyard Sauvignon Blanc, a fuller-bodied, rounder style with delicious depth of lush, tropical fruit flavours.

For many years, Collards' Achilles heel was the lack of a top-class red. That weakness has recently been eliminated by the release of the sturdy, chocolatey, spicy Rothesay Vineyard Cabernet Sauvignon and the classy, mouthfilling, deliciously rich and supple Marlborough Pinot Noir.

*****	Hawke's Bay Chenin Blanc, Marlborough Riesling, Rothesay Vineyard Chardonnay
****½	Marlborough Pinot Noir, Rhine Riesling, Rothesay Vineyard Sauvignon Blanc
****	Barrique Fermented Sémillon, Rothesay Vineyard Cabernet Sauvignon
***½	Blakes Mill Chardonnay, Hawke's Bay Chardonnay, Marlborough Chardonnay, Marlborough Sauvignon Blanc
**½	Private Bin Dry White
**	Cabernet/Merlot

CORBANS WINES

426-448 Great North Road, Henderson. Est 1902. Owner: DB Group Limited. Production (NZ wine, estimated): 18,000 tonnes (equivalent to 1,350,000 cases, but much is packaged in casks).

The sturdy figure of Assid Abraham ('A.A.') Corban, with his magnificent walrus moustache and trademark waistcoat and chains, gazes sternly down from the wall in the entrance to Corbans' head office at Henderson. For much of the first half of this century the winery he founded dominated the New Zealand wine scene. Today, still ranking as the country's second-largest wine giant, Corbans is a subsidiary of DB Group Limited and through shareholding links is ultimately controlled by the Dutch brewer Heineken NV.

Spurred by tales of the riches amassed by emigrants to the

New World, Corban, a Lebanese stonemason, arrived in New Zealand in 1892. The origin of Corbans Wines lies in Corban's purchase in 1902 of a 10-acre (4-hectare) block of scrub-covered Henderson gumland. After planting 'Mt Lebanon Vineyards' in such *vinifera* grapes as Syrah, Chasselas and Cabernet Sauvignon, Corban's first vintage in the new land flowed in 1908.

With Assid Abraham's sons also involved – Wadier as wine-maker and Khaleel as a tireless travelling salesman – Corbans prospered through prohibition and depression. By the time of the patriarch's death in 1941 Corbans had become a household name. In the 1950s and 1960s his grandson, Alex, kept Corbans in the vanguard of the industry's quality advances by pioneering the use of cold fermentation, selected fermentation yeasts and bulk fermentation of sparkling wines.

Hand in hand with the wine boom of the 1960s, however, came Montana's challenge to Corbans' longstanding industry dominance. To strengthen the company's financial clout, 10 wine and spirit merchants were admitted to a 19 percent shareholding in 1964. The outside-ownership wedge had been inserted and was to be driven home deeper in the early 1970s when Rothmans acquired a 25 percent shareholding. In 1979 Rothmans (later renamed Magnum Corporation, and then DB Group Limited) gained absolute control.

Then followed a period of massive investment in new wine-making equipment and the planting of the extensive company-owned vineyards in Marlborough, notably Stoneleigh. The quality of wines bearing the Corbans label, which had stood still during the 1970s, rose sharply. Then in 1987 Corbans, itself a subsidiary of Brierley Investments Limited, bought another Brierley-owned wine firm, Cooks/McWilliam's, giving Corbans an estimated 30 percent share of the market for New Zealand wine.

In the most recent ownership change, Brierley sold its major-ity stake in DB Group Limited in 1993 to Singapore-based Asia Pacific Breweries Limited, itself controlled by Heineken NV.

A widely dispersed operation, Corbans owns vineyards in Hawke's Bay and Marlborough, wineries at Te Kauwhata, Gisborne, Hawke's Bay and Marlborough, and a final blending, bottling and warehousing complex at East Tamaki, on the other side of Auckland city from its head office.

The majority of Corbans' grapes are purchased from contract growers in Gisborne, Hawke's Bay and Marlborough (although its cask wines and cheaper bottled wines are sometimes a blend of New Zealand and imported wine). However, about 50 percent of its premium varietal grapes are grown in the company's Stoneleigh and Moorlands vineyards (150 hectares) adjoining Corbans Marlborough Winery, and in the three Longridge vine-yards (120 hectares) in Hawke's Bay.

Under general manager Noel Scanlan – 28 years with the company – Corbans markets a diverse array of brands, including

Corbans, Cooks, Stoneleigh Vineyard, Longridge of Hawke's Bay, Robard & Butler and Huntaway. About 250,000 cases are exported annually, principally to the UK but also in significant volumes to Sweden, Finland, the Netherlands, Belgium, Germany, Canada and the eastern USA.

At the summit of Corbans' range are the Cottage Block wines, 'handcrafted from hand-picked grapes [and] made in the true style of boutique winemaking'. The label was launched in 1994, so few vintages of each wine have been released, but the powerful, arrestingly fragrant, flavour-drenched Cottage Block Gisborne Chardonnay has swiftly established itself as one of New Zealand's most memorable Chardonnays. Another standout is the thrillingly perfumed and intense, raisiny, honey-sweet Cottage Block Marlborough Noble Rhine Riesling.

Under the buff-coloured Private Bin label – until recently reserved for the top bottlings – can be found several highly impressive wines, notably the steely, biscuity Marlborough Chardonnay, enticingly fragrant, lush, citrusy and soft Gisborne Chardonnay and rich, spicy, honeyish Amberley Riesling, grown at Waipara in North Canterbury.

Under the Cooks Winemakers Reserve label, Corbans produces a lush, buttery, strongly oak-influenced Hawke's Bay Chardonnay and a dark, chunky, rewardingly full-flavoured Hawke's Bay Cabernet Sauvignon. The recently introduced Huntaway Reserve range, restricted to Gisborne wines, includes a highly fragrant, vibrantly fruity Chardonnay, perfumed, rich and supple Merlot and a Pinot Gris with ripe, rounded, peachy, spicy flavours.

The highlight of the Stoneleigh Vineyard selection of Marlborough wines is the Riesling, a full-bloomed wine with concentrated lemony, limey, slighty honeyish flavours that build in the bottle for a decade; even longer. The Sauvignon Blanc is fresh, aromatic and cuttingly herbaceous; the Chardonnay appley, nutty and crisp. The weakness in the range is the typically light and green-edged Cabernet Sauvignon.

Corbans' North Island equivalent of the Stoneleigh Vineyard selection is its Longridge of Hawke's Bay range. The Chardonnay, French and American oak-aged, is a sound wine with a touch of complexity, and the Sauvignon Blanc Oak Aged is a skilfully balanced wine with fresh, limey, tangy flavours. Depending on the year, the Cabernet Sauvignon/Merlot veers from light and green-edged to full-bodied and ripely flavoured, but the multiple award-winning Gewürztraminer is consistently perfumed, peppery and pungent.

The Corbans Estate range – marketed in the UK under the Cooks label – offers a range of well priced, consistently sound wines with clearcut varietal characters and pleasing flavour depth.

For many years, Corbans appeared content to let Montana

dominate the bottle-fermented sparkling wine field in New Zealand. No longer. Amadeus, a very stylish and lively, nutty, yeasty blend of Hawke's Bay Pinot Noir and Chardonnay, is one of the country's classiest sparklings – and bargain-priced. The notably refined Verde, similarly based on Hawke's Bay Pinot Noir and Chardonnay and even cheaper than Amadeus, swept all other sparklings aside at the 1996 Air New Zealand Wine Awards.

(A note on abbreviations: CB stands for Corbans Cottage Block; PB for Corbans Private Bin; Longridge for Longridge of Hawke's Bay; R & B for Robard & Butler; Stoneleigh for Stoneleigh Vineyard.)

*****	CB Gisborne Chardonnay, CB Noble Rhine Riesling, PB Amberley Riesling, PB Gisborne Chardonnay, PB Marlborough Chardonnay, Stoneleigh Riesling
****½	Amadeus Méthode Champenoise, Longridge Gewürztraminer
(****½)	CB Marlborough Chardonnay, CB Marlborough Merlot/Cabernet Sauvignon, CB Marlborough Pinot Noir, Cooks Winemakers Reserve Hawke's Bay Cabernet Sauvignon, Huntaway Reserve Gisborne Chardonnay, Huntaway Reserve Matawhero Merlot, Verde Méthode Traditionnelle
****	Cooks Winemakers Reserve Chardonnay, Stoneleigh Sauvignon Blanc
(****)	CB Hawke's Bay Cabernet Sauvignon/Franc, CB Hawke's Bay Chardonnay, Huntaway Reserve Gisborne Pinot Gris, Huntaway Reserve Gisborne Sémillon, PB Hawke's Bay Cabernet Sauvignon/Merlot
***½	Longridge Sauvignon Blanc Oak Aged, R & B Gisborne Mendoza Chardonnay, Stoneleigh Chardonnay
(***½)	Cooks Winemakers Reserve Hawke's Bay Pinot Noir
***	Cooks Gisborne Chardonnay, Cooks Gisborne Sauvignon Blanc, Estate Gisborne Chardonnay, Estate Gisborne Sauvignon Blanc, Estate Marlborough Gewürztraminer, Estate Marlborough Rhine Riesling, Longridge Cabernet Sauvignon/Merlot, Longridge Chardonnay, PB Hawke's Bay Pinot Noir
(***)	R & B Hawke's Bay Chardonnay, R & B Marlborough Dry Riesling
**½	Stoneleigh Cabernet Sauvignon, White Label Johannisberg Riesling
**	White Label Chardonnay/Chenin Blanc, White Label Sauvignon Blanc/Sémillon

DELEGAT'S WINE ESTATE

Hepburn Road, Henderson. Est 1947. Owners: Jim and Rose Delegat.
Production: 120,000 cases.

The stocky, ambitious Jim Delegat and his popular sister, Rose, are the only brother and sister team to head a major New Zealand winery. Delegat's, like Babich and Selaks, is a quality-orientated, medium-sized winery of Croatian roots.

Nikola (Nick) Delegat purchased the property in 1947 and within a year had planted 4 hectares of vines. In the early decades Delegat's fortified wines enjoyed a strong following. Following the founder's death in 1973, Jim assumed control, bringing table wines much more to the fore, and by the early 1980s Delegat's had built a strong reputation for its bold, buttery Chardonnays.

The third key figure is winemaker Brent Marris, who since his 1986 arrival at Delegat's has won a host of top awards in competitions, especially for his striking Proprietors Reserve Chardonnay. (Marris also releases a pair of top-flight wines under his own Wither Hills label, discussed in the Marlborough section.)

Unlike most other New Zealand wineries of a comparable size, Delegat's specialises in just four grape varieties – Chardonnay, Sauvignon Blanc, Merlot and Cabernet Sauvignon – from just two regions – Hawke's Bay and Marlborough. In Hawke's Bay the company owns a 25-hectare vineyard in the Gimblett Road shingle country, and another 20-hectare vineyard on State Highway 50, backing onto Gimblett Road. In the upper Wairau Valley of Marlborough, the sweeping 55-hectare Oyster Bay vineyard has also recently been established.

Only the Hawke's Bay wines are marketed under the Delegat's brand, with the top models designated as Proprietors Reserve; the Marlborough wines are labelled as Oyster Bay. (In 1997 Delegat's also purchased Conders Bend, a small Marlborough-based company, acquiring its stocks and brand.)

Unlike most of New Zealand's leading Chardonnays, Delegat's Proprietors Reserve is not fully barrel-fermented; Marris wants to preserve its splendidly rich, ripe fruit character. Half the final blend is tank-fermented and then matured on its yeast lees for nine months in new and one-year-old French oak barriques; the rest is handled in oak throughout, with regular lees stirring. Very powerful, sustained and downright delicious, this is one of Hawke's Bay's greatest Chardonnays.

The mid-priced, lightly oaked Hawke's Bay Chardonnay is a fruity, uncomplicated style, attractive in its youth. It is overshadowed by the classy Oyster Bay Chardonnay (75 percent barrel-fermented) with its pure, incisive fruit flavours, touch of mealy richness and fresh, appetising acidity.

The unwooded Hawke's Bay Sauvignon Blanc is a full-bodied, tropical fruit-flavoured, well-rounded wine in an easy-drinking style. The pick of the winery's Hawke's Bay fruit, however, is reserved for the Proprietors Reserve Sauvignon Blanc Oak Aged. Half barrel-fermented and all oak-aged, this is a highly seductive wine bursting with ripe, pineapple and melon-evoking fruit flavours, enhanced by judicious use of oak. The Oyster Bay Sauvignon Blanc is also typically chock-full of zingy, tropical fruit and fresh-cut grass flavour.

Delegat's mid-priced Hawke's Bay Cabernet/Merlot, matured in seasoned oak barrels, is a medium-bodied style with fresh, berryish, plummy, slightly green-leafy flavours. The two premium Hawke's Bay reds – Proprietors Reserve Cabernet Sauvignon and Proprietors Reserve Merlot – are both substantial, full-flavoured and complex, but particularly in cooler vintages the riper-tasting, more supple Merlot has the edge.

*****	**Proprietors Reserve Chardonnay, Proprietors Reserve, Oak Aged Sauvignon Blanc**
****½	**Oyster Bay Chardonnay, Proprietors Reserve, Merlot**
****	**Oyster Bay Sauvignon Blanc, Proprietors Reserve, Cabernet Sauvignon**
***½	Hawke's Bay Sauvignon Blanc
***	Hawke's Bay Chardonnay
**½	Hawke's Bay Cabernet/Merlot

LINCOLN VINEYARDS

130 Lincoln Road, Henderson. Est 1937. Owners: The Fredatovich family. Production: 45,000 cases.

Lincoln is one of the larger family-owned wineries of Croatian origin in West Auckland, although the wines have yet to reach the heights of such comparable companies as Delegat's and Babich.

Peter Fredatovich Jnr and his brother, John, who assumed control of the winery in the late 1980s, exude the gentleness and easy warmth typical of the Fredatovich family. Their father, Peter Snr, until his retirement, held the reins at Lincoln for three decades. His own father, Petar, who established Lincoln on its present, now house-encircled, property in 1937, coopered casks out of native timber to accommodate the wine grown on his half-hectare, overhead-trellised vineyard.

Winemaker Ian Trembath, who joined Lincoln following the departure of Nick Chan, who made the 1985 to 1994 vintages, works with grapes grown in Auckland, Gisborne, Hawke's Bay and Marlborough. The Home Vineyard, a 2.5-hectare block alongside the winery, is planted principally in Cabernet Sauvignon, with a smaller plot of Merlot and Muscat vines over 40 years old.

Gold medals for the 1992 Vintage Selection Chardonnay (grown in Gisborne) and 1993 Vintage Selection Cabernet/Merlot (grown in Kumeu and Henderson) are among the recent highlights, but overall the wines are sound rather than spectacular.

Three low-priced, easy-drinking wines – Chardonnay,

Merlot/Cabernet and Classic, a blended medium-dry white – are
produced under the Manuka Hill label. Chenin Blanc and – to a
lesser extent – Chenin Blanc/Chardonnay blends are a winery
specialty, typically fresh, lively and tart. But above all, Lincoln is
known for its rich, citrusy, soft Gisborne Chardonnays.

The budget-priced Lincoln Gisborne Chardonnay, briefly
matured in French and American oak casks, is a straightforward,
drink-young style. The very fragrant, fruity, American oak-fermented and matured Lincoln Parklands Chardonnay is delicious
in its youth – soft and creamy. At its best – and its quality has
been variable – the top-end-of-the-range Vintage Selection
Chardonnay is even more elegant and concentrated.

The aged ports – Anniversary Show Reserve and Old Tawny –
are both rich, raisiny and creamy-smooth. The reds are typically
chunky and flavoursome, although not refined, but the richly
coloured, fragrant and flavour-packed Vintage Selection
Cabernet/Merlot 1993 represents Lincoln's finest red-wine hour.

****   Anniversary Show Reserve Port, Old Tawny Port,
         Vintage Selection Chardonnay
***½   Parklands Chardonnay, Vintage Selection Cabernet/
         Merlot
***   Marlborough Sauvignon Blanc, The Home Vineyard
         Cabernet/Merlot
(***) Gewürztraminer, Hawke's Bay Cabernet Sauvignon,
         Hawke's Bay Chenin Blanc/Chardonnay
**½   Gisborne Chardonnay, Hawke's Bay Chenin Blanc,
         Manuka Hill Classic
(**½) Hawke's Bay Rhine Riesling, Hawke's Bay Sauvignon
         Blanc, Manuka Hill Merlot/Cabernet
(**)   Manuka Hill Chardonnay

MAZURAN'S VINEYARD

*255 Lincoln Road, Henderson. Est 1939. Owner: Rado Hladilo.
Production: 1,500 cases.*

This small Henderson winery preserves almost intact the now
largely vanished traditions of 'sherry' and 'port' production.
George Mazuran, the Croatian founder, enjoyed a highly successful career as a political lobbyist representing small family-owned
vineyards, and 25 to 40 years ago his dark, treacley, creamy-
smooth, liqueur-like fortified wines dominated New Zealand
competitions. However, the current owner, Rado Hladilo –
Mazuran's son-in-law – has not engaged seriously in table wine
production and the winery has now slipped into obscurity.

***   Old Tawny Port 1954
**½   Dry Sherry

PACIFIC VINEYARDS

90 McLeod Road, Henderson. Est 1936. Owners: Michael and Millie Erceg. Production: 250 tonnes (equivalent to 18,750 cases, but some is packaged in casks).

A decade ago Pacific was one of New Zealand's larger wineries, with a production accent on low-priced wine casks and wine coolers. Today its output is heavily reduced, but in some vintages it includes one of the country's most arresting Gewürztraminers.

The Croatian founder, Mijo (Mick) Erceg, planted his first vines on the now densely suburban property in Henderson in 1936. His timing was perfect; war soon broke out and alcoholic beverages of any kind became scarce, sending the demand for New Zealand wine skyrocketing. 'I sold some wine to an American serviceman for ten shillings a gallon – he was very happy. Then a fortnight later I heard that wine was being sold for 30 shillings a gallon. So I bought a distillery, put in a cellar and planted five or six acres in grapes. In 1943 in went another five acres ...'

After Mijo Erceg's death in 1983, control of Pacific passed to his widow, Millie. She still runs the winery shop and its adjacent vineyard, but today the majority shareholder is their son, Michael (holder of an American PhD in mathematics), who markets Pacific wines through his importing, production and distribution company, Independent Liquor.

The utilitarian winery backs onto the 4-hectare estate vineyard, planted in Cabernet Sauvignon and Merlot. Winemaker Steve Tubic, who joined Pacific in 1987, works with grapes sourced from Auckland, Gisborne and Hawke's Bay.

The premium varietal wines carry the Phoenix brand. Phoenix Chardonnay, grown in Hawke's Bay and two-thirds fermented and matured in French and American oak barriques (the rest is handled in stainless steel) is a decent wine – fresh, crisp, ripe and toasty. The estate-grown, French and American oak-aged Phoenix Cabernet Sauvignon and Phoenix Merlot are reasonably flavoursome but slightly green-edged and rustic.

These are workmanlike wines, with one exception – the full-bloomed, highly concentrated Phoenix Gewürztraminer. Grown in the Thomas vineyard in Gisborne, the wine is not consistently outstanding, but at its best offers a voluminous fragrance and a riveting intensity of peppery, lychee-like, honeyish flavour.

****Phoenix Gewürztraminer
**½ Phoenix Cabernet Sauvignon, Phoenix Merlot

PLEASANT VALLEY WINES

322 Henderson Valley Road, Henderson. Est 1902. Owner: Stephan Yelas. Production: 11,000 cases.

The resurgence of Pleasant Valley, a much-respected winery in the 1960s whose prestige was later eroded, is one of the most heartening aspects of the current Henderson wine scene. Pleasant Valley ranks as the oldest surviving winery in New Zealand under the continuous ownership of the same family.

Stipan Jelich (Stephan Yelas), a Croatian immigrant, made the first wine at his hillside vineyard in 1902 from vines planted in the late nineteenth century. Under his son Moscow's direction between 1939 and 1984, Pleasant Valley carved out a strong reputation for its Château Yelas Pinotage, Riesling-Sylvaner, Pinot Chardonnay, Hock, 'sherries' and 'ports'.

The winery stagnated, however, during the last decade of Moscow's stewardship; only since his son, Stephan, took over the reins in 1984 has Pleasant Valley again sought to compete on quality terms with its competitors. The original kauri winery, still housing 'sherry' and 'port'-filled barrels from Moscow's era, has been modernised and a qualified winemaker, Rebecca Salmond, employed (Salmond also produces consistently attractive Hawke's Bay Sauvignon Blancs, Chardonnays and Cabernet/Merlots under her own Odyssey label).

The 12-hectare, sloping estate vineyard on the southern flanks of the Henderson Valley is planted in Pinotage, Cabernet Sauvignon, Merlot and Chardonnay. Fruit is also purchased from growers in Auckland (Kumeu), Gisborne and Hawke's Bay.

Of the top-tier Signature Selection wines, the best-known is the Pinotage, a vibrantly fruity, berryish and savoury red, full of Beaujolais-like charm. Why is it so good? 'It's where it's grown,' says Stephan Yelas. 'The vines are in a bowl on a steep, sunny, north-facing hillside. It's sheltered from the wind and gets really, really hot.' This is one of New Zealand's finest Pinotages.

The Signature Selection Cabernet/Merlot, also estate-grown, has impressively concentrated cassis, plum and oak flavours, braced by firm tannins. The lower-priced Auckland Cabernet Sauvignon is another characterful, chewy Henderson red with good depth of blackcurrant and mint flavours.

Two Chardonnays are produced – a deliciously fragrant, fresh and buoyant, lightly wooded Gisborne Chardonnay that drinks well within months of the vintage; and the more complex and slowly evolving Signature Selection model, a stylish, barrel-fermented Hawke's Bay wine with tight, persistent, mealy flavours. Also worth discovering are the barrel-matured 'sherries' – Amontillado, Amoroso and Oloroso – which are notably rich, mellow and lingering, and the Aged Founders, a fifteen-year-old, notably rich and mellow tawny 'port'.

**** Aged Founders, Signature Selection Cabernet/Merlot, Signature Selection Pinotage
***½ Auckland Cabernet Sauvignon, Signature Selection Brut, Signature Selection Chardonnay
*** Gisborne Chardonnay, Signature Selection Sauvignon Blanc
**½ Gisborne Gewürztraminer

SEIBEL WINES

113-117 Sturges Road, Henderson. Est 1987. Owners: Norbert and Silvia Seibel. Production: 2,250 cases.

Norbert Seibel is a quiet man, not given to screaming the merits of his own wines. Born in Mainz, Germany, he graduated from the Geisenheim Institute and later worked in South Africa, as chief winemaker for Nederburg and then The Bergkelder, before he came to New Zealand in 1980 as chief winemaker for Corbans.

'Working in these large firms,' recalls Seibel, 'I began to develop the conviction that the true potential of any vineyard or grape variety is best realised on a small scale, with individual and expert attention.' He resisted becoming a 'flying winemaker' – flying, that is, around New Zealand's wine regions. After resigning from Corbans in 1986, Seibel worked as a consultant winemaker before giving birth to his own label in 1987.

For the first few years, Seibel had no winery, but in 1993 he and his wife, Silvia, bought the old Bellamour Winery (once called Balic Estate and, before that, Golden Sunset), founded by Joseph Balic in 1912. The grapes are all purchased from growers in Gisborne, Hawke's Bay and Marlborough.

Not surprisingly for a German winemaker, Seibel is captivated by Riesling. His White Riesling Medium-Dry is a dryish wine which captures well the inimitable delicacy and lemon and lime-like flavours of Riesling. The White Riesling Classic Dry, matured on its yeast lees in 'wine sweetened' (old) barrels, is a complex wine mingling fruit flavours with slightly nutty oak.

The barrel-fermented, strongly 'malo'-influenced Marlborough Chardonnay is designed for early drinking – full and soft, with good depth of citrusy, buttery, rounded flavour. Its stablemate, the Limited Edition Marlborough Chardonnay, is a bolder, more complex style with loads of crisp, peachy, citrusy, mealy flavour.

The dry to medium-dry Chenin Blancs (a favourite variety of Seibel since he worked in South Africa and later made the famous Corbans Tolaga Bay Chenin Blanc 1976) and bone-dry Sauvignon Blancs are characterful wines that age well. At the bottom of the range the two Long River wines, white and red, which in different vintages have been based on different varieties, both offer good value.

****   Limited Edition Marlborough Chardonnay
***½   White Riesling Classic Dry, White Riesling Medium-Dry
***   Gewürztraminer Semi-Dry, Hawke's Bay Chardonnay, Hawke's Bay Chenin Blanc, Hawke's Bay Sauvignon Blanc, Long River Cabernet Sauvignon/Pinotage, Marlborough Chardonnay, Marlborough Sauvignon Blanc
**½   Hawke's Bay Cabernet/Merlot, Long River Sauvignon Blanc

SOLJANS WINES

263 Lincoln Road, Henderson. Est 1937. Owner: Tony Soljan.
Production: 7,500 cases.

There's a lot going on at Soljans. Apart from producing a wide array of white, red and fortified wines, proprietor Tony Soljan caters for social functions in his popular 'wine garden' and offers a contract bottling service (and complete riddling, disgorging and packaging service for bottle-fermented sparkling wines) to other wineries.

Frank Soljan, a Croatian immigrant, bought the property in 1937 and established Soljans Wines. His two sons, Tony and Rex, ran the company for many years until 1994, when Rex withdrew from the partnership.

The original winery today serves as the vineyard shop. The long-term winemaker, Tony Soljan, a sunny extrovert, has shared the winemaking duties since 1993 with Sarah Hennessy, one of several women to hold senior positions in the company. The 3-hectare estate vineyard, with its beautiful overhead-trellised vines, is planted principally in Cabernet Sauvignon, Merlot and Seibel 5455 (for 'port'). Red-wine grapes are purchased from Kumeu and white-wine varieties from Gisborne, Hawke's Bay and Marlborough.

Long respected as a producer of high quality fortified wines, Soljans is now pursuing the table wine market. My favourite wines are the nutty-brown, raisiny Pergola Sherry, a mellow, ten- to fifteen-year-old with impressive *rancio* complexity, and the West Auckland-grown, briefly French oak-matured Pinotage, typically mouthfilling, supple and packed with berryish, plummy, meaty flavour.

The estate-grown Barrique Selection Cabernet/Merlot is a fragrant wine with subtle French oak influence, delicate, ripe flavours and a smooth finish. The Hawke's Bay Chardonnays are pleasantly soft in their youth but tend to peak early. Both the Rhine Riesling and Gewürztraminer are fresh, slightly sweet and flavoursome.

Two sparklings are produced. Momento is an unabashedly sweet, Muscat-based, Asti Spumante look-alike of high quality. Legacy, a vintage-dated, bottle-fermented blend of Hawke's Bay Pinot Noir and Chardonnay, is a full-flavoured style with citrusy, buttery, moderately complex flavours.

****   Pergola Sherry, Pinotage
***½ Barrique Selection Cabernet/Merlot, Momento
***   Barrique Selection Chardonnay, Gewürztraminer,
       Legacy, Rhine Riesling
**½   Sauvignon Blanc
**   Chardonnay

ST JEROME WINES

219 Metcalfe Road, Henderson. Est 1963. Owners: The Ozich family. Production: 7,500 cases.

The small St Jerome winery lies in the foothills of the Waitakere Ranges, only a kilometre from Babich. Founded in the 1960s by Mate Ozich (and originally called Nova, then Ozich), St Jerome is known principally for its muscular, concentrated, tautly structured Cabernet Sauvignon/Merlot.

Today Mate's sons, Davorin and Miro, run the company. Miro focuses on the vineyard; Davorin, who has an MSc in biochemistry and worked the 1987 vintage at the fabled Bordeaux châteaux, Margaux and Cos d'Estournel, handles the administration and winemaking.

The sunny, 8-hectare estate vineyard behind the winery, sloping steeply to the north, is planted in 60 percent Cabernet Sauvignon and 40 percent Merlot. The Ozich brothers also buy white-wine grapes and fruit for their lower-tier reds from growers, principally in Hawke's Bay.

The soft, well-spiced Gewürztraminer and citrusy, slightly honeyed Rhine Riesling are both characterful, full-flavoured wines. The barrel-fermented Hawke's Bay Chardonnay is typically full-bodied, with plenty of peachy, ripe flavour.

St Jerome's claim to fame rests squarely with its strapping, estate-grown Cabernet Sauvignon/Merlot. Davorin Ozich, who was powerfully influenced by his Médocian sojourn, reports he came away 'confident about how to handle red wine'. The fermenting juice is hand-plunged four times daily; after the fermentation the skins are kept submerged in the wine for three weeks, boosting its colour, flavour and tannins; and the wine is matured in French oak barriques for a very long time – up to three years.

The result is an almost opaque, notably robust red with a powerful surge of blackcurrant and cedarwood flavours, buttressed by firm tannins. Past vintages were often austere, with more chunky, raw power than finesse, but the 1991 and subsequent releases have kept the flavour concentration for which the wine is known while exhibiting greater fragrance, delicacy and suppleness.

**** **Cabernet Sauvignon/Merlot**
***   **Chardonnay Sauvignon Blanc, Gewürztraminer, Rhine Riesling**
** ½ **Cabernet Sauvignon, Estate Dry White**
**   **Dry Red**

WEST BROOK WINERY

34 Awaroa Road, Henderson. Est 1935. Owner: Anthony Ivicevich.
Production: 11,250 cases.

Tucked away unobtrusively amidst a sea of houses in Henderson, not far from Delegat's, West Brook is a small, traditionally low profile winery with a fast-improving array of sharply priced wines.

Originally called Panorama, the winery was founded by Mick and Tony Ivicevich, father and son Croatian immigrants who modestly marketed their first 'sherry' and 'port' in 1937 in unlabelled beer bottles. Tony's rangy, amiable son Anthony and his wife, Sue, who now run the company, have steered it away from its past emphasis on fortified wines to varietal table wines, and in 1987 changed the winery's name to West Brook to underline the change of direction. Anthony and Sue's son, Michael, who is studying winemaking while gathering experience at other wineries, also has crucial input.

White-wine grapes are sourced from Gisborne, Hawke's Bay and Marlborough. The 2.5-hectare home vineyard behind the winery is planted predominantly in Cabernet Sauvignon, with some Merlot and Chardonnay.

Of the top-tier wines, which carry the Blue Ridge label, the best so far is the fresh, frisky, penetratingly flavoured Marlborough Sauvignon Blanc. The estate-grown Blue Ridge Cabernet/Merlot typically displays ripe fruit and good flavour concentration, but less fragrance and finesse. The straight Merlot, not labelled as Blue Ridge, is a pleasant, plummy, supple Henderson red, designed for early consumption.

Other satisfying West Brook white wines are the Barrique Fermented Chardonnay, at its best impressively robust, deep-flavoured, mealy and rounded, and the rich, slightly sweet, well-spiced Gewürztraminer.

***½   Barrique Fermented Chardonnay, Blue Ridge
        Marlborough Sauvignon Blanc, Gewürztraminer
***   Hawke's Bay Sauvignon Blanc, Merlot
**½   Blue Ridge Cabernet/Merlot, Chenin Blanc, Riesling

Waiheke Island

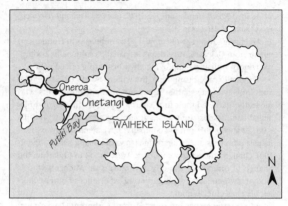

The pocket-sized red-wine specialists on Waiheke Island have fired the imagination of New Zealand's wine lovers as much as any other vineyards to have emerged in recent years. The magical ingredients are the stunning beauty of the island itself, set in Auckland's Hauraki Gulf, and the sheer power and richness of such celebrated reds as Goldwater Estate Cabernet Sauvignon/Merlot, Stonyridge Larose Cabernets and Te Motu Cabernet/Merlot.

Waiheke's typically warm, dry ripening season (not markedly warmer than the mainland, but decidedly drier) is a key factor in the wines' success. As Stephen White, owner of Stonyridge Vineyard, has written: 'Like France, New Zealand has a marginal climate for growing Cabernet Sauvignon, so I was looking for an area with higher summer temperatures (26-32°C), a maritime influence, low rainfall in January, February and March, and a poor but free-draining soil ... I chose Waiheke.'

Waiheke is set to play a crucial role in New Zealand's red-wine future. More than twenty small vineyards have been established, mostly at the western, more heavily populated end of the island. The top Cabernet-based wines rival those of Hawke's Bay for quality – and offer greater vintage-to-vintage consistency.

GOLDWATER ESTATE

Causeway Road, Putiki Bay, Waiheke Island. Est 1978. Owners: Kim and Jeanette Goldwater. Production: 10,500 cases.

Goldwater Estate, which pioneered the production of quality reds on Waiheke Island, today produces one of New Zealand's most prestigious Cabernet Sauvignon/Merlots – dark, weighty, concentrated and classy.

Kim Goldwater, a sandy-haired engineer turned fashion photographer turned winemaker, and his wife, Jeanette, planted their first vines on Waiheke in 1978. Their sloping vineyard, over-looking placid Putiki Bay on the island's south-west coast, was originally established entirely in Bordeaux varieties: Cabernet Sauvignon, Merlot and Cabernet Franc for a blended, claret-style red and Sauvignon Blanc for an estate white (since replaced by Chardonnay.) By 1982 they had their debut – a Cabernet-based red of arresting colour and flavour intensity.

The Goldwaters' vineyards on Waiheke now cover 12 hectares. The Goldwaters also purchase Sauvignon Blanc and Chardonnay from Marlborough to satisfy their UK agent's request for the region's white wines.

The celebrated Cabernet Sauvignon/Merlot is one of New Zealand's most Bordeaux-like reds – intense, complex, tightly structured. 'Classic Bordeaux techniques used by the top châteaux,' is how Kim Goldwater describes the vinification. The fermenting juice is pumped over its skins rather than hand-plunged; the wine is held on its skins for 15 to 25 days after the ferment has subsided to soften its tannins; and then matured for a year to 18 months in French oak barriques, typically half new. In its youth powerful, brambly and strongly oak-influenced, it overflows with rich, ripe, blackcurrant-and-spice flavours framed by taut tannins.

The Roseland Marlborough Chardonnay offers fresh, ripe cit-rus and melon-like fruit flavours wrapped in toasty oak. The Dog Point Marlborough Sauvignon Blanc also shows the typical Goldwater characters of mouthfilling body and ultra-ripe flavour.

***** Cabernet Sauvignon/Merlot
(****) Dog Point Marlborough Sauvignon Blanc
***½ Roseland Marlborough Chardonnay

PENINSULA ESTATE

52 Korora Road, Oneroa, Waiheke Island. Est 1986. Owners: Doug and Anne Hamilton. Production: 1,500 cases.
On an elevated, windy site with a striking view over Big Oneroa Beach, Peninsula Estate produces an impressively sturdy, bram-bly, flavour-packed Cabernet/Merlot, in its youth cloaked with tannin.

Doug Hamilton, a former mechanic, and his wife, Anne – who has lived on the island all her life – planted their first vines in 1986. The exposed vineyard has been established on one of Waiheke's cooler sites, typically ripening its 2.5 hectares of Cabernet Sauvignon, Merlot, Cabernet Franc and Malbec grapes two weeks later than most of the other vineyards. Chardonnay, Syrah and red Bordeaux varieties have also recently started com-ing on stream from a neighbouring 2.5-hectare vineyard owned by Robert and Emerald Gilmour.

Winemaker Christopher Lush produces two reds. Robust, chewy and flavourful, Oneroa Bay Cabernet/Merlot is designed for early drinking or short-term aging. The flagship Cabernet Sauvignon/Merlot, matured for a year in French oak barriques (one-third new each year), is an even burlier wine with deep colour, masses of blackcurrant fruit and grippy tannins, ideal for cellaring.

****½ Cabernet Sauvignon/Merlot
***½ Oneroa Bay Cabernet/Merlot

STONYRIDGE VINEYARD

Onetangi Road, Waiheke Island. Est 1982. Owner: Stephen White. Production: 1,275 cases.

If auction prices are an accurate guide, New Zealand's greatest reds are Te Mata Coleraine Cabernet/Merlot, from Hawke's Bay, and a bold, dark, seductively perfumed red with smashing fruit flavours grown near Onetangi Beach on Waiheke – Stonyridge Larose Cabernets.

Stephen White, the driving force behind Stonyridge, has a clear goal: 'to make one of the best Médoc-style reds in the world.' After graduating from Lincoln University with a diploma in horticulture, White worked in Tuscan and Californian vineyards, and at Châteaux d'Angludet and Palmer in Bordeaux, before his first vines sank root in Stonyridge's poor, free-draining clay soils in 1982.

A hill quarry called Stonyridge looms to the west of the property. The 4.5-hectare, low-yielding (average 5 tonnes per hectare) vineyard, sloping gently to the north, is planted principally in Cabernet Sauvignon, with smaller plots of Merlot, Cabernet Franc, Malbec, Petit Verdot, Montepulciano, Syrah (for a future Rhône-style red) and Chardonnay (for the future Stonyridge white). In his stylish terracotta, concrete and timber winery, White pursues a 'simple and traditionally French' approach to winemaking, including long skin maceration, a second label to enable 'selection', maturation in French oak barriques and selling *en primeur*.

Estate-grown since 1995 (before that based on bought-in grapes), the second-tier Airfield red is named after the landing strip that divides Stonyridge from its neighbour, Waiheke Vineyards. Based on fruit from younger vines, but also used as the only label in a lesser vintage like 1992, Airfield Cabernet is typically an impressive red in its own right, full of sweet-fruit charm, with less oak influence, softer tannins and more drink-young appeal than Larose.

Not that Larose isn't accessible in its youth – this ravishingly perfumed, deep-flavoured and supple red can be pure pleasure to drink at two years old. In other vintages, the wine is denser and tighter, needing five years to unfold. It is matured for a year in 70 to 100 percent new French oak barriques, but the wine is essentially a celebration of spicy, minty, superbly ripe, extraordinarily intense berry fruit flavours. Only a few hundred cases of Larose are produced each year, and the *en primeur* offer is typically fully subscribed within three days.

***** Larose Cabernets
****   Airfield Cabernets

TWIN BAYS

56 Korora Road, Oneroa. Est 1988. Owners: Barry and Meg Fenton. Production: 150 cases.

One of Waiheke's rarest reds is grown by Barry and Meg Fenton at Oneroa on a headland flanked by two bays. Fruit from the 2.5-hectare vineyard, planted in Cabernet Sauvignon, Merlot and Cabernet Franc, is processed at nearby Peninsula Estate by consultant winemaker Kim Crawford. A good although not memorable wine simply called 'The Red' appears in lesser vintages. Fenton, the top wine, can be irresistible at just two years old – dark and ravishingly fragrant, with a wealth of rich, sweet-tasting blackcurrant and spice flavours, wrapped in quality oak.

(*****) Fenton
(***½) The Red

WAIHEKE VINEYARDS

Onetangi Road, Waiheke Island. Est 1989. Owners: The Dunleavy and Buffalora families. Production: 1,600 cases. No winery sales.

It took only one vintage – the arrestingly dark, fragrant and flavour-packed Te Motu Cabernet/Merlot 1993 – to establish this fledgling producer as a Waiheke Island heavyweight. In fact, the company itself is often referred to by the name of its flagship red, Te Motu – an abbreviated version of the Maori name for Waiheke Island, Te Motu-Arai-Roa ('the island-sheltering-long').

Owned by the Dunleavy and Buffalora families, the venture is run on a day-to-day basis by three Dunleavys – John, who oversees the vineyard; his brother, Paul, who administers the finances; and their father, Terry, who handles the distribution and promotion and carved out a high profile (as 'Mr Wine') while executive officer of the Wine Institute from 1975 to 1990.

The first vines were planted in 1989. Today, the 4-hectare vineyard near Stonyridge, only half a kilometre from the coast at Onetangi, is established in 80 percent Cabernet Sauvignon, 15 percent Merlot and 5 percent Cabernet Franc. The wine is crushed, fermented and pressed at the vineyard, then transported to Matua Valley's winery in West Auckland to be matured and bottled by consultant winemaker Mark Robertson. An on-site winery is on the drawing boards.

A lower-tier, less oak-influenced red designed for early consumption is labelled Dunleavy Cabernet/Merlot. Its big brother, Te Motu Cabernet/Merlot, is a notably rich wine with rare breed.

Matured in French and American oak barriques, it is densely coloured and sturdy, with tight-knit, brambly, nutty flavours. This is a classic claret-style red, taut, concentrated and complex.

***** **Te Motu Cabernet/Merlot**
(***½) **Dunleavy Cabernet/Merlot**

Great Barrier Island

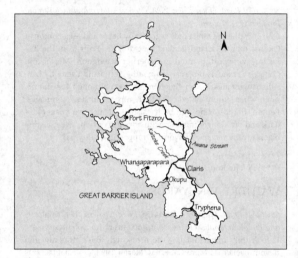

JOHN MELLARS OF GREAT BARRIER ISLAND

Okupu Beach, Great Barrier Island. Est 1990. Owner: John Mellars. Production: 150 cases. Winery sales by appointment.

Further out in Auckland's Hauraki Gulf than Waiheke, on the larger, more rugged Great Barrier Island, John Mellars makes one of New Zealand's rarest reds. After a twenty-year career as an owner of a computer company, Mellars built a tiny winery and tends a hectare of Cabernet Sauvignon and Merlot vines on his steep, north-facing slope overlooking Okupu Beach. The 1994 and 1995 vintages proved slightly flawed, but the first 1993 vintage yielded 156 bottles of hearty, warm red with loads of rich, ripe, smooth-flowing flavour and great drinkability. The 1996 vintage is also impressively fragrant, subtle and full-flavoured.

(*****) **Great Barrier Cabernet**

Central and South Auckland

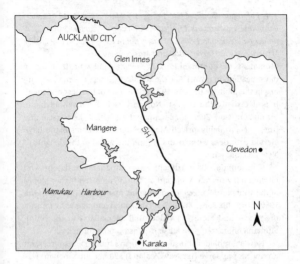

ARAHURA VINEYARD

Ness Valley Road, Clevedon. Est 1991. Owners: Ken and Diane Mason. Production: 350 cases. Winery sales by appointment.

The recent release of 40 cases of powerful, chewy, complex Arahura Merlot 1994 marked the emergence not only of a new winery in South Auckland, but of the historic first wine from the Clevedon area.

Ken Mason, a retired judge, and his wife, Diane, intend to produce a single, claret-style red. Their son, Tim, who worked for five years as a cellarhand at Montana, and has worked vintages for other companies in Hawke's Bay and California, is also heavily involved. In the family's 2-hectare clay vineyard, first planted in 1991, the major varieties are Merlot (50 percent) and Cabernet Sauvignon (30 percent), with smaller plots of Cabernet Franc and Malbec.

A winery was erected for the 1997 vintage, and the Masons expect production to climb to about 1,000 cases. The first 'commercial' release will be of 1996 Merlot/Cabernet Franc/Malbec in early 1998. The scarce 1994 Merlot, produced with the aid of consultant winemaker Mark Robertson, and matured for eighteen months in French and American oak casks, is an auspicious debut – powerful but highly approachable, with concentrated cassis/plum flavours, sweet oak, an earthy, savoury complexity and strong but supple tannins.

(****½) Merlot

MONTANA

171 Pilkington Road, Glen Innes, Auckland. Est 1944. Owner: Corporate Investments Limited. Production (NZ wine, est): 25,000 tonnes (equivalent to 1,875,000 cases, but much is packaged in casks). Winery sales in Hawke's Bay and Marlborough.

Montana is the dominant force in New Zealand wine. In the early days, nestled on a West Auckland hillside, it was the highest winery in the land; by the late 1970s it was one of the best and today it is decisively the largest. Not only is it a household name throughout New Zealand; such popular labels as its consistently fine, yet affordably priced Marlborough Sauvignon Blanc have alerted countless wine lovers around the world to the delights of New Zealand wine.

The founder, Ivan Yukich, was a Croatian immigrant who planted a 0.2-hectare vineyard at Titirangi, on the higher slopes of the Waitakere Ranges, producing his first wines in 1944. In the 1960s, with his sons, Frank – a far-sighted and aggressive entrepreneur – and Mate – a viticultural specialist – at the helm, Montana embarked on a crash expansion programme.

New shareholders bolstered the firm's financial resources; an unprecedently large (for New Zealand) 120-hectare vineyard was planted at Mangatangi, in the Waikato; Gisborne farmers were contracted to supply additional fruit; and in 1972 Montana opened a gleaming new winery at Gisborne. A year later, Seagram, the multinational distilling and winemaking company, purchased a 40 percent shareholding and Montana was listed on the stock exchange; simultaneously came the historic thrust of new vineyards into Marlborough.

Montana and the hard-driving Frank Yukich parted company in 1974, when the relationship between Yukich and Seagram turned sour. A decade later, during the wine industry's ferocious price war, Seagram itself pulled out. The listed Corporate Investments Limited – whose largest shareholder is Peter Masfen, one of New Zealand's wealthiest men – gained effective control in 1985. A year later, Montana purchased Penfolds Wines (NZ) Limited, absorbing its key staff and equipment. In the late 1980s, Montana made a decisive move into Hawke's Bay, snapping up hundreds of hectares of established vineyards and the old McDonald winery.

Montana is a leviathan, with company-owned vineyards and wineries in Gisborne, Hawke's Bay and Marlborough. Last year it claimed a 44 percent share of the domestic market for New Zealand wine. It is discussed in the Auckland section of this book because its head office and principal blending, bottling and warehousing facilities are based there (refer also to The McDonald Winery in the Hawke's Bay section).

Montana grows about half of its grape requirements. Much of the crop for its lower priced wines is purchased from contract growers; bulk wine from such countries as Australia, Spain and Chile is also imported and blended with New Zealand wine for sale in everyday-drinking bottled wines and casks. However, Montana has 'management control' over 1,000 hectares of grapes (including 250 hectares of vineyards it sold in 1995 but leased back for 60 years), and about 75 percent of the grapes for its premium varietal wines are sourced from its own vineyards.

At Montana's Marlborough winery, on the outskirts of Blenheim, looms a tank farm with a storage capacity of 20 million litres; the largest tanks hold the equivalent of almost three quarters of a million bottles of wine. From the regions, much wine then rolls north by rail to Auckland for its final blending, bottling and maturing under the direction of Auckland-based chief winemaker, Jeff Clarke.

Montana made some of the country's finest wines in the early to mid-1980s, with its readily available Marlborough Sauvignon Blanc and Marlborough Rhine Riesling frequent gold medal winners. Then followed a five-year period when Montana, seemingly content to produce large volumes of good, but rarely memorable wines, was surpassed in quality terms by the more complex Chardonnays and premium reds produced by its smaller rivals. The 1990s, however, have brought a new wave of top-flight wines from Montana.

Most of the best white and red wines are marketed under the Montana Estates, Church Road and Saints labels. The flagship Estates range, based on grapes cultivated in Montana's own vineyards, includes a lush, savoury Ormond Estate Chardonnay from Gisborne, a citrusy, nutty, steelier Renwick Estate Chardonnay from Marlborough; a gingery, deliciously rich-flavoured Patutahi Estate Gewürztraminer from Gisborne; the lush, tropical fruit-flavoured, subtlely oaked Brancott Estate Sauvignon Blanc from Marlborough; and the impressively mouthfilling and minty Fairhall Estate Cabernet Sauvignon, also Marlborough-grown.

Montana's greatest appeal for wine lovers, however, is its ability to produce stylish, satisfying wines at sharp prices that clearly reflect the company's economies of scale. The Church Road wines (discussed under The McDonald Winery in the Hawke's Bay section) and Saints range surpass the quality of many boutique wines, yet are almost all very affordably priced.

The Saints selection includes a mouthfilling, soft Gisborne Chardonnay packed with ripe, peachy, toasty flavour; a full, zingy, gently oaked Marlborough Sauvignon Blanc with ripe, searching flavours; a generous, dark, rich-flavoured, American oak-aged Hawke's Bay Cabernet/Merlot that would be the envy of many Australian wineries; and a luscious, raisiny, richly botrytised Marlborough Noble Riesling.

The recently launched Montana Reserve range of Marlborough wines includes a fresh, appley, slightly creamy, American oak-aged Reserve Chardonnay; a deep-scented, ripely flavoured

Reserve Sauvignon Blanc; and a rich, chewy, fairly complex Reserve Pinot Noir.

At the core of the company's wide selection of table wines lie the hugely popular varietals marketed under the Montana brand – Marlborough Sauvignon Blanc, Marlborough Riesling, Gisborne Chardonnay, Marlborough Chardonnay and Cabernet Sauvignon/Merlot.

Oak plays no part in the handling of Montana's world famous Marlborough Sauvignon Blanc, which places its accent squarely on the explosive flavours of slowly ripened Marlborough grapes. Grown in the sweeping Brancott vineyard, machine-harvested and cool-fermented in stainless steel tanks, this is a zesty, assertive style of Sauvignon Blanc, packed with green capsicum-like flavour, appetisingly crisp and fresh. After five to fifteen years' cellaring it offers mellow, toasty drinking, but is much less exciting than in its punchy, verdant youth.

The fresh, citrusy, uncomplicated Gisborne Chardonnay (New Zealand's biggest selling Chardonnay) and richer, more complex, more oak-influenced Marlborough Chardonnay both offer great value. So does the fragrant, strong flavoured and tangy, slightly sweet Marlborough Riesling. For many years a weak point in Montana's range was its light, herbaceous Marlborough Cabernet Sauvignon, but since the 1994 vintage, blending with Hawke's Bay fruit and Merlot has produced a much more satisfying, darker, riper Cabernet Sauvignon/Merlot.

Don't overlook the bubblies. From its Asti Spumante look-alike, Bernadino Spumante, to the exceptionally stylish Deutz Marlborough Cuvée (produced with technical guidance from the Champagne house of Deutz and Geldermann), Montana is the key force in New Zealand's sparkling wine production. The famous Lindauer Brut is a blend of Pinot Noir (60 percent-plus), Chardonnay and Chenin Blanc, grown in Marlborough and Gisborne, and matured on its yeast lees for eighteen months. It's easy to drink a lot of this crisp, yeasty, delicately flavoured wine, especially at its bargain price.

*****	Church Road Reserve Chardonnay, Deutz Marlborough Cuvée
(*****)	Church Road Reserve Cabernet/Merlot
****½	Church Road Cabernet/Merlot, Deutz Marlborough Cuvée Blanc de Blancs, Fairhall Estate Cabernet Sauvignon, Ormond Estate Chardonnay, Patutahi Estate Gewürztraminer, Saints Noble Riesling
(****½)	Saints Marlborough Sauvignon Blanc
****	Brancott Estate Sauvignon Blanc, Church Road Chardonnay, Lindauer Brut, Lindauer Special Reserve, Marlborough Rhine Riesling, Marlborough Sauvignon Blanc, Renwick Estate Chardonnay, Saints Gisborne Chardonnay, Saints Hawke's Bay Cabernet/Merlot

(****)	Reserve Chardonnay, Reserve Pinot Noir, Reserve Sauvignon Blanc, Saints Gisborne Gewürztraminer, Saints Hawke's Bay Pinotage
***½	Bernadino Spumante, Cabernet Sauvignon/Merlot, Marlborough Chardonnay
(***½)	Azure Bay Cabernet Sauvignon, Late Harvest Selection
(***)	Azure Bay Sauvignon/Sémillon, Jackman Ridge Cabernet Sauvignon, Timara Riesling
***	Lindauer Rosé, Lindauer Sec
**½	Azure Bay Chardonnay/Chenin Blanc, Gisborne Chardonnay, Timara Cabernet/Merlot
**	Jackman Ridge Chardonnay, Jackman Ridge Riesling, Jackman Ridge Sémillon/Sauvignon Blanc, Timara Chardonnay/Sémillon

ST NESBIT WINERY

Hingaia Road, Karaka. Est 1981. Owner: Dr Tony Molloy QC. Production: No 1996 vintage. No winery sales.

Always rare, the exceptional claret-style red from St Nesbit will be totally unprocurable for a few years; the release in 1997 of the 1991 vintage marked the winery's last release until the year 2001 or 2002.

Dr Tony Molloy QC, a distinguished tax lawyer, planted his first vines in fertile, loamy soils on an arm of the Manukau Harbour at Karaka, not far from Auckland's southern motorway, in 1981. It is a cool site by Auckland standards, where in some vintages the fruit ripens several weeks later than on Waiheke Island.

For many years, Molloy's vines came under assault by rabbits and birds. After the original block of Cabernet Sauvignon was found to be infected by leafroll virus, the vines were levelled with a chainsaw. A new, 3-hectare vineyard has been planted in Merlot (70 percent), Petit Verdot (which Molloy was the first to import into New Zealand), Malbec and Cabernet Franc.

Molloy makes the wine himself. In a bid to maximise its individuality, he uses only natural, 'wild' yeasts, does not chaptalise, and adds minimal amounts of sulphur dioxide. The wine (in the past mostly but not always Cabernet Sauvignon-predominant) has typically had a strong new French oak influence, been wood-matured for about three years, and then bottle-aged until its release at about five or six years old.

With their notable delicacy and breed, the 1984 to 1991 vintages of St Nesbit established themselves among New Zealand's classiest reds, in a spicy, subtle, complex and firm style highly reminiscent of true claret. Given Molloy's track record, his future Merlot-based reds will be well worth waiting for.

*****   St Nesbit

VILLA MARIA ESTATE

5 Kirkbride Road, Mangere. Est 1961. Owner: George Fistonich and family. Production: 277,500 cases.

Villa Maria boasts not only a range of good, sometimes excellent, 'private bin' (in reality widely available) wines, but also 'reserve' whites and reds equal in quality to any other wines in the country. Its extraordinary avalanche of gold medals and trophies in the past decade tells its own story of wine quality.

A winery of Croatian origin, Villa Maria has grown to become New Zealand's third largest wine company. (The Vidal and Esk Valley wineries, both part of the Villa Maria empire, are treated separately in the Hawke's Bay section.) In 1949 Andrew Fistonich made his first wine at Mountain Vineyards in Mangere, South Auckland. Fistonich's son, George, later took over the reins, formed a new company, and in 1961 launched his first wine – Villa Maria Hock.

Villa Maria grew apace through the 1960s and 1970s, absorbing the old Vidal winery in 1976. George Fistonich, now in his mid-fifties, is a quiet man whose outward restraint gives little hint of his lifelong passion for Villa Maria.

Villa Maria was severely knocked by the wine industry's pitched price battle of a decade ago, and in late 1985 slid into receivership. The subsequent phoenix-like rise from the ashes of 1985 has been extremely heartening. A major capital injection by Grant Adams enabled Villa Maria to eliminate its debts swiftly and even, in 1987, to buy the ailing Glenvale winery – since renamed Esk Valley. The company stopped producing price-sensitive cask wines and placed far greater emphasis on expanding its share of the more profitable bottled wine market.

Today, Villa Maria (with its subsidiaries) claims a 9 percent share of the domestic market for New Zealand wine, and an over 20 percent share of the bottled white and red wine market. Grant Adams sold his shareholding to Mangere farmer and grapegrower Ian Montgomerie in 1991, but in 1996 Montgomerie sold his shares to the Fistonich family, restoring Villa Maria fully to Fistonich control.

The vast majority of Villa Maria's grapes are grown by contract grapegrowers, with whom the company's team of viticulturists, headed by Steve Smith, Master of Wine, liaises closely. However the company does own the estate vineyard at Esk Valley, and has recently established the 20-hectare, densely planted, principally red-wine Ngakirikiri vineyard in shingle country near Gimblett Road in Hawke's Bay. Villa Maria also manages and buys the grapes from a 42-hectare block of Sauvignon Blanc, Chardonnay and Riesling, established in the Awatere Valley by a group of small investors, Seddon Vineyards.

Under winemaker Michelle Richardson, Villa Maria produces a brilliant array of wines, with strength right through the ranks.

The top wines, labelled 'reserve', include the strikingly powerful, rich and creamy Reserve Barrique Fermented Chardonnay, based on 'super-ripe' fruit matured in 70 percent new oak; the slightly leaner, steelier, more slowly evolving Reserve Marlborough Chardonnay; two thrillingly intense Reserve Marlborough Sauvignon Blancs, labelled as Wairau Valley and Clifford Bay (Awatere Valley); the dark, robust, flavour-packed, firmly structured Reserve Cabernet Sauvignon/Merlot, grown in Hawke's Bay and matured in French and American oak casks; and the gloriously perfumed and succulent Reserve Noble Riesling, usually grown in Marlborough, which is New Zealand's top sweet white on the show circuit.

The second-tier Cellar Selection range is designed to show-case fruit flavours, with less use of oak than in the Reserve range. The Cellar Selection Chardonnay places its emphasis on fresh, strong citrus/melon flavours, crisp and lively, with subtle wood and lees-aging characters adding a touch of complexity. The Cellar Selection Sauvignon Blanc, faintly oaked, is essentially a celebration of fresh, crisp, gooseberry and green capsicum-flavoured Marlborough fruit. Plummy, slightly toasty, rich-flavoured and supple, the Cellar Selection Merlot/Cabernet Sauvignon has strong drink-young appeal.

The standard of the third-tier Private Bin range has risen sharply in the past few years. The earlier focus on regional wines has been partly replaced by a policy of widespread blending across regions, in a bid to achieve even higher quality. The Private Bin Chardonnay, for instance, blends the fragrant, soft, tropical fruit flavours of Gisborne grapes with the fresh, tangy characters of Marlborough grapes. The Private Bin Sauvignon Blanc marries the ripe, easy-drinking nature of Gisborne and/or Hawke's Bay fruit with the herbaceous style of Marlborough. The Private Bin Gewürztraminer, Müller-Thurgau, Riesling (especial-ly), Chenin Blanc/Chardonnay and Cabernet Sauvignon/Merlot are all consistently attractive – and bargain-priced.

*****	Reserve Barrique Fermented Chardonnay, Reserve Cabernet Sauvignon/Merlot, Reserve Noble Riesling
(*****)	Reserve Marlborough Riesling, Reserve Clifford Bay Sauvignon Blanc, Reserve Wairau Valley Sauvignon Blanc
****½	Reserve Marlborough Chardonnay
(****½)	Cellar Selection Riesling
****	Cellar Selection Chardonnay, Cellar Selection Merlot/Cabernet Sauvignon, Cellar Selection Sauvignon Blanc, Private Bin Riesling
***½	Private Bin Gewürztraminer, Private Bin Sauvignon Blanc
***	Private Bin Cabernet Sauvignon/Merlot, Private Bin Chardonnay, Private Bin Chenin Blanc/Chardonnay, Private Bin Müller-Thurgau

Waikato/Bay Of Plenty

South and over the low Bombay Hills from Auckland, about a dozen wineries are scattered thinly across the Waikato and Bay of Plenty regions. The wineries here are an eclectic mix of medium-sized high fliers like Morton Estate, upmarket boutiques and more humble producers.

Grape yields are lower in the Waikato's loam-clay soils than in Gisborne and the region, although warm and sunny, also shares Auckland's drawbacks for grapegrowing of high rainfall and humidity. With the southwards shift of viticulture, since 1986 the area in vines has plummeted from 206 hectares (5.3 percent of total plantings) to only 117 hectares (1.9 percent of the total producing area) in 1996. Chardonnay, Sauvignon Blanc and Cabernet Sauvignon are the most common varieties.

From 1897, the presence of the government viticultural research station at Te Kauwhata provided a focal point for Waikato grape-growers, but the historic station closed several years ago and was sold to Rongopai. The Cooks winery at Te Kauwhata, viewed in the early 1970s as a triumph of 'space age' technology, is now used by Corbans for bulk wine storage.

In the Bay of Plenty to the east, the area in vines is tiny, but Morton Estate and Mills Reef (both heavily reliant on Hawke's Bay grapes) are sizeable, prestigious producers.

Waikato

DE REDCLIFFE ESTATES

Lyons Road, Mangatawhiri. Est 1976. Owner: Otaka Holdings (NZ) Limited. Production: 20,000 cases.

It sounds French and it's Japanese-owned, but the handsome, stone-walled De Redcliffe winery sits in the isolated Mangatawhiri Valley, 45 minutes south of Auckland by road, 'much less by helicopter'.

Chris Canning, the founder, planted his first vines in 1976, and soon won a following for his light but elegant Cabernet/Merlot. A self-described 'marketing entrepreneur', Canning also master-minded, in the late 1980s, the erection of Hotel du Vin, New Zealand's only vineyard hotel, just a stone's throw from the winery. To fund this $NZ8 million venture, De Redcliffe Group Limited, which owned the hotel, winery and vineyard, was launched on the stock exchange in 1987. After reporting a major trading loss in 1989, in early 1990 the company was sold to the Japanese-owned Otaka (NZ) Limited; Canning soon after ended his involvement.

Winemaker Mark Compton, who joined De Redcliffe in 1987, works with grapes drawn from the ravishingly beautiful,

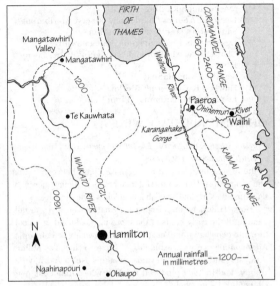

rose-bordered estate vineyard, planted in alluvial soils overlying gravels. This 6-hectare vineyard is planted principally in Chardonnay, with lesser amounts of Pinot Noir and Sémillon. However, the majority of De Redcliffe's grapes are purchased from growers in Auckland, the Waikato, Hawke's Bay and Marlborough. Three new vineyards are being developed on a joint venture basis in Hawke's Bay and Marlborough, enabling the company to boost its production while maximising its control over fruit quality.

The Marlborough Riesling is attractively scented, full and tangy, with lots of fresh, delicate, lemon/lime flavour, a sliver of sweetness and long finish. The Reserve Marlborough Sauvignon Blanc is notably weighty, ripe and rich. The top-tier, fully barrel-fermented Dedication Series Chardonnay, grown in Hawke's Bay, is a stylish wine with excellent concentration of citrusy, nutty, complex flavour.

Sémillon is a De Redcliffe specialty. The lightly oaked Reserve Sémillon, grown in Auckland (predominantly) and Mangatawhiri, offers very good depth of ripe, melon and capsicum-like flavours. The lower-priced Sémillon/Chardonnay is a crisp, refreshing wine, lemony and slightly grassy.

The recent vintages of De Redcliffe's red wines have been plain, lacking full ripeness and flavour depth, but can be expected to improve as its new vineyards come on stream in Hawke's Bay. However, the dark, soft, sweet and pruney Dessert Cabernet Sauvignon and perfumed, creamy-smooth Tawny Port both rank among New Zealand's better fortified wines.

**** Marlborough Riesling
(****) Dedication Series Chardonnay, Reserve Marlborough
Sauvignon Blanc, Reserve Sémillon
***½ Dessert Cabernet Sauvignon, Mangatawhiri
Chardonnay, Marlborough Sauvignon Blanc, Tawny
Port
*** Sémillon/Chardonnay
(***) Hawke's Bay Cabernet/Merlot
** Lyons Road Chardonnay, Pinot Noir

OHINEMURI ESTATE WINES

*Moresby Street, Karangahake. Est 1989. Owners: Horst and Wendy
Hillerich. Production: 1,500 cases.*

In the rugged, bush-tangled Karangahake Gorge, between Paeroa
and Waihi, Horst and Wendy Hillerich produce a tangy, incisively
flavoured Riesling and charming Beaujolais-style Pinotage.

Horst Hillerich, an engaging personality who loves to talk
wine until the early hours of the morning, graduated in viticul-
ture and oenology from Veitshochheim University in Franconia.
After coming to New Zealand in 1987, he worked at The Millton
Vineyard and Totara Vineyards, met his Nelson-born wife,
Wendy, and in 1989 produced the first wines under his own
Ohinemuri Estate label.

Ohinemuri Estate is a winery, not a vineyard. The distinctive,
richly atmospheric collection of buildings, modelled on a Latvian
chalet, sit on a bank of the Ohinemuri River. The gorge is too
steep and rainy for growing quality grapes on a commercial scale,
so the Hillerichs buy their fruit, mostly from Gisborne and
Hawke's Bay.

Most of Ohinemuri Estate's small output is sold directly to the
public, over the counter or in its popular winery café. The
Sauvignon Blanc offers a touch of oak and lees-aging complexity
amidst its crisp, ripely herbal flavours, but the barrel-fermented
Chardonnay has varied in quality and style. A winery specialty is
the partly whole bunch-fermented Pinotage Primeur, a light
ruby, fresh and lively, Beaujolais-style charmer with soft, raspberryish flavour.

Hillerich's real forte, naturally, is the Germanic varieties
like Riesling and Gewürztraminer. The slightly sweet
Gewürztraminer is typically perfumed and full of varietal character, and the off-dry Riesling – briefly matured on its yeast lees – is
consistently satisfying, with plenty of fresh, lively lemon-lime
flavour and racy acidity.

***½ Gewürztraminer, Riesling, Sauvignon Blanc
*** Pinotage Primeur
**½ Chardonnay

QUARRY ROAD ESTATE

Waerenga Road, Te Kauwhata. Est 1996. Owners: Toby Cooper, Jenny Gander, Nikki Cooper and Peter West. Production: 4,500 cases.
Until recently known as Aspen Ridge, this small winery east of Te Kauwhata township was established in 1963 by Alister McCissock, who won a following for grape jellies and grape juices but enjoyed much less success with table wines.

In 1996, McCissock sold the 5-hectare vineyard and winery to Toby Cooper and his wife, Jenny Gander, in partnership with Toby's sister, Nikki Cooper and her husband, Peter West. The traditional 'sherries', 'ports' and grape juices will still be produced, alongside a range of premium table wines – Sauvignon Blanc, Chardonnay, Riesling, Cabernet Rosé and Cabernet Sauvignon.

From the new owners I have tasted a light, crisp, green-edged 1996 Merlot and a much classier 1995 Cabernet Sauvignon with deep colour and well-concentrated, plummy, firm flavour.

(***½) Cabernet Sauvignon
(**) Merlot

RONGOPAI WINES

Wayside Road, Te Kauwhata. Est 1982. Owners: Tom and Faith van Dam and partner. Production: 17,000 cases.
Rongopai means 'good taste' – a fitting name for a winery which produces some of New Zealand's most opulent, rampantly botrytised sweet white wines.

Rongopai was founded in 1982 by Dr Rainer Eschenbruch and Tom van Dam, who had worked together at the government viticultural research station. In the mid-to-late 1980s, a stream of stunning Riesling Ausleses (forerunners of today's Reserve Botrytised Riesling) earned the winery a strong reputation, but four years ago Eschenbruch withdrew from the partnership. Van Dam and his wife, Faith, now control the company, with an over-seas-based investor also having a one-third stake.

In 1994, Rongopai purchased the white-walled, cavernous winery at the old viticultural research station, complete with a three-storey-high copper-pot still and a host of casks dating back to the First World War. Here, van Dam processes grapes grown in Rongopai's pair of 2-hectare vineyards at Te Kauwhata: its 5-hectare, joint venture vineyard opposite the 'Station' winery; and a larger joint venture vineyard in Hawke's Bay.

Rongopai Reserve Botrytised Riesling is an alluring beauty, with a gorgeous perfume and splendid depth of honey-sweet flavour, threaded with steely acidity. Promoted as 'the ultimate aphrodisiac', the Reserve Botrytised Chardonnay is liquid nectar, with great weight and rich, treacly, everlasting flavour. These are great wines by any standard. Other impressive sweet wines – usually based on such early-ripening German varieties as Müller-

Thurgau, Scheurebe and Wurzer, late-harvested with soaring sugar levels and a degree of shrivelling and botrytis – are released under the Botrytis Reserve and Botrytised Selection labels.

The Winemakers Selection Chardonnay and Winemakers Selection Sauvignon Blanc, both grown at Te Kauwhata, reflect the northern warmth in their fullness of body, ripeness and roundness. These are fat, rich-flavoured, softly structured wines of consistently high quality.

The reds, based on Syrah, Pinot Noir and Merlot, are more of a mixed bag, sometimes failing to justify their high price, but the Winemakers Selection Merlot/Malbec is full of character – weighty, gamey, leathery and supple.

*****	**Reserve Botrytised Chardonnay, Reserve Botrytised Riesling**
****½	**Botrytis Reserve, Winemakers Selection Sauvignon Blanc**
****	**Winemakers Selection Chardonnay, Winemakers Selection Merlot/Malbec**
***½	**Botrytised Selection**
(***)	**Chenin Blanc, Riesling, Sauvignon Blanc, Winemakers Selection Syrah**
(**½)	**Chardonnay, Winemakers Selection Pinot Noir**

TOTARA VINEYARDS SYC

Main Road, Thames. Est 1950. Owners: The Chan family and Kevin Honiss.

Totara is a distinctive winery. Geographically out on a limb, just south of Thames at the base of the Coromandel Peninsula, it is also the only predominantly Chinese-owned wine company in New Zealand.

Stanley Chan, whose initials still form part of the company's official name, founded Totara in 1950. He purchased the property – then bearing a plot of table grapes planted by Ah Chan (no relation) in 1925 – and plunged into commercial winemaking. Today the company is owned by the Chan family in partnership with Kevin Honiss.

Totara has languished in the past decade. Hard-hit by the 1985–86 price war, it soon after uprooted almost all its vineyards and now buys its grapes from North Island growers. The slightly sweet, blended Fu Gai has been popular in Chinese restaurants, and the kiwifruit and coffee-based liqueurs have enjoyed export success. The table wines are not widely seen, but the partly barrel-aged Winemakers Reserve Sauvignon Blanc and oaky Winemakers Reserve Chardonnay can be of award-winning quality.

(***)	**Winemakers Reserve Chardonnay, Winemakers Reserve Sauvignon Blanc**
**	**Chardonnay**

VILAGRAD WINES

Rukuhia Road, Ohaupo. Est 1922. Owners: The Nooyen family.
Production: 3,000 cases.

Guests at weddings, conferences and other social functions
staged at this small winery consume most of its output. Founded
by Ivan Milicich at Ngahinapouri, south of the city of Hamilton,
in 1922, the 5-hectare vineyard and winery are now in the hands
of third-generation family members Nelda and Pieter Nooyen.
The premium Nooyen Reserve range includes a barrel-fermented
Chardonnay of solid – occasionally excellent – quality and a full-
flavoured but slightly green-edged Pinot Noir and
Cabernet/Merlot/Malbec.

**½   Nooyen Reserve Chardonnay
(**½)   Nooyen Reserve Cabernet/Merlot/Malbec, Nooyen
         Reserve Pinot Noir

Bay of Plenty

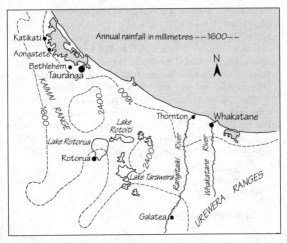

COVELL ESTATE

Troutbeck Road, Galatea. Est 1981. Owners: The Covell family.
Production: 1,000 cases.

Far from the major wine trails, one of New Zealand's rarest Pinot
Noirs and Chardonnays flow from Bob and Des Covell's tiny winery on the frost-prone flanks of the Urewera Ranges in the inland,
eastern Bay of Plenty.

The Covells, beef and pig farmers, planted their first vines in
1981 and produced their first experimental wine in 1987, but did

not process their first 'commercial' wine until 1991. The Covells' son, Robert, and his wife, Diane, are also involved in the venture.

Pinot Noir and Chardonnay are the key varieties in the 5-hectare vineyard, with smaller plots of Gewürztraminer, Riesling, Cabernet Sauvignon and Merlot. Spring frosts, caused by cold air spilling down the mountains, are a constant danger after the vines' buds have burst, causing severe crop losses about two years in five. Cultivated at 200 metres above sea level, the grapes always retain high acidity.

In their tiny on-site winery, the Covells produce distinctive wines. Oak-aged for two years, the Pinot Noir is light in colour and body but clearly varietal, with a perfumed bouquet and subtle, mellow flavours. The slightly austere but flavoursome Chardonnay, fermented and lees-aged in new French oak barriques, is appley, citrusy, buttery and yeasty, with racy acidity.

***   Chardonnay
**½ Pinot Noir

KANUKA FOREST WINES

Moore Road, Thornton, Whakatane. Est 1988. Owners: Tony and Julia Hassall. Production: 535 cases.
Behind the sand dunes at Thornton, on the coast 15 kilometres west of Whakatane, Tony and Julia Hassall are unravelling the winemaking potential of the eastern Bay of Plenty. A Whakatane accountant, Hassall and his wife, Julia, planted their first vines in 1988 and processed their first commercial vintage in 1993.

The sandy, 3-hectare vineyard is planted primarily in Cabernet Sauvignon, Merlot, Sauvignon Blanc and Chardonnay. The early releases of Chardonnay and Fumé Blanc have been very assertively oak-influenced, but the claret-style red is an enjoyable middle-weight, with moderately ripe flavour.

(**½) Cabernet Sauvignon/Merlot
(**)   Chardonnay
(*½)   Fumé Blanc

MILLS REEF WINERY

Moffat Road, Bethlehem. Est 1989. Owners: The Preston family. Production: 22,500 cases.
New Zealand's most architecturally striking and sumptuous winery lies at Bethlehem, on the outskirts of the city of Tauranga. Here Warren ('Paddy') Preston and his family produce an impressive lineup of Hawke's Bay wines, with a special focus on Chardonnay and sparkling wines.

A gentle, unassuming personality, Paddy Preston is a former kiwifruit winemaker who for many years enjoyed spectacular success in fruit winemakers' competitions in New Zealand. Under the Preston's label, the family still exports large volumes of kiwifruit wine to Japan and Taiwan. In 1989, however, Paddy switched to grape winemaking – with instant success.

With Paddy's wife, Helen, their sons, Warren and Tim, and daughter, Melissa, all involved, Mills Reef is truly a family affair. Grapes are drawn from the company's own 8-hectare vineyard in Mere Road, Hawke's Bay, and other growers based in Hawke's Bay.

The top wines are labelled Elspeth (in honour of Paddy Preston's mother), followed by a mid-tier Reserve range, and everyday-drinking varietals under the Moffat Road Selection label. Elspeth Chardonnay is consistently outstanding, with layers of citrusy, figgy, oaky, mealy flavour, a deliciously creamy texture and lingering finish. Partly barrel-fermented, Elspeth Sauvignon Blanc is chock full of ripe, herbal flavours in a rich, mouthfilling style. The Elspeth Riesling is a powerful, deliciously perfumed and poised wine that flourishes with cellaring.

The reds are less memorable than the whites, but fast improving. Elspeth Cabernet/Merlot is bold and brambly, with rich fruit, quality oak and tight tannins; the Reserve Pinot Noir is chewy, cherryish, smoky and supple, with depth of flavour, complexity and lots of drink-young appeal.

Paddy Preston's infatuation with Chardonnay also extends to his top sparkling wine, Mills Reef Traditional Method. A vintage-dated, Chardonnay-predominant wine, barrel and bottle-fermented, in the past it placed its accent on rich, creamy fruit characters, but is now evolving to a more subtle, tight and yeasty style. Its cheaper stablemate, the Pinot Noir-based, non-vintage Charisma, is a biscuity, yeasty, flinty wine, bargain-priced.

*****	Elspeth Chardonnay
****½	Elspeth Sauvignon Blanc, Mills Reef Traditional Method
****	Elspeth Cabernet/Merlot, Elspeth Riesling, Reserve Chardonnay
(****)	Charisma, Reserve Pinot Noir
(***½)	Reserve Riesling, Reserve Sauvignon Blanc
***	Moffat Road Cabernet Sauvignon, Moffat Road Chardonnay
**½	Moffat Road Riesling, Moffat Road Sauvignon Blanc
(**)	Moffat Road Pinot Noir

MORTON ESTATE WINERY

State Highway 2, Aongatete, via Katikati. Est 1982. Owners: John and Alison Coney. Production: 97,500 cases.

Think Morton Estate – think Chardonnay. The handsome Cape Dutch-style winery near Katikati, on the Auckland side of Tauranga, won a gold medal with its debut 1983 Chardonnay; its popular White Label Hawke's Bay Chardonnay accounts for over a third of its total sales; its refined, weighty, tightly structured Black Label Hawke's Bay Chardonnay is one of the most celebrated of all New Zealand Chardonnays.

The winery was founded by Morton Brown, an entrepreneur who, after a series of financial manoeuvres, withdrew from the company in 1988, leaving Mildara Wines of Australia with full control. Following the collapse of the Appellation Vineyards venture – which briefly merged Morton Estate, Cellier Le Brun and Allan Scott – Morton Estate was acquired in mid-1995 by John Coney, a New Zealand property developer and financier, and his wife, Alison. The winemaker from the start was John Hancock, an extroverted Australian with a passion for Chardonnay. The blend of Morton Estate, Hancock and Chardonnay achieved a high profile, but in 1996 Hancock departed to establish a new company, Trinity Hill, in Hawke's Bay. Into Hancock's shoes stepped Evan Ward, previously winemaker at Corbans Hawke's Bay Winery, with a particularly strong reputation for such classy bottle-fermented sparklings as Amadeus and Verde.

Of critical importance to Morton Estate's recent successes has been its development of the 70-hectare Riverview vineyard at Mangatahi, an elevated, relatively cool site inland from Ngatarawa in Hawke's Bay. Chardonnay covers half the vineyard, with smaller plots of Sauvignon Blanc, Pinot Noir, Cabernet Sauvignon, Merlot, Meunier and Syrah. Riverview has yielded brilliant Chardonnay and high quality Cabernet Sauvignon, Merlot and Pinot Noir. The firm also owns the nearby 25-hectare Colefield vineyard and the 17-hectare Mill Road vineyard at Haumoana, and in 1997 planted a new, 40-hectare block of Chardonnay and Merlot in the Ngatarawa district. Morton Estate's Hawke's Bay grapes are all crushed and dejuiced at Riverview before (in most cases) the juice is sent to the Bay of Plenty for fermentation. The company also owns the 41-hectare Stone Creek vineyard in Marlborough.

Morton Estate's most prestigious wines carry a Black Label, with White Label (often high quality) wines positioned in the middle, and the Mill Road selection of everyday-drinking wines at the bottom. Until recently, the Marlborough wines were marketed under a separate Stone Creek brand, but this label is being phased out and in future the Marlborough wines will all be labelled as Morton Estate.

Morton Estate's greatest wine is the powerful, exceptionally rich Black Label Hawke's Bay Chardonnay, a tightly structured, mealy, grapefruit and melon-flavoured beauty, fermented and matured in all-new French oak barriques. In top vintages, the standard of the fully barrel-fermented, deep-flavoured and biscuity White Label Hawke's Bay Chardonnay approaches that of its big brother (at half the price), although in lesser years the gap widens.

Of the Sauvignon Blancs, the White Label Hawke's Bay is typically fresh and lively, with gently herbaceous flavours and a sliver of sweetness. Its Marlborough stablemate, launched in 1994, is fleshy and ripe, with lush fruit flavours.

The Riverview vineyard produces superb reds in warm vintages – scented, silky Pinot Noirs (among Hawke's Bay's finest) and fragrant, sturdy, full-flavoured Cabernet Sauvignon and Merlot-based reds that can be deliciously ripe and rich. In cooler years, the wines are less distinguished, lacking body and concentration. Sparklings are also an important part of the range, especially the lower-tier, non-vintage, delicately yeasty and creamy Morton Brut and the richer, Pinot Noir-dominant Vintage Méthode Champenoise.

*****	Black Label Hawke's Bay Chardonnay
(*****)	Black Label Hawke's Bay Pinot Noir
****½	Black Label Hawke's Bay Cabernet/Merlot
****	White Label Hawke's Bay Chardonnay
(****)	Black Label Hawke's Bay Merlot, White Label Marlborough Chardonnay
***½	Morton Brut NV, Vintage Méthode Champenoise, White Label Hawke's Bay Pinot Noir, White Label Marlborough Riesling, White Label Marlborough Sauvignon Blanc
(***½)	Black Label Méthode Champenoise
***	White Label Hawke's Bay Cabernet/Merlot
**½	Mill Road Cabernet/Merlot, Mill Road Chardonnay, Mill Road Sauvigon Blanc, White Label Hawke's Bay Sauvignon Blanc

Gisborne

Chardonnays are the Gisborne region's greatest gift to the wine world – freshly scented, ripe-tasting and rounded Chardonnays that can offer delicious drinking six months after they were a bunch of grapes. Most of the vines are grown on the highly fertile Poverty Bay flats (a misnomer if ever there was one) near the city of Gisborne, with smaller outposts of grape-growing further up the mountainous East Cape at Tolaga Bay and Tikitiki, and to the south near Wairoa.

Gisborne is New Zealand's third-largest wine region, with 18 percent of all plantings. It used to be the largest – in 1986, it contained 36 percent of the country's vineyard area. Since then, most viticultural expansion has been concentrated in the drier, and often less fertile, soils to the south. Yet the naturally productive Gisborne region produced over 30 percent of New Zealand's total grape harvest in 1997. In Gisborne's warm, sunny climate, the combination of rich soils and abundant autumn rainfall encourages dense vine-foliage growth and bumper crops. During the critical February to April harvest period, the average rainfall is 33 percent higher than in Hawke's Bay and 70 percent higher than in Marlborough.

Friedrich Wohnsiedler, a German butcher whose main street shop was ransacked by patriots on New Year's Eve 1914, pioneered winemaking in Gisborne. Wohnsiedler produced his first Waihirere wines in the 1920s. By the time of his death in 1958, his 10-acre (4-hectare) vineyard enjoyed a nationwide reputation for its 'sherries', 'ports' and 'madeira'.

During the 1960s, after Montana and Corbans arranged grape-growing contracts with local farmers, vineyards swept across the fertile Gisborne plains. Müller-Thurgau was heavily planted, yielding bumper crops of grapes for the larger wineries' cask and everyday-drinking bottled wines.

Today, Gisborne is white wine country. Chardonnay (now the most common variety) and Müller-Thurgau account for over half the planted area, followed by Muscat Dr Hogg, Reichensteiner (for bulk wines), Sauvignon Blanc, Sémillon and Chenin Blanc. In the past, most of the Cabernet Sauvignon-based reds lacked body and flavour richness, but the new breed of claret-style reds – notably the Merlots – is much riper and chunkier; some would not be out of place in a lineup of Hawke's Bay reds.

The Gisborne wine trail is remarkably short, with only seven wineries (not including Montana's and Corbans' giant wineries in the city's industrial zone) open to visitors. Of the smaller producers, the best known are Matawhero, which burst into the limelight in the 1970s with a string of spicy Gewürztraminers, and The Millton Vineyard, famous as an organic producer but also the source of superb Rieslings and Chenin Blancs.

In recent years, quality-orientated growers have begun to explore more fully Gisborne's potential for fine-wine production. By planting on less fertile sites on the margins of the plains, and using a range of viticultural techniques to produce higher quality grapes – devigorating rootstocks; improved clones; virus-free vines; leaf-plucking to reduce fruit shading; later harvesting – winemakers have succeeded in producing some outstanding wines – Chardonnays that captivate in their youth with their full-bloomed fragrance and lush, vibrantly fruity flavour; pungent, peppery Gewürztraminers; even ripe and supple Merlots.

HARVEST WINE COMPANY

Customhouse Street, Gisborne. Est 1990. Owners: Wi Pere Trust and Brian Shanks. Production: 900 cases. Winery sales by appointment.
This large cider producer also produces a trickle of grape wines. It is owned by general manager Brian Shanks and the Wi Pere Trust (a group of farmers with extensive vineyards contracted to Corbans). Among the early releases have been a Riesling, Chardonnay, Müller-Thurgau and a decent, carbonated, off-dry Sparkling Chardonnay marketed in a 330 ml, screw-top bottle.

(**½) **Sparkling Chardonnay**

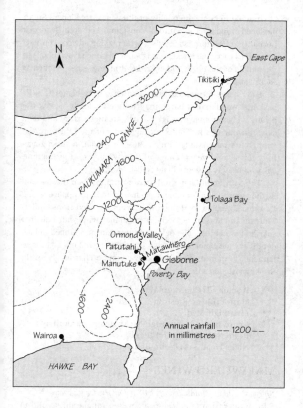

LONGBUSH WINES

State Highway 2, Manutuke. Est 1989. Owners: John and Bill Thorpe.
Production: 15,000 cases.

Soft, peachy-ripe, toasty, buttery Chardonnays are the most notable achievement to date at this fast-growing winery on the main highway at Manutuke, just south of the city of Gisborne.

Previously known as Landfall, and before that White Cliffs, the winery has experienced a series of major changes since its first vintage in 1989. The founding partners were Ross Revington and John Thorpe, but following Revington's departure in 1993 (see Revington Vineyard), Longbush is now controlled by the Thorpe brothers, John and Bill.

The silty, 8-hectare estate vineyard, planted in Pinot Noir and Gewürztraminer, has been granted transitional Bio-Gro (certified organic) status. The Thorpe brothers also buy grapes from other Gisborne growers.

In a bid to boost the quality of the wines, Dr Richard Smart has been hired as a viticultural consultant and John Hancock (formerly of Morton Estate) gives winemaking advice. The flagship wines carry the Woodlands label, with Longbush varietals in the middle of the range and everyday-drinking wines branded as Nicks Head.

Fully barrel-fermented, with a buttery, oaky bouquet, at its best the Woodlands Chardonnay rolls effortlessly across the palate, with impressive weight, a soft, creamy texture and delicious flavour depth. The other highlights of the range are the strongly flavoured, tangy Rhine Riesling, which matures gracefully for several years, and – in drier vintages – the fragrant, spicy, delicately flavoured and stylish Merlot.

The Sauvignon Blancs are more restrained than those found further south, with rounded, ripe, melon and pineapple-evoking flavours. The pale, perfumed Kahurangi, blended from Müller-Thurgau and Muscat, is a light, fresh, grapey wine with a distinct splash of sweetness. The oak-aged Pinot Noir has tended to lack depth, but the Pinot Noir-based, Beaujolais-style First Light Red, launched a month after the vintage, can be charmingly fresh, raspberryish and soft.

****	Woodlands Chardonnay
***	Merlot, Rhine Riesling
(***)	First Light Red
**½	Chardonnay, Kahurangi, Nicks Head Chardonnay, Pinot Noir, Sauvignon Blanc
**	Nicks Head Sauvignon Blanc

MATAWHERO WINES

Riverpoint Road, Matawhero. Est 1976. Owner: Denis Irwin.

Fifteen years ago Matawhero enjoyed a reputation second to none in New Zealand for its handling of the Gewürztraminer variety. Today Matawhero's star has dimmed, but the wines flowing from the end of Riverpoint Road can still be absorbing.

Matawhero emerged in 1976 when Denis Irwin, then a grape-grower's son working in a converted chicken-shed, produced wine from the pick of his family's Gewürztraminer crop. Vintage after vintage proved successful, abounding with this variety's perfume and flavour spiciness. A stream of gold and silver medals followed.

The mid-1980s, however, proved a flat patch. Endeavouring to establish a second winery at Gisborne, Victoria, Irwin was for several years more often than not absent from Matawhero. The wines suffered, becoming erratic in quality. In 1989, Irwin retreated from Australia and has since been fully engaged at Matawhero.

The 30-hectare estate vineyard encircling the winery is planted principally in Gewürztraminer and Chardonnay, with smaller amounts of Chenin Blanc, Sauvignon Blanc, Cabernet Sauvignon, Merlot, Malbec, Pinot Noir and Syrah. The nearby Bridge Estate vineyard is devoted exclusively to red-wine varieties.

No longer interested in producing wines that display intense varietal characters, Irwin now pursues other qualities. 'There are a lot of more pungent, obvious Gewürztraminers on the market than mine now,' he says. 'That's great – there's no challenge for me in that. I want structure, subtlety, complexity. Varietal character is the last point I'm interested in, although it does come as the wines age.' The famous Gewürztraminer is today much less arrestingly perfumed and penetratingly spicy than its predecessors, but still weighty, with rich flavours – musky, peachy, gingery, honeyish and soft.

The oak-matured Sauvignon Blanc is fleshy and ripe, with good depth of non-herbaceous, slightly honeyish and toasty, well-rounded flavour. However, the Reserve Chardonnay has been of inconsistent quality – sometimes tired and dull, sometimes robust, with impressive depth of savoury, figgy, mealy, complex flavour. The lower-tier Estate Chardonnay is typically broad and rounded in a ripe, soft, easy-drinking style.

Over the past decade, Matawhero's reds have been the finest in Gisborne, with a power and richness that sit oddly with the region's modest red-wine reputation. Most consistently rewarding are the Cabernet Sauvignon/Merlot, a dark, gutsy, brambly, spicy, tannic wine, full of character; and Bridge Estate, a bold and beefy, single-vineyard blend of Merlot, Malbec, Cabernet Sauvignon and Cabernet Franc packed with rich, chocolatey, firm flavour.

**** **Bridge Estate, Cabernet Sauvignon/Merlot**
***½ **Gewürztraminer, Pinot Noir, Reserve Chardonnay,**
       Sauvignon Blanc
***   **Estate Chardonnay**
½   **Estate Cabernet

PARKER MÉTHODE CHAMPENOISE

91 Banks Street, Gisborne. Est 1987. Owner: Phil Parker. Production: 450 cases.

Phil Parker is a charismatic entrepreneur with a passion for bottle-fermented sparkling wines. At the launch of his first wine, a toy yacht was broken across a 6-litre bottle of Parker Classical Brut 1987.

Parker runs the popular Smash Palace tavern, near Corbans' mammoth winery in the heart of Gisborne's industrial area. In his small winery out the back, each year Parker produces a few hundred cases of 'designer sparkling wines', whereby individual customers are encouraged to order the amount of sugar and brandy they want in the dosage (final topping up after disgorging).

The Classical Brut, a Pinot Noir/Chardonnay blend, is often

not disgorged until it is five or six years old, but it is typically still fresh and lively, with appley, biscuity, yeasty flavours in a bone-dry, slightly austere style. The non-vintage Dry Flint, based on Sémillon and Chenin Blanc, is herbal, tangy and yeasty. The salmon-pink Rosé Brut, blended from Pinotage, Pinot Noir and Chardonnay, is robust, full-flavoured and dry.

Parker also created First Light Red, the cleverly named (given Gisborne's closeness to the international dateline) Beaujolais-style wine now produced by other Gisborne winemakers. His own wine, based on whole bunch-fermented Pinot Noir and released only a few weeks after the harvest, is a light, fresh, buoyantly fruity red, raspberryish and soft.

***½ Classical Brut
***   Dry Flint, Rosé Brut
**½   First Light Red

POUPARAE PARK

Bushmere Road, Gisborne. Est 1994. Owner: Alec Cameron. Production: 1,000 cases.
Attracted by the chance to 'add value', in 1994 kiwifruit grower Alec Cameron entered the wine industry by purchasing grapes and producing his first wines at the nearby Longbush winery. Sold at Cameron's property in Bushmere Road, the wines have included a lightly wooded Chardonnay, a slightly sweet Riesling, Sauvignon Blanc, Pinotage and First Light Red – all solid but unmemorable.

(**½) Pinotage
(**)   Chardonnay, Riesling

REVINGTON VINEYARD

c/- 110 Stout Street, Gisborne. Est 1987. Owners: Ross and Mary Jane Revington. Production: 1,500 cases. No winery sales.
Revington Vineyard, despite an impressive string of competition successes, does not enjoy a high profile; Ross Revington, the co-owner, is absorbed in his career as a Gisborne lawyer. Yet his Gewürztraminer and Chardonnay are often exceptional.

Revington Vineyard lies in the Ormond Valley, north of the city. When Revington and his wife, Mary Jane, purchased the vineyard in 1987, it had previously supplied the fruit for several gold medal-winning wines under the Cooks label. What is the key to the site's magic? 'Kerry Hitchcock, then winemaker for Cooks, used to say "the fairies live there",' recalls Revington.

Today the 4-hectare vineyard of flat, sandy loams over clay is planted in Chardonnay (predominantly) and Gewürztraminer. Managed organically, it has been awarded transitional Bio-Gro status. The Revingtons do not own a winery, so the grapes are crushed in Gisborne and then the juice is trucked to Marlborough to be fermented and matured by David Pearce of Grove Mill (who made the Revingtons' first wine in 1988 when he was still based at Corbans' Gisborne winery). For several years, when Ross Revington was a partner in the Landfall (now Longbush) winery, Revington Vineyard wines were marketed as part of the Landfall range. Since Revington's withdrawal from Landfall in 1993, however, they have been marketed separately.

The Chardonnay is consistently classy, with mouthfilling body, superbly rich grapefruit and melon-like flavours, strong new oak influence and a crisp, tight finish. An immaculate wine, it flourishes in the cellar for several years. The Gewürztraminer at its best ranks among New Zealand's finest, with great weight and an arresting intensity of peppery, slightly earthy, dry flavour. These are rare wines, but worth tracking down.

***** Chardonnay
****½ Gewürztraminer

SHALIMAR ESTATE

Wharekopae Road, Patutahi. Est 1992. Owners: Alec and Helen Stuart. Production: 1,000 cases.

As a contract grape-grower, in the past Alec Stuart cultivated some of the finest Pinotage crushed by Montana. Now, having fulfilled his dream to build his own winery, he's determined to scotch the idea that Gisborne cannot produce quality reds.

Shalimar Estate's sunny, terraced vineyard lies at Patutahi, on the inland edge of the plains. After growing grapes for Montana from 1969 until the vine-pull scheme in 1986, Stuart grew other crops for a few years, then in 1992 began planting vines again. Today the 4-hectare vineyard, on terraced and flat land, is established in numerous varieties – Cabernet Sauvignon, Merlot, Pinotage, Sauvignon Blanc, Chardonnay, Pinot Gris, Sémillon and Riesling.

Launched from the 1994 vintage, the initial wines tended to lack freshness and depth, but the 1995 Reserve Chardonnay was a big step forward, with plenty of ripe buttery flavour. A consultant winemaker, Evert Nijzink, has been appointed and, tasted in their infancy, the 1996 and 1997 wines looked very solid.

(***) Reserve Chardonnay
(** ½) Cabernet/Merlot
(**) Pinot Gris

THE MILLTON VINEYARD

Papatu Road, Manutuke. Est 1984. Owners: James and Annie Millton. Production: 11,250 cases.

Gisborne's leading small winery is renowned both for the quality and organically-grown nature of its wines. At Manutuke, kilometres south of the city, James and Annie Millton produce consistently outstanding Rieslings, Chenin Blancs and botrytised sweet whites.

James Millton worked for Montana for two years and later in the Rheinhessen, before he returned to New Zealand to work briefly for Corbans and then John Clark (Annie's father), who had grown vines at Manutuke since the late 1960s. After building a winery, the Milltons' first wines flowed in 1984. Today they own four vineyards covering 22 hectares in the Manutuke and Matawhero districts; no grapes are sold and none are purchased from elsewhere.

At Britain's National Organic Wine Fair in 1993, the trophy for the Best Wine of the Show was awarded to The Millton Vineyard Chardonnay Barrel Fermented 1992; the second and third prizes also went to Millton. Gisborne's warm, moist climate is not ideally suited to organic viticulture, but the Milltons do not use herbicides, non-selective insecticides, systemic chemicals or artificial fertilisers. The quality of the land is enhanced by bio-dynamic herbal preparations; weed control is by mechanical means; insect pests are biologically controlled by parasites and predators. For fungus control, a limited use is made of copper sulphate and sulphur sprays, and sulphur dioxide is added in small amounts to the wine as a preservative.

The Chenin Blanc Dry vies with Collards' for the title of New Zealand's champion Chenin Blanc. Hand-harvested at three different ripeness levels, with some botrytis infection, and partly fermented in old French oak, it is a robust, succulent, fractionally off-dry wine, awash with pineappley, honeyish flavours.

The medium-sweet Riesling Opou Vineyard is a more opulent, slightly softer style than the freshly acidic Rieslings of the south, with a ravishing perfume and delicious surge of lemony, honeyish flavour. About one year in two, it is partnered by a treacly, rampantly botrytised Riesling Late Harvest Individual Bunch Selection. Stunning 'Sauternes-style' oak-aged sweet whites, based on such varieties as Chenin Blanc and Sémillon, are also produced under the Tête de Cuvée (top selection of the harvest) label.

The Chardonnay Barrel Fermented (lees-stirred every full moon) is typically an elegant, vibrantly fruity wine with very good depth of citrusy, nutty, soft flavour. In top vintages (about one year in three) the flagship Clos de Ste Anne Chardonnay is produced. A single-vineyard wine fermented with natural yeasts in all-new oak and given a full malolactic fermentation, it is deliciously fat, nutty, peachy-ripe and mealy, with a buttery-soft finish.

The fresh, scented, ripely flavoured Te Arai River Sauvignon Blanc (Gisborne's finest) and chewy, full-flavoured and complex Te Arai River Cabernet Sauvignon/Merlot are both of high quality. Easily overlooked but consistently delightful is the Cabernet

Rosé, a bright copper-pink, Cabernet Franc-based wine with delicate, strawberryish, lively, lingering flavours.

***** Chenin Blanc Dry, Riesling Opou Vineyard, Tête du
         Cuvée
****½ Cabernet Rosé, Clos de Ste Anne Chardonnay,
         Riesling Late Harvest Individual Bunch Selection
****   Chardonnay Barrel Fermented, Te Arai River
         Sauvignon Blanc
(****) Te Arai River Cabernet Sauvignon/Merlot
***   Estate Chardonnay

WAIMATA VINEYARD

Upper Stout Street, Gisborne, Est. 1989. Owner: Tairawhiti Polytechnic. Production: 1,000 cases.

Waimata Vineyard wines (previously known as Tai-Ara-Rau) are produced by students studying for the one-year wine industry certificate offered by Gisborne's Tairawhiti Polytechnic, which owns the 2.5-hectare Waimata Vineyard, on the banks of the Waimata River, and a small winery. The wines sold to the public include an easy-drinking Merlot and Pinot Noir and a barrel-fermented, deliciously fragrant, fat and ripe Reserve Chardonnay.

(***½) Reserve Chardonnay

Hawke's Bay

Hawke's Bay's heritage of quality table winemaking and notable success with such classic grape varieties as Chardonnay and Cabernet Sauvignon have earned it the status of an aristocrat among New Zealand wine regions. Although now overtaken in area terms by Marlborough, it is by far the largest wine region in the North Island, and in terms of prestige closely rivals Marlborough.

Marist missionaries planted the first vines in Hawke's Bay in 1851. During the 1890s, the Mission made its first recorded sales and several wealthy landowners produced and sold table wines from classic *vinifera* grape varieties. By 1909, Bernard Chambers' 14-hectare Te Mata vineyard of Meunier, Syrah, Cabernet Sauvignon, Riesling and Verdelho was the largest in the country, annually producing 12,000 gallons (54,552 litres) of wine.

Today wine is booming in the Bay: between 1990 and 1997, the number of wine companies leapt from 12 to 36. Between 1992 and 1995, vine plantings expanded by over 40 percent. Chardonnay is the most widely planted variety, followed by Cabernet Sauvignon, Müller-Thurgau, Sauvignon Blanc and Merlot.

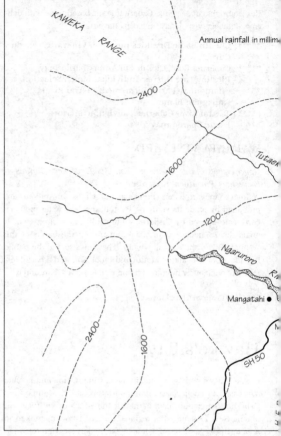

Sheltered from the prevailing westerly winds by rugged inland ranges climbing to over 1,600 metres, Hawke's Bay enjoys a warm, sunny climate; the city of Napier has similar sunshine hours and temperatures to Bordeaux. During summer, anticyclonic conditions lead to droughts in such years as 1994 (and early 1995), although easterly cyclonic depressions can also bring heavy autumn rains (as in 1988 and 1995).

On the Heretaunga Plains, where almost all of the vines are planted, there is a wide range of soil types. In the many vineyards planted in fertile alluvial soils with a high water table – especially those between the city of Hastings and the coast – the vines grow vigorously, yielding heavy crops of inadequately ripened and poorly balanced grapes. 'In Hawke's Bay we can grow the best Cabernet Sauvignon in New Zealand, but less than 10 miles [16 kilometres] away, we can also produce the worst,'

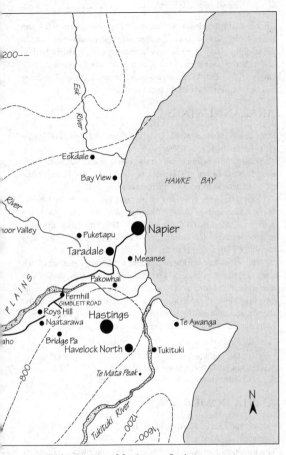

says Dr Alan Limmer of the Stonecroft winery.

The favoured districts for premium grape-growing include the Taradale Hills, river terraces along the Tukituki and Ngaruroro rivers, Havelock North and Ngatarawa. In the past decade, most expansion has been on low-vigour sites, especially in the shingly, arid Gimblett Road area inland from Hastings. Here, in extremely free-draining soils and high summer temperatures (less affected by cooling coastal breezes) the vines grow less vigorously, producing light crops harbouring ripe, concentrated flavours. The viticultural potential of the hill-country is still largely unexplored, but Morton Estate's relatively cool, slightly elevated site at Mangatahi, inland from Ngatarawa, has yielded numerous outstanding Chardonnays.

A diverse array of wine styles flow from Hawke's Bay, including a few shining examples of Riesling, Gewürztraminer, Pinot Gris,

Chenin Blanc, bottle-fermented sparkling, sweet white wine and Pinot Noir. The region's greatest strengths, however, are its mouthfilling, slowly evolving Chardonnays, rich, ripely herbal, oak-matured Sauvignon Blancs, and impressively fragrant, delicately flavoured claret-style reds blended from Cabernet Sauvignon, Merlot and Cabernet Franc.

AKARANGI WINES

River Road, Havelock North. Est 1987. Owners: Morton and Vivien Osborne. Production: 1,125 cases.

This low-profile winery sits on the banks of the Tukituki River, near Te Mata Estate in Havelock North. Morton Osborne, a clinical psychologist, produced his first wines in 1987.

The 5-hectare vineyard is planted principally in Chenin Blanc, Sauvignon Blanc, Chardonnay, Riesling, Cabernet Sauvignon, Merlot and Cabernet Franc. Osborne makes the wine in a converted boat-building shed, and stores and sells it in a century-old Presbyterian church.

The wines have rarely risen above mediocrity, tending to lack body and flavour richness. The Chenin Blanc is typically an austere style with biting acidity and moderate depth of green apple flavours. The Cabernet/Merlot is a decent quaffer, smooth and slightly green-edged. However, the richly coloured, ripe, vibrantly fruity and supple 1995 Merlot is an encouraging sign.

(***) Merlot
**   Cabernet/Merlot
*½   Chenin Blanc, Sauvignon Blanc
*   Chardonnay

ALPHA DOMUS

Maraekakaho Road, Hastings. Est 1991. Owners: The Ham family. Production: 2,775 cases.

The public face of Alpha Domus is winemaker Grant Edmonds, formerly winemaker at Esk Valley and then chief winemaker for Villa Maria. The company is owned, however, by the Ham family – Dutch immigrants and Palmerston North nursery owners Anthonius ('Ton') and Lea Ham, and their three sons, Paul, Henry and Anthony. The name 'Alpha' is derived from the first letter of each of their names, 'domus' is Latin for 'house' or 'family'.

Chardonnay, Sauvignon Blanc and Bordeaux-style reds are the key wines flowing from Alpha Domus' 20-hectare vineyard and winery at Maraekakaho, near Hastings, where planting began in 1991. For the first few vintages, some of the grapes are being sold to another winery. The initial release was of second-tier wines from the 1995 and 1996 vintages, followed by a reserve AD Chardonnay 1996 and reserve AD Cabernet/Merlot/Malbec 1996. The future holds small volumes of Pinot Noir, barrel-fermented Sémillon and botrytised Sémillon.

The Sauvignon Blanc is fresh and lively in a ripe, flavoursome, very easy-drinking style. The Rosé, based on Merlot, Malbec and Cabernet Franc, is fresh, mouthfilling, berryish and dry. The Cabernet Sauvignon/Merlot is a smooth-flowing red with generous blackcurrant and plum-like flavours, very appealing in its youth.

The AD Chardonnay is a powerful yet refined wine, richly fragrant, with a lovely balance of intense, ripe melon and peach flavours and nutty oak, finishing crisp, slightly buttery and long. The strapping AD Cabernet/Merlot/Malbec 1996, tasted as a one-year-old barrel sample, was a bold, lush wine with dark, almost impenetrable colour, overflowing with sweet, supple, brambly, dark plum flavours.

(*****) AD Chardonnay
(****½) AD Cabernet/Merlot/Malbec
(***½) Cabernet Sauvignon/Merlot, Rosé, Sauvignon
        Blanc

BRADSHAW ESTATE

291 Te Mata Road, Havelock North. Est 1994. Owners: Wayne and Judy Bradshaw. Production: 2,000 cases.
Accountant Wayne Bradshaw and his wife, Judy, own this small winery and restaurant on the site of Vidal's original 'No 1' vineyard, just across the road from Lombardi at Havelock North.

The 1994 to 1996 vintages were based on bought-in grapes because the Bradshaws' own 4-hectare vineyard of Sauvignon Blanc and Merlot was contracted to another winery. Dutch winemaker Hans Peet makes a 'really popular' Non-Wooded Chardonnay with good depth of fresh, crisp, apple and lemon flavours, a fragrant, full-bodied and lively Sauvignon Blanc, and a buoyant, firm, raspberry and spice-flavoured Merlot.

*** Non-Wooded Chardonnay
(***) Merlot, Sauvignon Blanc

BROOKFIELDS VINEYARDS

Brookfields Road, Meeanee. Est 1977. Owner: Peter Robertson. Production: 9,500 cases.
An exceptional 'gold label' Cabernet/Merlot and Reserve Chardonnay, backed up by a consistently rewarding Gewürztraminer and oak-aged Sauvignon Blanc, make Peter Robertson's range one of the most satisfying in the Bay.

Robertson, a biochemistry graduate, bought Brookfields in a run-down state from the Ellis family in 1977. Founded by Richard Ellis in 1937, Brookfields had for four decades specialised in fortified-wine production.

Robertson, who picked up some of his early winemaking

experience during a two-year spell with the legendary Tom McDonald at McWilliam's in Hawke's Bay, firmly altered Brookfields' course by upgrading the winery equipment and replanting the 2.5-hectare, silty-loam estate vineyard in Sauvignon Blanc and Chardonnay. Most of the grapes, however, are purchased from growers in Ohiti Road, behind Roy's Hill, and at Tukituki and Fernhill.

The winery lies only a couple of kilometres from the sea at Meeanee, south of Napier. The richly atmospheric winery, built in 1937 from handmade concrete blocks, is full of rustic dark wooden tables and benches. The winery restaurant opens for lunch on Fridays and at weekends. 'My wines are made to be drunk with food,' says Robertson. 'They're mouthfilling, with firm alcohol and acidity.'

The outstanding Reserve Chardonnay has a robust, complex, distinctly Burgundian style with ripe, intense citrusy fruit and biscuity, buttery, French oak characters. The French and American oak-aged Estate Chardonnay (Robertson's 'house wine') is an easy-drinking, forward wine with lots of ripe, soft flavour.

The Sauvignon Blanc, Gewürztraminer and Pinot Gris are all absorbing. Briefly oak-aged, the Sauvignon Blanc is typically a powerful wine with rich gooseberry and passionfruit flavours and a subtle backdrop of wood. The Gewürztraminer, a drier, weightier style than most New Zealand Gewürztraminers, is less pungently aromatic than Gisborne wines but gingery, spicy and deep-flavoured. The dry Pinot Gris has been of variable quality – sometimes dull – but at its best offers an Alsace-like richness of savoury, spicy, peachy flavour.

Brookfields' 'gold label' Cabernet/Merlot (matured in all-new French oak barriques) and strapping, chewy, tannin-laden Reserve Cabernet Sauvignon must be ranked among the Bay's most delicious reds. The virtues of splendidly ripe fruit are reflected, as Robertson puts it, in their 'lovely ripe jammy flavours'. These are notably dark, fragrant, powerful reds that unfold well over a decade.

*****   **Cabernet/Merlot, Reserve Chardonnay**
****½ **Reserve Cabernet Sauvignon**
****   **Gewürztraminer, Sauvignon Blanc**
***   **Estate Cabernet, Estate Chardonnay, Pinot Gris**

C.J. PASK WINERY

Omahu Road, Hastings. Est 1985. Owners: Chris Pask and the Berriman family. Production: 28,500 cases.

'C.J.' (Chris) Pask, a burly top-dressing pilot-turned-grape-grower, in 1985 kept the pick of his crop, converted his tractor shed into a winery, and plunged into commercial wine production. Today the company enjoys a strong reputation for its very elegant and concentrated Reserve Chardonnay and rich claret-style reds.

Muscular Cabernet Sauvignon, bursting with the taste delights of sweet ripe fruit, first shot the winery to prominence in the mid-to-late 1980s. However, Chris Pask's white wines did not stand out, so in 1990 a specialist winemaker was hired. Kate Radburnd (formerly Marris) is a Roseworthy College graduate who built a high profile during her 1987–1990 spell as winemaker at Vidal. Radburnd joined Pask because she 'wanted to see how a smaller winery works, especially one where you grow your own grapes'.

A key advantage for the winery is Chris Pask's stake in 45 hectares of vineyards in the stony Gimblett Road district, planted principally in Chardonnay, Sauvignon Blanc, Cabernet Sauvignon, Cabernet Franc and Merlot. The original vineyard and winery at Fernhill were sold to Montana in 1989; soon after, a new concrete Mediterranean-style winery with stained glass and prominent columns rose on the north side of Hastings. Radburnd and her Australian family, the Berrimans, bought a minority shareholding in the company in 1993.

At their best, the Cabernet Sauvignon and Merlot-based reds are strikingly fragrant, rich and supple, but they can also disappoint; a number of recent releases have been light and strongly herbaceous. The top Reserve reds are typically perfumed, fleshy and seductively full-flavoured, yet even here a distinctly green-edged character can intrude. Recent vintages of the lower-tier, non-Reserve reds have ranged in quality from mediocre to memorable.

Roy's Hill White, an unwooded, dry Chenin Blanc, and the smooth, fresh, berryish Roy's Hill Red (a lightly oaked blend of Bordeaux grapes) both offer solid, no-fuss drinking. The Pinot Noir is a sound, strawberryish red, but lacks real excitement.

The Sauvignon Blanc is attractively fresh and lively, with ripe fruit aromas and flavours and a sliver of sweetness to broaden its popular appeal. The Chardonnays have gone from strength to strength in recent vintages. Tank-fermented and barrel-aged, the standard Chardonnay offers strong, ripe grapefruit-lemon flavours and a touch of nutty oak in a crisp, elegant, drink-young style. Fully barrel-fermented, the Reserve Chardonnay is consistently outstanding, with mouthfilling body and concentrated, mealy, complex flavours.

*****	Reserve Chardonnay
(****½)	Reserve Cabernet/Merlot/Malbec, Reserve Merlot
****	Merlot
***½	Cabernet Sauvignon, Chardonnay, Sauvignon Blanc
***	Cabernet/Merlot
**½	Pinot Noir, Roy's Hill Red, Roy's Hill White

CLEARVIEW ESTATE WINERY

Clifton Road, Te Awanga. Est 1988. Owners: Tim Turvey, Helma van den Berg, David and Betty Ward. Production: 3,700 cases.

With an impressive collection of gold medals and trophies, a glorious site right on the coast and an acclaimed vineyard restaurant, in just a few vintages this small winery has made a big splash. Tim Turvey graduated with a BA and then worked on the land before he purchased his Te Awanga property – with three trees, a hedge and a dilapidated house – in 1985. The first vines were planted in 1988 and a year later Turvey produced his first wine, based on bought-in grapes.

Helma van den Berg, Turvey's partner, runs the shingly, 'amazingly well-drained' estate vineyard, an old Vidal block originally planted in 1916. Five hectares of Chardonnay, Cabernet Sauvignon, Merlot and Cabernet Franc vines have been established, and the couple also manage another six hectares of vineyards at Te Awanga.

Chardonnay and claret-style reds are the major strings to Clearview Estate's bow. Above all, the winery is renowned for its strapping, succulent Reserve Chardonnay, made from ultra-ripe fruit ('never below 25 brix,' says Turvey). Fermented in all-new French oak barriques and wood-matured for up to a year, with regular lees-stirring, this is a strikingly bold wine with a bottomless depth of peachy, oaky, mealy flavour.

The second-tier Beach Head Chardonnay is robust, ripe, oaky and full-flavoured, although typically less intense than its Reserve big brother. Black Reef Riesling is a slightly sweet style with lively, lemony, incisive flavour. At its best, the Reserve Fumé Blanc is packed with ripe, tropical fruit and toasty oak flavours, although in some vintages the wood influence is too assertive, dominating the fruit flavours.

The lower-tier Cape Kidnappers Cabernet Sauvignon is a chunky red with plenty of warm, ripe flavour. The Reserve Cabernet Franc and Reserve Merlot are both dark, mouthfilling reds crammed with sweet fruit flavours; these are exuberantly fruity wines with oak complexity and long-term cellaring potential. Even finer is the Reserve Old Olive Block, a powerful, sensuous blend of Cabernet Sauvignon, Cabernet Franc and Merlot with a seductive fragrance, lush blackcurrant, plum and spice flavours and silky tannins.

*****	Reserve Chardonnay
(*****)	Reserve Old Olive Block
****½	Reserve Cabernet Franc, Reserve Merlot
***½	Beach Head Chardonnay, Black Reef Riesling, Blush, Cape Kidnappers Cabernet Sauvignon, Reserve Fumé Blanc
(**)	Te Awanga Sauvignon Blanc

CRAB FARM WINERY

125 Main Road North, Bay View, Napier. Est 1987. Owner: James Jardine. Production: 3,000 cases.

Not for this winery a predictable logo on its label featuring an ancestor's coat-of-arms or tranquil vineyard scene. Rather, a giant menacing crab straddles the label, recalling how this coastal property, after it rose from the sea during the 1931 Napier earthquake, was for years littered with dead crabs.

James Jardine, a Rotorua surgeon, planted his first vines on the state highway north of Napier in 1980. The grapes were for several years sold to local winemakers, but in 1987 an implements shed was converted into a winery and James's son Hamish – who gathered his early winemaking experience at Matawhero in Gisborne and Château Reynella in Australia – was appointed winemaker. A tiny batch of Pinot Noir flowed from the 1987 vintage; the first white wine followed in 1988; in 1989 the winery opened to the public.

The 12-hectare estate vineyard, with pockets of shingle and silt, is established principally in Chardonnay and Gewürztraminer, supplemented by Cabernet Sauvignon, Merlot and Pinot Noir. Jardine's wines do not scale the heights, but are reliable and often full-flavoured and characterful.

Gewürztraminer is made in two styles: a weighty, lemony, well-spiced Gewürztraminer Dry and a fresh, flavour-packed, slightly sweet Late Harvest model. The Sauvignon Blanc is a typical Hawke's Bay style – full-bodied and ripely herbal. Aiming for a 'fat, tropical-flavoured' style of Chardonnay, fermented and lees-aged in French oak, Jardine produces a mouthfilling, ripe, flavourful wine with lots of drink-young appeal.

The Pinot Noir is typically a sturdy, savoury wine with earthy, mushroomy nuances. The Cabernet/Merlot is full, with restrained oak and supple red berry-plum flavours. In top vintages a more intense and complex red, Jardine Cabernet Sauvignon, appears with strong blackcurrant and mint flavours.

***½ Jardine Cabernet Sauvignon, Late Harvest
    Gewürztraminer
***   Cabernet/Merlot, Chardonnay, Gewürztraminer Dry,
    Pinot Noir
**½ Sauvignon Blanc

CROSS ROADS WINE COMPANY

Korokipo Road, Fernhill. Est 1990. Owners: Lester O'Brien and Malcolm Reeves. Production: 10,500 cases.

Malcolm Reeves and Lester O'Brien first met in the early 1970s when both were lecturing at Massey University in Palmerston North. When their paths crossed again in Paris in 1981, Reeves

suggested to O'Brien that they establish a winery. Hence the
company name: Cross Roads.

The Spanish mission-style winery, where doves and ducks
wander the grounds, rose on the main highway at Fernhill prior
to the 1993 vintage. The earlier 1990–92 vintages were produced
at a variety of premises. The 5-hectare estate vineyard is planted
in Riesling and various red-wine varieties which the partners prefer not to identify. Most of the grapes, however, are purchased
from Hawke's Bay growers.

Lester O'Brien, a chemistry graduate who later founded a
computer company in Belgium, is the general manager. Malcolm
Reeves, wine columnist for *The Evening Standard* in Palmerston
North, and formerly a senior lecturer in food technology, specialising in sensory evaluation and fermentation technology, is the
winemaker.

The bottom-tier wines are sold under the Springwood label.
Cross Roads Riesling Dry and Gewürztraminer are decent,
clearly varietal wines, impressive in top vintages. The
Cabernet/Merlot is a generous, smooth red, full of berryish,
spicy, minty fruit.

The Chardonnay is a full, citrusy, slightly buttery wine with a
touch of complexity. The Sauvignon Oak Aged mingles ripe tropical-fruit and moderately herbal flavours with subtle barrel-fermented characters. The Pinot Noir is typically scented and
supple, with vibrant, cherryish, spicy flavours and lots of charm –
one of the best in the Bay. The Reserve Cabernet/Merlot is
fleshy and soft, with good depth of blackcurrant, plum and oak
flavours.

The Reserve Hawke's Bay Chardonnay is stylish and tight,
with excellent depth of citrusy, figgy, mealy flavour. However,
Cross Road's most distinguished wine is The Talisman, an estate-
grown blend of six red grapes whose identities the partners
delight in concealing, but say were chosen after studying the
varietal components of Châteauneuf-du-Pape, Chianti, the super-
Tuscan reds and Bordeaux. Whatever its varietal makeup, The
Talisman is a boldly coloured, highly fragrant, voluptuous red
bursting with ripe-plum, spice and new French oak flavours.

(*****) The Talisman
(****) Reserve Hawke's Bay Chardonnay
***½   Chardonnay, Pinot Noir, Reserve Cabernet/Merlot,
         Sauvignon Oak Aged
***   Cabernet/Merlot, Gewürztraminer, Riesling Dry
**½   Sauvignon
(**½)   Springwood Merlot/Cabernet
(*)   Springwood Chardonnay

ESK VALLEY ESTATE

Main Road, Bay View, Napier. Est 1987. Owner: Villa Maria Estate.
Production: 75,000 cases.

Lush, silky, Merlot-based reds and robust, rich yet elegant Reserve Chardonnays are the chief attractions at this old, recently rejuvenated winery overlooking the Pacific Ocean at Bay View.

Esk Valley, under its earlier name, Glenvale, was founded in 1933 by English-born Robert Bird, who produced his first wines from the Albany Surprise table variety in a cellar tunnelled out of the hillside. Glenvale's production was for several decades focused on fortified wines, with its Extra Strength Sherry enjoying a throng of enthusiasts.

After the founder's grandsons, Robbie and Don Bird, took over the reins in 1979, Glenvale changed tack, marketing a range of solid varietal wines and a flood of wine casks. Hit hard, however, by the industry's pitched 1985–86 price battle, in 1987 the Bird brothers sold their winery to Villa Maria.

The new regime promptly unveiled a 'boutique' marketing strategy, slashed production, upgraded the winery and announced plans to transform Esk Valley into a tourist drawcard. A steep, north-facing terraced hillside bordering the winery, originally planted with vines in the 1940s but later established in pines, was replanted in Merlot, Malbec, Cabernet Sauvignon and Cabernet Franc.

Today this densely planted, drought-prone, irrigated vineyard each year yields about 250 cases of exceptional red wine, labelled The Terraces. Another half-hectare of Chardonnay is estate-grown, but the vast majority of Esk Valley's grapes are drawn from growers around Hawke's Bay.

Gordon Russell, who joined Esk Valley as assistant winemaker in 1990 and rose to the top job in 1993, delights in producing a 'mouth-watering, not mouth-puckering' style of Merlot. The straight varietal Merlot, oak-aged for a year, is a hugely drinkable red with an abundance of berryish, meaty, plummy flavour, supple and sustained. Its blended, Merlot-predominant stablemate, which includes a minority proportion of Cabernet Sauvignon and/or Cabernet Franc, is equally generous, full-flavoured and satisfying. Esk Valley also makes a deliciously aromatic, fresh, lively and dry Merlot Rosé that ranks among the country's finest.

The Sauvignon Blanc is fresh-scented and clearly varietal, with limey fruit characters to the fore in cool years and riper, softer flavours redolent of melon and passionfruit in warm vintages. The bargain-priced Wood Aged Chenin Blanc is vibrantly fruity and tangy, with good flavour depth, a touch of nutty oak and controlled acids. The Chardonnay, half barrel-fermented and all oak-aged, is flavoursome, citrusy and buttery, with a creamy finish.

The three jewels in the Esk Valley crown are the Reserve Chardonnay, The Terraces and the Reserve Merlot-predominant blend. The latest vintages of the Reserve Chardonnay are power-ful, arrestingly deep-flavoured wines, mealy and complex, with strong new-oak influence.

The Terraces is an excitingly bold, dark red with a marvellous intensity of plummy, spicy, complex flavour, braced by firm yet supple tannins. Top vintages cry out for cellaring for at least five years. The softer, voluptuous Reserve Merlot-based blend is per-fumed and rich, with intense, plummy, sweet fruit flavours that give it great drink-young appeal, but also the power and structure to mature well for several years.

***** Reserve Chardonnay, Reserve Merlot-predominant blend, The Terraces
****½ Merlot Rosé
**** Merlot, Merlot-predominant blend
***½ Chardonnay, Wood Aged Chenin Blanc
*** Sauvignon Blanc

ESKDALE WINEGROWERS

State Highway 5, Eskdale. Est 1973. Owners: Kim and Trish Salonius. Production: 1,500 cases.

One of Hawke's Bay's best-kept wine secrets, known only to the more enquiring members of the wine-drinking fraternity, is the tiny, low profile Eskdale winery. Kim Salonius is one of the wine industry's staunchest individualists.

Canadian-born Salonius arrived in New Zealand as a history student in 1964. After his passion for wine was aroused while pursuing graduate studies in Germany, he returned to New Zealand and in 1973 planted his first vines north of Napier along-side the highway through the Esk Valley. Today the silty 4-hectare estate vineyard, planted in Chardonnay, Gewürztraminer and Cabernet Sauvignon, is Eskdale's only source of fruit.

Salonius's aim is 'to keep life uncomplicated'. He is reluctant to advertise his wine and does not enter competitions. He pro-duces only about 1,500 cases of wine each year, which he says leaves plenty of spare time to pursue his ardent love affair with books. He loves conversing with customers who appreciate his mouthfilling dry wines, but has little patience with the 'Müller-Thurgau brigade'.

In the richly atmospheric, church-like winery (which he built himself), Salonius's goal is to produce robust, strong-flavoured wine ('as big as I can get it') that is ready to drink when he sells it. The grapes are hand-picked at advanced sugar levels; the unfer-mented juice is held on its skins for a long period to boost its flavour; the wine is barrel-aged for an extraordinarily long period – two years for Chardonnay, three for Cabernet Sauvignon – and then bottle-aged prior to release.

Eskdale Cabernet Sauvignon is a dark, sturdy red with

excellent depth of berryish, herbal, spicy, chocolatey flavours and well-rounded tannins. The Chardonnay is concentrated, slightly yeasty, savoury and complex. The fleshy, pungently spicy Gewürztraminer ranges in style from dry to medium-dry, depending on the vintage, and sometimes achieves great heights, with a botrytis-derived honeyed richness. These are hand-crafted wines of much appeal.

****½ Gewürztraminer
****   Cabernet Sauvignon, Chardonnay

GUNN ESTATE

85 Ohiti Road, Fernhill. Est 1994. Owners: Alan and Denis Gunn. Production: 2,000 cases.

An opulent, richly expressive, downright delicious Reserve Chardonnay is the greatest achievement of this small winery on the banks of the Ngaruroro River in Ohiti Road, Fernhill.

Two brothers run the company. Alan Gunn, a contract grape-grower since 1982, owns 14 hectares of Chardonnay, Sauvignon Blanc, Riesling, Merlot and Cabernet Sauvignon vines in Ohiti Road, planted in silty loams overlying free-draining gravels. Denis Gunn, a Roseworthy College graduate, previously worked as an assistant winemaker at Villa Maria and then at Kemblefield.

Gunn Estate's wine production started in 1994 and is planned to stay small, rising to only about 4,000 cases, principally of Chardonnay and Merlot. The Chardonnay, given 'short' oak maturation, is a weighty wine with crisp, ripe citrus/peach flavours. The Reserve Chardonnay, fermented in oak (half new), is a more powerful style with layers of lush fruit and toasty oak flavours, rich, mealy and complex. The Merlot/Cabernet Sauvignon is a vibrantly fruity, soft, berryish wine, not highly complex but flavoursome and very easy drinking in its youth.

(****½) Reserve Chardonnay
(***)   Chardonnay, Merlot/Cabernet Sauvignon

HUTHLEE ESTATE VINEYARD

Montana Road, Bridge Pa. Est 1991. Owners: Devon and Estelle Lee. Production: 1,000 cases.

Ripe, supple reds are the key attraction at Devon and Estelle Lee's small Bridge Pa winery. The vineyard name blends Estelle's maiden name, Huthnance, and the couple's married name, Lee.

The Lees bought their 'lifestyle block', planted in peaches and 2 hectares of neglected Merlot and Cabernet Franc vines, in 1984, while Devon was working as a building inspector for the local council. For several years the grapes were sold (some still are), but inspired by a trip through the winelands of Europe, in 1991 the Lees kept some of their grapes and arranged with a local winery to produce their first wine under the Huthlee Estate label.

In free-draining sandy loams overlying river shingles (described by Devon Lee as 'only good for grazing sheep or growing grapes'), the Lees have 8 hectares of Cabernet Franc, Merlot, Cabernet Sauvignon, Pinot Gris and Sauvignon Blanc. In the small on-site winery, built prior to the 1994 vintage, the first wines have all been red or rosé, but 1997 brought the first white wines – a Pinot Gris and Sauvignon Blanc.

The blended Kaweka Red is a decent oak-aged quaffer. The Reserve Cabernet Savignon reveals deep colour, plenty of stuffing and strong, spicy flavour, framed by firm tannins. The Merlot, in contrast, is fresh, raspberryish and plummy in a vibrantly fruity, easy-drinking style.

***½ Reserve Cabernet Sauvignon
***   Merlot
**½   Kaweka Red, Rosé

KEMBLEFIELD ESTATE WINERY

Aorangi Road, Mangatahi. Est 1993. Owners: John Kemble and Kaar Field. Production: 18,750 cases.

The American-financed Kemblefield winery nestles on the banks of the Ngaruroro River, 25 kilometres inland from Hastings, with sweeping views over the terraced valley to the Kaweka Ranges. For part-owner John Kemble, the US market beckons: 'There's very little New Zealand wine sold in the States,' he notes, 'but we've got the distribution contacts.'

Kemble's partner, Californian tax attorney Kaar Field (the 'field' in Kemblefield), still lives in the US. Kemble, the winemaker, graduated in viticulture from the University of California, Davis, in 1983 and for the next nine years was assistant winemaker at the Ravenswood Winery in Sonoma, best known for its hefty Zinfandels. Visiting New Zealand in 1992, he was impressed with Morton Estate's Riverview vineyard, and soon after bought the nearby property on which the Kemblefield winery and 44 hectares of Chardonnay, Sauvignon Blanc, Merlot and Cabernet Sauvignon have since been established.

The first wine, based on bought-in grapes, flowed in 1993 and in 1996 the estate vineyard yielded its first small crop. By the year 2000, production is projected to reach 25,000 cases, which will rank Kemblefield among New Zealand's middle-sized wineries.

The initial Cabernet Sauvignon and Merlot-based reds, based on bought-in fruit, have been plain, light and green-edged. However, the barrel-fermented, lees-aged Chardonnay is stylish and tight-structured, with strong, ripe, lemony fruit and nutty oak. The unwooded Sauvignon Blanc is fresh, ripe and flavoursome, and the Reserve Sauvignon Blanc – the star so far – is a mouthfilling wine with impressive depth of quince and melon-like flavours, oak complexity and a slightly creamy texture.

****   Reserve Sauvignon Blanc
***½ Chardonnay
***   Sauvignon Blanc
**½   Cabernet Sauvignon/Merlot, Gewürztraminer, Merlot

LINDEN ESTATE

State Highway 5, Eskdale. Est 1991. Owners: The van der Linden family. Production: 11,250 cases.
In the heart of the Esk Valley, Linden Estate produces fat, ripe, toasty, buttery-soft Chardonnays of strong drink-young appeal.

The Dutch founder, Wim van der Linden, is a former engineer who emigrated to New Zealand in 1951. Twenty years later, he planted Palomino and Müller-Thurgau vines to supply the fast-expanding McWilliam's (NZ) winery. After Wim's son, John, a tutor in viticulture at the local polytechnic, started growing classic *vinifera* varieties, in 1991 the van der Lindens launched their own wine.

The 22-hectare vineyard, run by another son, Stephen, is planted in Sauvignon Blanc, Chardonnay, Cabernet Sauvignon and Merlot. The majority of the vines are cultivated on the sandy, silty valley floor, but the van der Lindens have also carved a warm, sheltered, north-facing site with hard limestone soils out of the adjacent hills. Known as the Dam Block, this 3-hectare vineyard is yielding markedly darker and more concentrated reserve reds.

Winemaker Nick Chan, formerly of Lincoln Vineyards, who joined Linden Estate in 1995, produces a distinctive style of Chardonnay – high-flavoured, forward and soft, with the reserve label showing strong oak and 'malo' influence. The Reserve Gewürztraminer is a mouthfilling style with good depth of citrusy, spicy, lingering flavour. The Sauvignon Blanc is fresh, ripe and soft in an easy-drinking style; the American oak-aged Reserve Sauvignon Blanc offers ripe, sweet fruit flavours and a subtle seasoning of oak.

The reds have varied in quality. The Cabernet/Merlot has tended to lack fragrance and finesse, but the Merlot can be appealingly perfumed, plummy and supple. Linden Estate's flagship red is clearly the chunky, French oak-matured Reserve Cabernet/Merlot, which reveals excellent depth of ripe, blackcurrant/plum flavours and a firm, persistent finish.

(****) Reserve Cabernet/Merlot, Reserve Chardonnay
(***½) Reserve Sauvignon Blanc
***   Chardonnay, Merlot
(***)   Reserve Gewürztraminer
**½   Sauvignon Blanc
**   Cabernet/Merlot

LOMBARDI WINES

Te Mata Road, Havelock North. Est 1959. Owners: Andy Coltart and Kim Thorp. Production: 1,500 cases.

Lombardi, until recently, was an enigma: a fortified-wine special-ist operating in a region renowned for the quality of its white and red table wines. Now, under its new proprietor, Andy Coltart, the objective is 'to hold on to Lombardi's traditional clientele, while developing a new following for table wines'.

For many years, the winery's *raison d'être* was its Italian-style liqueurs and vermouths. In 1948 English-born W.H. Green and his wife, Tina, born in Italy, planted a 1.2-hectare vineyard near Te Mata Winery in Havelock North. The first Lombardi wine flowed in 1959. The founders' son, Tony, preserved the fortified-wine tradition, producing a wide range of liqueurs, vermouths, 'sherries' and 'ports', plus a small selection of sound but plain table wines.

The long-delayed but inevitable change of direction came in 1994, when the Greens sold the business to their neighbour, Andy Coltart (a self-described 'property developer and farmer') and his partner, Kim Thorp, a Wellington-based advertising agent. The estate vineyard has been replanted in Cabernet Franc, Riesling, Chardonnay and Sauvignon Blanc, with plots of Sangiovese and Montepulciano to preserve the Italian theme.

The first table wines under the new regime have included a robust, ripely herbal Sauvignon Blanc, citrusy, buttery, oak-aged Chardonnay and smooth, slightly herbal Merlot/Cabernet – all sound wines, sensibly priced. The wine-based liqueurs – which at 23 percent alcohol, the legal maximum, pack only a soft punch – include an assortment of flavours – orange, coffee, aniseed. The vermouth selection includes Dry (white), Di Torino (medium red) and Bianco (sweet white). The oak-aged Dessert Cabernet Special Reserve Port is rich, raisiny and creamy-sweet. Lombardi must be heaven for people with a sweet tooth.

(***½) Dessert Cabernet Special Reserve Port
(***)   Chardonnay
(**½) Merlot/Cabernet, Sauvignon Blanc

MISSION VINEYARDS

Church Road, Taradale. Est 1851. Owner: Greenmeadows Mission Trust Board. Production: 60,000 cases.

Mission occupies a special place in New Zealand wine. It is by far the oldest winemaking enterprise, and the country's only nineteenth-century wine producer still under the same manage-ment. The wines, until recently, tended to offer average quality at a below-average price, but during the 1990s the Mission has enjoyed mounting competition success, especially for its Chardonnays, claret-style reds and botrytised sweet whites under the premium Jewelstone label.

Nestled at Greenmeadows, at the foot of the Taradale Hills near Napier, the vineyards and winery are run by the Catholic Society of Mary to fund its Marist seminary, which after 80 years at Taradale shifted to Auckland in 1990. Set amidst peaceful lawns and trees on an elevated site overlooking the winery, the former seminary building now serves as a hostel for polytechnic students, a luncheon restaurant, and an ever-present reminder of the Mission's action-packed past.

French missionaries first based the Marist Hawke's Bay mission at Pakowhai in 1851, laying out orchards and vineyards until Maori intertribal warfare in 1857 forced a move to Meeanee. For several decades wine production stayed on a tiny scale, sufficient only to supply the fathers' sacramental and table wine needs. Not until the 1890s were the first sales recorded, principally of red wines.

After floodwaters swept across the Meeanee plains and inundated the Mission cellars in 1897, the Society of Mary was forced to move again, this time to higher ground. A new 4-hectare vineyard was soon planted at Greenmeadows, but it was not until 1910, after more ruinous flooding, that the seminary itself was cut into sections and hauled by steam engine to Greenmeadows.

Under the guidance of Brother John, the winemaker from the 1960s until 1982, Mission acquired a reputation for sound, although unspectacular, wines. Fontanella, Mission's bottle-fermented sparkling wine (long ago phased out of the range) was viewed as the country's finest, although rarest, bubbly.

Today Mission, a medium-sized winery by New Zealand standards, has its first lay winemaker – Paul Mooney, a BSc graduate who arrived in 1979. About half of the Mission's grapes are purchased from growers in Hawke's Bay (with especially good fruit flowing from vineyards in Ohiti Road, near Roy's Hill) and Gisborne. The company's own plantings include a fertile, 16-hectare block at Meeanee, viewed as a 'bulk' site; the less vigorous, 16-hectare Greenmeadows vineyard (including the 'Chanel block'), which yields outstanding Chardonnay; and a new 10-hectare vineyard in extremely shingly soils ('that won't even grow grass,' says Mooney) in Gimblett Road, where Cabernet Sauvignon, Syrah, Merlot and Petit Verdot have been planted.

The Mission markets a broad selection of wines, typically sharply priced. Chardonnay is a special strength, from the standard Chardonnay, a partly barrel-fermented wine with fresh, crisp fruit and a touch of oaky, buttery complexity; to the middle-tier St Peter Chanel Chardonnay, a sort of junior Jewelstone Chardonnay, grown in the same block but with less new oak influence; and finally to the powerful, high impact, splendidly concentrated and creamy Jewelstone Chardonnay.

The East Coast Sauvignon Blanc, blended from Hawke's Bay

and Gisborne fruit, is a pleasant, light wine, fractionally off-dry. I prefer the Reserve Sauvignon Blanc, a partly barrel-fermented Hawke's Bay wine with loads of fresh, green-edged, slightly nutty flavour. Other attractive white wines include the slightly sweet, full-bodied, peachy and earthy Pinot Gris; the well-spiced, gingery, flavoursome Gewürztraminer, also made in a medium-dry style; and the deep-scented, incisively flavoured, mouth-wateringly crisp Rhine Riesling. Of the trio of sweet whites, the standout is the intense and treacly Jewelstone Noble Riesling.

The lower-tier reds, Cabernet Sauvignon and Cabernet Sauvignon/Merlot, are matured in seasoned oak casks. In lesser years, they can be unripe and thin, but in warm, dry years they offer quite good depth of attractive, blackcurrant-and-spice flavours and rounded tannins, with the straight Cabernet Sauvignon typically offering slightly greater flavour richness. Mission's top red, however, is clearly the enticingly perfumed, ripely fruity and complex Jewelstone Merlot/Cabernet Sauvignon.

*****   Jewelstone Noble Riesling
****½   Jewelstone Chardonnay, Jewelstone Merlot/ Cabernet Sauvignon
****   Jewelstone Botrytised Riesling, Rhine Riesling
***½   St Peter Chanel Chardonnay
(***½) Jewelstone Pinot Grigio Dry
***   Cabernet Franc, Cabernet Sauvignon, Chardonnay, Gewürztraminer, Ice Wine, Pinot Gris, Reserve Sauvignon Blanc
**½   Cabernet Sauvignon/Merlot, East Coast Sauvignon Blanc, Mirage, Sémillon/Sauvignon Blanc, White Mirage

NGATARAWA WINES

Ngatarawa Road, Bridge Pa, Hastings. Est 1981. Owners: Alwyn Corban and Garry Glazebrook. Production: 30,000 cases.
This fast-growing winery produces an impressive Chardonnay and Cabernet/Merlot under its flagship Glazebrook label, but winemaker Alwyn Corban's greatest achievement is his gorgeously botrytised sweet Rieslings.

Corban is a reserved, amiable personality, one of the industry's gentlemen. The son of Alex Corban – Corbans' production manager from 1952 to 1976 and the Wine Institute's first chairman – Alwyn graduated from the University of California, Davis, with a master's degree in oenology, and later worked for four years at McWilliam's in Napier, before forming the Ngatarawa partnership with Garry Glazebrook, owner of the large Washpool sheep station, in 1981.

The charmingly rustic winery at Bridge Pa, inland from Hastings, is based partly in the Glazebrooks' former racing stables, built in the late nineteenth century. Eighteen hectares of vines have been planted in the 'Hastings dry belt', an area known for its relatively low rainfall. In the estate vineyard, Riesling, Sauvignon Blanc and Cabernet Sauvignon are grown in sandy loams over alluvial gravels; further to the west, another block is established in Chardonnay, Cabernet Sauvignon, Merlot, Malbec and Cabernet Franc. Grapes are also purchased from Hawke's Bay growers.

The wines are marketed under a three-tier system. The top wines are labelled Glazebrook, mid-priced varietals carry the Stables label, and everyday-drinking wines are designated Classic. Launched from the 1996 vintage, the Classic range includes a peachy, buttery-soft Chardonnay, a weighty, ripe and smooth Sauvignon Blanc and a full-bodied, fresh Cabernet/Merlot with smooth berry/spice flowers.

Stables Chardonnay is a barrel-fermented wine with quite good body and flavour depth and a touch of complexity in a forward, soft style. Stables Sauvignon Blanc is full-bodied, with fresh, crisp tropical-fruit flavours. Riesling-based but not heavily botrytised, Stables Late Harvest is a floral, medium-sweet wine with fresh, delicate, lemony, slightly honeyish flavour. Designed for early consumption, Stables Cabernet/Merlot is a sturdy, lightly oaked red with pleasing depth of blackcurrant/plum flavour and a smooth finish.

Under its Old Saddlers label, Ngatarawa produces a solid tawny 'port' and a superior, mellow and complex medium-sweet 'sherry', barrel-aged for over a decade.

Glazebrook Reserve Chardonnay, fermented and lees-aged in predominantly new French oak barriques, is a mouthfilling, rich, mealy, oaky, citrusy wine with a taut acid spine. Glazebrook Cabernet/Merlot is typically concentrated and firm, with the latest vintages (more Merlot-influenced) notably more fragrant and supple than the relatively austere wines of the past.

Based on shrivelled, nobly rotten Riesling grapes, for which the hand-pickers make several separate sweeps through the vineyard, Glazebrook Noble Harvest is a beautifully poised and searching wine with a highly concentrated, honey-sweet fragrance and flavour; one of New Zealand's greatest 'stickies'.

In 1994, Corban set aside a tiny amount of ultra-ripe (42 brix) Riesling with 100 percent noble rot infection. Searching for 'an extra dimension and complexity', he barrel-fermented the wine and matured it in wood for eighteen months. Light gold, with a ravishing, honeyed perfume, it is powerful and succulent, with great weight through the palate. Yet it is not a Sauternes style – the wood adds richness, but the fruit flavours show the finesse and acid spine of Riesling. At $NZ60 per 375 ml bottle, Alwyn Noble Harvest is by far New Zealand's most expensive wine.

***** **Glazebrook Noble Harvest**
(*****)**Alwyn Noble Harvest**

**** ½ Glazebrook Reserve Cabernet/Merlot, Glazebrook
Reserve Chardonnay
*** ½ Old Saddlers Sherry
*** Stables Cabernet/Merlot, Stables Chardonnay,
Stables Late Harvest, Stables Sauvignon Blanc/
Classic Cabernet/ Merlot, Classic Chardonnay,
Classic Sauvignon Blanc
** ½ Old Saddlers Port

RIVERSIDE WINES

*Dartmoor Road, Puketapu. Est 1989. Owners: Ian and Rachel
Cadwallader. Production: 3,750 cases.*

There's a lot happening at Ian and Rachel Cadwallader's farm,
Rosemount, in the peaceful Dartmoor Valley, inland from Napier.
The family graze sheep and cattle, grow crops, including grapes,
and since 1989 have made wine under the Riverside label.

Ian Cadwallader's family has farmed in the Dartmoor for 146
years. The couple planted their first vines in 1981 but for the first
few years sold the grapes to established wineries. The early
Riverside wines were made in a converted boatshed, but in 1993
a purpose-built winery was erected, and three years later an
experienced winemaker, Nigel Davies, formerly of Villa Maria
and Babich, was hired.

Cabernet Sauvignon, Merlot, Sauvignon Blanc and
Chardonnay are cultivated on alluvial river flats below the slightly elevated winery, and on a nearby river terrace with lighter red
metal soils, Cabernet Sauvignon, Pinotage and Sémillon have
been planted. Much of the crop from the Cadwalladers'
20 hectares of vineyards is still sold to other wineries.

The wines to date have been plain, with few highlights. The
Chardonnays are sometimes enjoyable in their youth, but have
been of varying quality and have not always matured gracefully.
However, the full-bodied, flavoursome Chardonnay from 1996
and the stylish, ripe and mealy 1996 Reserve Chardonnay are a
big step forward. The Barrel Fermented Sauvignon Blanc has
lacked the flavour richness and finesse expected of a wine in its
high price bracket. The reds and rosé are typically medium-bodied, with slightly green-edged flavours of moderate depth.

(***) Reserve Chardonnay
(**½) Cabernet/Merlot, Chardonnay
** Barrel Fermented Sauvignon Blanc, Merlot, Rosé

SACRED HILL WINERY

*Dartmoor Road, Puketapu. Est 1986. Owners: The Mason family.
Production: 22,500 cases.*

Named after nearby Puketapu ('sacred hill'), this deceptively rustic winery lies at the head of the Dartmoor Valley in the back-
country hills. Seemingly content in the past to produce solid but

plain wines, in recent years Sacred Hill has started to make some superb Chardonnays, reds, and sweet whites.

The winery is run by David and Mark Mason; David controls the administration and Mark focuses on the vineyards. Four years after their father began planting vines, in 1986 the brothers reserved the pick of the crop and made the first Sacred Hill wine. The early years proved a financial struggle, but lately production has expanded swiftly and the brothers have become part-owners of Rockwood Cellars, a contract crushing facility in Hastings which produces several wines (notably fresh, smooth reds and a strapping, deeply flavoured Reserve Selection Chardonnay) under its own label.

The fertile, silty, 12-hectare vineyard near the winery is planted in Sauvignon Blanc, Chardonnay, Gewürztraminer, Pinot Noir, Cabernet Sauvignon, Cabernet Franc and Syrah. Further up the valley, on a stunning site above sheer white cliffs carved by the Tutaekuri River, the much less fertile, lower-cropping 7.5-hectare Whitecliff vineyard is planted in a wide selection of grapes.

With winemaker Tony Bish (formerly of French Farm Vineyards and Rippon Vineyard) at the helm, and further input from consultant winemaker Jenny Dobson (who spent twelve years as *maître-de-chais* at Château Sénéjac, a *cru bourgeois* in the Haut-Médoc region of Bordeaux), in the mid-to-late 1990s the standard of Sacred Hill wines has soared.

From the start, Sauvignon Blanc has been a mainstay of the range and is now produced in various styles – unwooded, barrel-fermented, honey-sweet. Whitecliff Sauvignon Blanc is a fresh, crisp, straightforward wine with melon and lime-like flavours. The Barrel Fermented Sauvignon Blanc shows richer, lusher fruit flavours with a backdrop of nutty oak. Sauvage, fermented with natural yeasts in all-new French oak casks, is a robust, ripely flavoured, boldly-wooded Sauvignon Blanc that demands cellaring. A lovely, slightly Sauternes-like, French oak-fermented Late Harvest Sauvignon Blanc has also been produced with fullness of body and fresh, ripe, honeyish, oaky, complex flavours.

Whitecliff Chardonnay is a fruit-driven style, fresh and crisp, for early drinking. The Reserve Barrel Fermented Chardonnay reveals impressive weight and depth of rich, tropical and citrus fruit flavours, fleshed out with toasty wood. Huge in body, the outstanding Rifleman's Chardonnay is a richly fragrant wine with a powerful, creamy palate and very intense grapefruit and fig-like flavours.

Of Sacred Hill's extensive range, one of the recent highlights has been the substantial, strong-flavoured, plummy, slightly minty and well-rounded Basket Press Merlot/Cabernet Sauvignon. From the 1995 vintage, Brokenstone Merlot is a highly perfumed red with ripe, sweet-fruit characters and impressive richness. XS Noble Selection, a Riesling-based sticky with a fun name, is a golden, weighty beauty with mouth-encircling, lemony, honeyish, botrytis-enriched flavour and a long, succulent finish.

(*****) Rifleman's Chardonnay, XS Noble Selection
(****½) Brokenstone Merlot
****   Reserve Barrel Fermented Chardonnay, Reserve
          Barrel Fermented Sauvignon Blanc
(****) Basket Press Merlot/Cabernet Sauvignon, Late
          Harvest Sauvignon Blanc, Sauvage
***   Whitecliff Cabernet Rosé, Pinot Noir
(***)   Late Harvest Gewürztraminer
**½   Whitecliff Chardonnay, Whitecliff Gewürztraminer,
          Whitecliff Sauvignon Blanc
(**½)   Whitecliff Merlot

ST GEORGE ESTATE

St George's Road South, Hastings. Est 1985. Owners: Martin and Gillian Elliott. Production: 675 cases.

Only a trickle flows from this Cape Dutch-style winery on the Havelock North–Hastings Highway. Martin Elliott sells his entire output directly from the winery – over the counter, by mail order, or in the cosy, often crowded vineyard restaurant.

Founded in 1985, St George Estate was originally a partnership between Martin Elliott (formerly owner of the local wine shop), and Michael Bennett, who gained his early winemaking experience at Villa Maria, Vidal and Te Mata. When Bennett left the company in 1993, Elliott and his wife, Gillian, emerged as the sole owners.

The 2-hectare estate vineyard, on flat, silty soils adjacent to the winery, is planted in Muscat, Merlot and Cabernet Franc; other grapes are purchased from Hawke's Bay growers. The wines, made by Elliott with the assistance of a local winemaking consultant, are typically workmanlike, with the full-bloomed, slightly sweet and soft, totally undemanding July Muscat the most popular.

**½ July Muscat, Sauvignon Blanc
**   Rosé
(*)   Chardonnay

STONECROFT WINES

Mere Road, Hastings. Est 1983. Owner: Dr Alan Limmer. Production: 2,250 cases.

'Wine is created in the vineyard,' says Dr Alan Limmer, a former agricultural chemist who runs the small Stonecroft Winery in Mere Road, near Hastings. Stonecroft's combination of a hot vineyard site and low-vigour soils produce bold, ripe wines with notable colour and flavour depth, including New Zealand's most acclaimed Syrah.

Limmer studied earth sciences and chemistry at Waikato University, where he earned a PhD, then worked in an agricultural laboratory in Hawke's Bay. After scouring the Heretaunga Plains for six months for an 'ideal plot of dirt', in 1983 he planted his first vines in Mere Road and four years later made his first wine.

Behind the winery, in silty, sandy gravels running 10 metres deep, Limmer has planted 4 hectares of Chardonnay, Gewürztraminer, Sauvignon Blanc, Cabernet Sauvignon, Merlot and Syrah. At about 6 tonnes per hectare, the vines crop lightly. In a sheltered, north-facing bowl at the base of Roy's Hill, a second, exclusively red-wine vineyard has been planted in Syrah, Merlot, and experimental plots of Zinfandel, Cinsaut and Mourvèdre.

New Zealand's first winemaker to master Syrah, Limmer looks to France rather than Australia for his inspiration. 'The Australian wines are big, upfront, with jammy fruit and American oak, but they tend to be one-dimensional [whereas] the reds of the northern Rhône have everything – fragrance, structure, aging ability.' Limmer avoids American oak, preferring to mature his Syrah for 18 months in French oak barriques (50–60 percent new), and with its flashing purple-black hues, rich, peppery perfume, generous body and powerful surge of red-berry, plum and spice flavours, his wine can be highly reminiscent of a good Crozes-Hermitage.

Ruhanui, launched from the 1994 vintage, is a richly fragrant, densely coloured blend of Cabernet Sauvignon, Merlot and Syrah, softly mouthfilling, with deep, warm blackcurrant and pepper flavours and a long, supple finish. (This replaces, and in quality surpasses, the former Cabernet/Merlot.) Berryish and plummy, with plenty of flavour, the lower-priced Crofters Red is made from a similar varietal blend to Ruhanui, but based on young vines and lesser barrels.

Stonecroft Chardonnay reveals lush, ripe grapefruit-like flavours, with new French oak adding complexity, and a long, soft finish. The Sauvignon Blanc is also a very ripe and rounded style, dry but with sweet, lush fruit flavours.

A 'Gewurz' fan, Limmer produces two styles: a powerful, weighty wine with a sliver of sweetness and strong, very ripe flavours of lychees and pepper; and the mouthfilling, sweet, barrel-fermented Late Harvest model, with a spicy, earthy, rather Alsace-like fragrance and rich, complex flavour.

*****   Syrah
(*****) Ruhanui
****½   Chardonnay, Gewürztraminer
****   Gewürztraminer Late Harvest, Sauvignon Blanc
(***½) Crofters Red

TE AWA FARM WINERY

State Highway 50, Roy's Hill. Est 1992. Owners: The Lawson family.
Production: 9,000 cases.

It's early days yet, but the initial wines to emerge from Ian and
Gus Lawson's vineyard at Roy's Hill have been classy enough to
suggest their five-year hunt for a premium red-wine and
Chardonnay site was not in vain.

Contract grape-growers since 1980, Ian Lawson and his son,
Angus ('Gus') purchased the 173-hectare Te Awa Farm, on the
corner of Ngatarawa Road and State Highway 50, near Gimblett
Road, in 1992. Gus Lawson manages the wine venture, and also
acts as a viticultural consultant to other growers and wineries in
the region.

Thirty-two hectares of close-spaced Cabernet Sauvignon,
Merlot, Syrah, Cabernet Franc, Malbec, Pinot Noir, Chardonnay
and Sauvignon Blanc vines have been planted in free-draining,
shallow alluvial soils. The wines, based on estate-grown, hand-
picked grapes, have initially been produced at a local winery, but
the Lawsons plan to build their own winery and employ a specialist winemaker.

Te Awa Farm's flagship wines carry the Boundary label and
the larger volume wines are called Longlands. Balanced for early
consumption, the partly French and American oak-fermented
Longlands Chardonnay is a smooth-flowing wine with ripe fruit
aromas, good depth of delicate, slightly buttery and nutty
flavours and a well-rounded finish. The top-tier Boundary
Chardonnay, 100 percent French oak-fermented, is an elegant,
firm wine with crisp grapefruit and nutty wood flavours in a
steely, slowly evolving style.

Longlands Cabernet/Merlot is full and smooth, with plenty of
ripe, plummy, spicy flavour. Even better is the silky, voluptuous
Boundary Merlot, a rich, ripely flavoured wine with deep colour
and a solid foundation of tannin.

(****) Boundary Chardonnay, Boundary Merlot
***½ Longlands Chardonnay
***   Longlands Cabernet/Merlot

TE AWANGA VINEYARDS

Parkhill Road, Te Awanga. Est 1995. Owners: Jim Scotland, Michael
Hewitt and partners. Production: 1,500 cases.

Two grape-growers with many years' experience are the key figures in this fast-growing venture. Jim Scotland has enjoyed particular success growing Riesling for Coopers Creek; Michael
Hewitt, a general practitioner, has supplied much of his fruit to
Morton Estate.

The company owns two vineyards. The Lawn Road Vineyard,
on the Tukituki River, is planted in Chardonnay, Sauvignon Blanc,

Cabernet Sauvignon, Merlot and Cabernet Franc. On the coast at Te Awanga, another 20-hectare vineyard is being established near Clearview Estate, in Chardonnay, Sauvignon Blanc, Sémillon, Merlot, Cabernet Franc, Pinot Noir and Cabernet Sauvignon.

The first 1995 wines were made at Morton Estate, but the company plans to erect its own winery in late 1997. The early releases have included a barrel-fermented, full flavoured and reasonably complex Hawke's Bay Chardonnay and a fruity, supple, very approachable Hawke's Bay Cabernet/Merlot 1995.

(***) **Hawke's Bay Cabernet/Merlot**
(**) **Hawke's Bay Chardonnay**

TE MATA ESTATE WINERY

Te Mata Road, Havelock North. Est 1896. Owner: Te Mata Estate Winery Limited. Production: 23,000 cases.

A pair of New Zealand's most distinguished reds (Coleraine and Awatea Cabernet/Merlots) plus one of its highest-flying Chardonnays (Elston) and two fine Sauvignon Blancs (Cape Crest and Castle Hill) flow from this historic Havelock North winery. John Buck, one of New Zealand's most knowledgeable and astute wine professionals, is the driving force behind Te Mata's resounding success.

Te Mata's roots lie in the late nineteenth century. A hobby vineyard, planted in 1892 by Bernard Chambers of the Te Mata Station, thrived, encouraging him to convert a stable built in 1872 into a cellar and, in 1896, to embark on commercial wine production. By 1909 Chambers' vineyard covered 14 hectares and was the largest in the country.

Following this early flourish Te Mata's fortunes entered a long period of decline. Its renaissance began in 1974 under the guidance of the current partners in the company: Michael Morris, a Wellington executive, and the short, sharp-witted and extroverted John Buck. Buck's lengthy wine career has embraced an unusual diversity of roles: retailer, author, merchant, columnist and now winery part-owner and general manager.

After restoring the old brick and native timber winery and purchasing new barrels and tanks, the new owners processed their first vintage in 1979. Success was swift. Te Mata Cabernet Sauvignon 1980 captured the trophy for the top red wine at the 1981 National Wine Competition, and a year later the 1981 vintage repeated the feat. Soon after, Te Mata withdrew from competitions.

The company leases and manages, rather than purchases, vineyards. However, its key personnel do own vineyards. At Maraekakaho, inland from Hastings, the 8-hectare Bullnose Vineyard has been planted by Buck, Morris and winemaker Peter Cowley in Cabernet Sauvignon, Merlot, Cabernet Franc and Syrah. The Woodthorpe Terraces project on the south side of the

Dartmoor Valley, which involves establishing 120 hectares of vines (principally Cabernet Sauvignon, Merlot and Chardonnay) and erecting a fully self-contained winery, is being funded by Te Mata Estate in a joint venture with an investment company in which Buck's wife, Wendy, has a stake.

Although primarily renowned for its reds, Te Mata also markets outstanding white wines. 'The Chardonnay fruit we get is fat and ripe with grapefruit flavours,' says Cowley, who trained with distinction at Roseworthy College in South Australia and then worked a couple of vintages at Delegat's before joining Te Mata in 1985. 'I want to keep that flavour but add to it with nine months in wood and some lees contact . . . some proportion of malolactic fermentation helps.' Elston Chardonnay stands out for its power and ability to flourish for several years in the bottle, evolving splendidly rich, complex, citrusy, savoury flavours. A lower-priced, partly barrel-fermented Chardonnay is also produced with fat, peachy-ripe, buttery flavours and lots of drink-young appeal.

Both of the Sauvignon Blancs are single-vineyard wines, mouthfilling, ripely herbal, dry and lingering. Te Mata seeks to produce Sauvignon Blancs which will improve in the bottle, peaking at eighteen months to three years old. Castle Hill is an unwooded style with fresh, limey, zingy varietal characters, whereas the fully barrel-fermented Cape Crest is typically slightly bigger, richer and more complex.

Te Mata's claret-style reds have deserved their acclaim. Single-vineyard wines from 1982 to 1988, since 1989 they have been blended from Te Mata's spectrum of vineyards and marketed in a tiered group, with Coleraine at the top, then Awatea, and finally a lower-priced Cabernet/Merlot. (A classy Bullnose Syrah with intense, delicate raspberry/black pepper flavours is also emerging.)

Awatea Cabernet/Merlot, oak-matured for eighteen months, is a dense-coloured, richly fragrant wine with a lovely surge of ripe, blackcurrant and spice flavours and a well-rounded finish. As Buck puts it, this is a 'more supple, more fragrant [in its youth], more forward style than Coleraine'. Delicious at two years old, overflowing with sweet fruit flavours, it can also age gracefully for several years.

Te Mata's highest-profile wine, Coleraine Cabernet/Merlot, is a deep-flavoured and tautly structured wine, fragrant and multi-dimensional. Typically more closed in its youth than Awatea, it is more new oak-influenced and in style bears a strong resemblance to a fine Médoc. Although during the 1980s it enjoyed a reputation second to none among New Zealand's reds, several vintages were disappointingly lean and green-edged. However, since 1989 the quality has been consistently high. Breed and delicacy, rather than sheer power, are the essence of Coleraine – the sublime 1991 vintage can hold its own in any company.

*****	Awatea Cabernet/Merlot, Cape Crest Sauvignon Blanc, Coleraine Cabernet/Merlot, Elston Chardonnay
(****½)	Bullnose Syrah
****	Castle Hill Sauvignon Blanc
(****)	Chardonnay
***½	Cabernet/Merlot
***	Oak Aged Dry White, Rosé

THE McDONALD WINERY

200 Church Road, Taradale. Est 1989. Owner: Montana Wines.

Tom McDonald was the first post-war winemaker to chart Hawke's Bay's red-wine potential, and the driving force behind New Zealand's first prestige red. It is thus fitting that Montana's recent production of some of Hawke's Bay's greatest reds has involved keeping the McDonald name alive.

Determined to upgrade its red wine quality, Montana, previously not heavily involved in the region, thrust into Hawke's Bay in 1988 and 1989, snapping up 238 hectares of established vineyards and the old McDonald Winery. After swiftly spending $NZ2 million to upgrade the building and its equipment for the 1990 vintage, Montana had the vineyard resources and a small-scale production facility ideal for making top-flight table wines.

The McDonald Winery, nestled against the flanks of the Taradale hills, was founded in 1897 by Bartholomew Steinmetz, a lay brother at the Mission who, the story goes, after falling in love left to plant his own 2-hectare Taradale Vineyards. Tom McDonald, aged fourteen, started labouring there in 1921 and five years later bought Steinmetz out.

After the (renamed) McDonald's Winery merged with McWilliam's (NZ) in 1962, Tom McDonald stepped into the powerful post of McWilliam's production director until his retirement in 1976. Under both the McDonald's and McWilliam's labels, McDonald proved the point that Hawke's Bay reds could achieve excellence. André Simon, the legendary wine writer, in 1964 praised the McDonald's Cabernet 1949 as 'a rare and convincing proof that New Zealand can bring forth table wines of a very high standard of quality'. In 1965 came the first vintage of the great 1965–75 series of white-labelled McWilliam's Cabernet Sauvignons that were so excitingly superior to anything else in the country.

In its current bid to produce outstanding reds in Hawke's Bay, Montana has enlisted the assistance of the Bordeaux house of Cordier, owner of several properties including the illustrious Châteaux Gruaud-Larose and Talbot in St Julien. 'Cordier has focused us on a narrow range of concerns,' reports winemaker Tony Prichard. 'The quality and amount of tannins, barrel handling [no American oak], blending and – the key thing – eliminating herbaceousness.'

Church Road Cabernet Sauvignon/Merlot is a wonderful buy. Distinctly Bordeaux-like in structure, it is chunky and spicy, nutty, warm and complex, with very good depth of fruit braced by firm but balanced tannins. This is a notably elegant and harmonious red. The Reserve model is a bolder, richer wine, sturdy and supple, with superb depth of brambly, chocolatey, spicy, cedary flavour and very fine-grained tannins.

The consistently impressive Church Road Chardonnay (fermented in one-third new French and American oak barriques) is typically fragrant, with rich, ripe, grapefruit-like, mealy, toasty flavour in a forward, rounded style. The more powerful Church Road Reserve Chardonnay, based on the 'pick' of the crop, fermented and lees-aged in French oak barriques (two-thirds new), is a very mouthfilling style with ripe stone-fruit flavours, impressive complexity and an oaky, buttery richness.

Produced in small volumes, Twin Rivers Cuvée Brut is a delicate, moderately yeasty, invigoratingly crisp bottle-fermented sparkling of good but not outstanding quality.

'Project Tom' (honouring Tom McDonald) is the name of Montana's bid to produce New Zealand's 'finest ever red wine'. The first 1995 vintage, a Hawke's Bay blend of Cabernet Sauvignon and Merlot, is being trumpeted by the company as 'a turning point for New Zealand reds'. Made at The McDonald Winery with assistance from Cordier, it will be released in 1998.

***** Church Road Reserve Chardonnay, Church Road
        Reserve Cabernet/Merlot
****½ Church Road Cabernet Sauvignon/Merlot
****   Church Road Chardonnay
***½   Twin Rivers Cuvée Brut

TRINITY HILL

2396 State Highway 50, Roy's Hill. Est 1993. Owners: John and Jennifer Hancock, Robert and Robyn Wilson, Hanne and Trevor Janes. Production: 2,000 cases.

John Hancock, the driving force behind this new winery on State Highway 50, west of Hastings, is best known for the string of superb Chardonnays he fashioned for over a decade at Morton Estate.

Trinity Hill was founded in 1993 by three families (hence the winery name): Robert and Robyn Wilson, London developers and restaurateurs; Auckland stockbroker Trevor Janes and his wife, Hanne (early shareholders in Morton Estate); and John and Jennifer Hancock. The company's 16-hectare vineyard in Gimblett Road has been planted in Chardonnay, Cabernet Sauvignon, Merlot and Syrah, and grapes are also purchased from Hawke's Bay growers.

When production reaches the planned 30,000 cases (at least half red) Trinity Hill will rank as a medium-sized producer. 'We're after finesse,' says Hancock. 'We're handling the juice gently, in small batches, to reduce phenolics.' The first 1996 wines were made at a local winery, but the company's own winery was up and running for the 1997 vintage.

Grown in the Shepherd's Croft vineyard in the Ngatarawa district, the Sauvignon Blanc is a fresh, lively wine with ripe melon/lime flavours and appetising acidity. Shepherd's Croft Chardonnay is tight and elegant, with excellent depth of citrusy, mealy, crisp flavour. Dark and smooth, Shepherd's Croft Syrah/Merlot/Cabernet Franc is a powerful, flavour-packed red, warm, supple and peppery.

(****) Shepherd's Croft Chardonnay, Shepherd's Croft
          Syrah/Merlot/Cabernet Franc
(***½) Shepherd's Croft Sauvignon Blanc

VIDAL ESTATE

913 St Aubyns Street East, Hastings. Est 1905. Owner: Villa Maria Estate. Production: 90,000 cases.

The Vidal and Esk Valley wineries lie at opposite ends of the Bay: Esk Valley north of Napier, Vidal in the heart of Hastings. Yet these sister wineries are both integral parts of the Villa Maria empire and produce outstanding Chardonnays and claret-style reds.

For more than half a century, the Vidal family controlled the company. The founder, Spanish-born Anthony Vidal, in 1905 purchased a half-hectare Hastings property, planted grapevines and converted the existing stables into a winery. After control passed to his three sons – Leslie, who concentrated on viticulture; Frank, the winemaker; and Cecil, who handled sales – Vidal continued to build a strong reputation. Its Burgundy and Claret, hybrid-based but incorporating some Cabernet Sauvignon, enjoyed national demand.

However, after Seppelt of Australia purchased a majority shareholding in 1972, Vidal's reputation declined, until Villa Maria acquired the winery in 1976. The wine quality swiftly rose and in 1979, amidst much publicity, New Zealand's first vineyard bar and restaurant was opened at Vidal.

Elise Montgomery, winemaker since 1990, works almost entirely with grapes grown on a contract basis in Hawke's Bay and, to a lesser extent, Gisborne. (Blends of these regions are labelled East Coast.) Vidal has a particularly illustrious reputation for its reserve reds: the Reserve Cabernet Sauvignon/Merlot 1990 won the trophy for Champion Wine of the Air New Zealand Wine Awards in 1992 and 1993.

The commercial range offers flavoursome, sharply priced wines, well-balanced for early drinking. The slightly sweet Gewürztraminer offers good depth of spicy/citric flavours; the Chenin Blanc/Chardonnay is a fleshy and flavourful, all-purpose dry white with a light seasoning of oak.

Two Sauvignon Blancs are made: the fresh, ripely aromatic and soft, unwooded East Coast Sauvignon Blanc and the full-bodied, passionfruit and lime-flavoured, lightly oaked East Coast Fumé Blanc. The moderately priced, briefly oak-matured East Coast Chardonnay and Hawke's Bay Chardonnay are both fresh, crisp, buoyantly fruity wines designed for early drinking, with good depth of apple/lemon flavours.

The Cabernet Sauvignon/Merlot is not highly concentrated, but typically flavoursome, ripe and smooth. The Pinot Noir is typically a floral, supple, middle-weight red with pleasant raspberry/cherry flavours, although the 1996 is more powerful, with excellent depth. The middle-tier range, labelled The Bays, includes a weighty, satisfyingly rich and subtle Chardonnay, fermented and matured in French and American oak barriques, and the sturdy Merlot/Cabernet Sauvignon, which reveals excellent depth of plummy, spicy, well-rounded flavour.

Vidal's reserve selection features some of Hawke's Bay's most outstanding wines. The Reserve Gewürztraminer is restrained in its youth, but after two or three years unfolds delicate, strongly spicy flavours. The Reserve Noble Sémillon, fermented in new French oak barriques, is a golden, mouthfilling, oily, honeyish wine of unusual richness and complexity.

The established jewels in the Vidal crown are the Reserve Chardonnay and Reserve Cabernet-based reds. The Reserve Chardonnay is a bold, lush wine with a lovely integration of rich, grapefruit-like flavours, nutty, biscuity oak and lees-aging characters. The top reds – the Reserve Cabernet Sauvignon and Reserve Cabernet Sauvignon/Merlot – are consistently outstanding, with deep colour and superbly concentrated and complex, tightly structured flavour. At ten years old, Vidal Reserve Cabernet Sauvignon/Merlot 1987, champion wine of the 1990 Sydney International Wine Competition, is in majestic form.

*****	Reserve Cabernet Sauvignon, Reserve Cabernet Sauvignon/Merlot, Reserve Chardonnay
(*****½)	Reserve Noble Sémillon
****	Reserve Fumé Blanc, Reserve Gewürztraminer
(****)	The Bays Chardonnay, The Bays Merlot/Cabernet Sauvignon
***½	Gewürztraminer, Merlot Rosé, Méthode Traditionnelle Brut, Müller-Thurgau, Pinot Noir
***	Cabernet Sauvignon/Merlot, Chenin Blanc/Chardonnay, East Coast Chardonnay, East Coast Fumé Blanc, East Coast Sauvignon Blanc, Hawke's Bay Chardonnay

WAIMARAMA ESTATE

267 Te Mata-Mangateretere Road, Havelock North. Est 1988. Owners: The Loughlin family. Production: 3,000 cases.

On his sheltered, north-facing slope overlooking the glistening

Tukituki River (Waimarama means 'moonlight on water'), John Loughlin has set out to produce 'the finest possible Bordeaux-style red wines'.

The vineyard and winery lie at the foot of Te Mata Peak, on the outskirts of Havelock North. Loughlin, a busy eye surgeon, purchased the property in 1972, but not until 1988 were the first vines planted. Four hectares of Cabernet Sauvignon, Merlot, Cabernet Franc and Malbec are now established in loamy soils of moderate fertility. Loughlin also manages and draws grapes from a neighbour's 2-hectare vineyard, planted wholly in Syrah.

Three kilometres away on Te Mata-Mangateretere Road, John Loughlin's son – also called John – and his wife, Kathryn, have established the 4-hectare Askern Vineyard, planted in white-wine grapes: Sémillon, Sauvignon Blanc, Riesling, Gewürztraminer and Chardonnay. Waimarama's retail outlet is based here.

Loughlin makes the wines himself, assisted by consultant Jenny Dobson, who returned to New Zealand in 1995 after twelve years as the *maître-de-chais* at Château Sénéjac, a *cru bourgeois* of the Haut-Médoc. The outstanding quality of the debut 1991 reds was not repeated until 1995, but at their best, Waimarama Estate's wines show a Bordeaux-like richness, delicacy and finesse.

French oak-aged, the Cabernet Sauvignon displays strong blackcurrant and cedary oak flavours, with chewy tannins. The Merlot is supple, spicy and harmonious, and top vintages of the Cabernet/Merlot are refined, complex and lingering. These are high quality reds, well-priced.

Undercliffe Cabernet/Merlot, the second-tier label, appears in lesser years. Waimarama Estate also makes a purple-black, fortified Dessert Cabernet with sweet, chocolatey flavours.

**** Cabernet/Merlot, Cabernet Sauvignon
(*****) Merlot
(***½) Dessert Cabernet
(**½) Undercliffe Cabernet/Merlot

Wairarapa

Seductively scented and silky Pinot Noirs that challenge those of California, Oregon and Victoria's Yarra Valley as the finest in the New World, are the most striking wines from New Zealand's fifth-largest wine region. The Wairarapa occupies the south-east corner of the North Island, with the cluster of vineyards in and around the township of Martinborough forming its most famous wine district.

The winemakers savouring the current excitement are not the first to explore the region's wine potential. William Beetham,

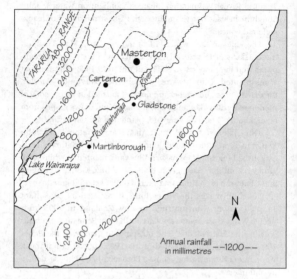

who first planted vines at his tiny Masterton vineyard, north of Martinborough, in 1883, produced a 'Hermitage' (Syrah) praised by visiting viticultural expert, Romeo Bragato, in 1895 as being of 'prime quality'. In 1985 Beetham's descendants broached a rare bottle of his Lansdowne Claret 1903. Geoff Kelly, then the highly respected wine columnist for *National Business Review*, enthused that the 82-year-old was 'alive and well ... with the oak standing firm, yet amazing fruit, body and freshness for the age. The finish is superb, long and lingering.'

The strong resurgence of viticultural interest in the Wairarapa came in the late 1970s, when Dr Derek Milne, a Wellington soil scientist, documented the close parallels between Martinborough's climate and those of top French wine regions, particularly Burgundy. Most (not all) of the initial wave of winemakers planted the Burgundian grapes, Pinot Noir and Chardonnay, but others later favoured a Bordeaux parallel and opted for Cabernet Sauvignon and Merlot. In 1996, the five most heavily planted bearing grape varieties were (in order): Pinot Noir (71 hectares), Chardonnay (67 hectares), Sauvignon Blanc (41 hectares), Riesling (29 hectares) and Cabernet Sauvignon (24 hectares).

In local terms, Martinborough's cool, dry climate during the pre-harvest months (the driest in the North Island) more closely resembles Marlborough's across Cook Strait than Hawke's Bay's in the north. Martinborough's wines also display the tense acidity and clear, deep flavours typical of Marlborough's. Wind is the chief weather problem, with regular north-westerly gales and strong, cold southerlies whipping in from Cook Strait damaging the vines' shoots and making shelter belts a necessity.

Pinot Noir, which prefers free-draining soils, thrives in the pockets of shallow loams over gravelly subsoils which border and penetrate the township. Although Pinot Noir is the highest-flying variety, Chardonnay, Sauvignon Blanc, Riesling, Gewürztraminer and Pinot Gris are also unleashing outstanding wines, high in extract and long in flavour.

ALEXANDER VINEYARD

Dublin Street Extension, Martinborough. Est 1990. Owners: Kingsley and Deborah Alexander. Production: 750 cases. Winery sales by appointment.

After eighteen years as a senior technician in the meteorological service, and with a deep interest in how climate influences viticulture and wine styles, Kingsley Alexander planted Bordeaux varieties rather than Pinot Noir in Martinborough. 'We didn't realise we were making a political statement by planting Cabernet Sauvignon,' he recalls.

Alexander and his wife, Deborah, both have a professional background in meteorology, and run a small met station on their vineyard. When they bought the property in 1989, with a small plot of vines already planted, the Alexanders planned only to grow grapes, but in 1994 they produced their first commercial wine (55 cases) and built their own winery prior to the 1996 vintage. Two hectares of high density, low-trellised, severely pruned Cabernet Sauvignon, Cabernet Franc and Merlot vines are now established in a mix of free-draining soils and heavier clays.

The early releases have been consistently rewarding. Dusty Road Cabernet Franc, based on Marlborough grapes, is a sappy, exuberantly fruity wine with deliciously strong, supple raspberryish flavours, full of drink-young charm. The estate-grown claret-style red, simply labelled Alexander, displays the freshness typical of the region's reds, with good weight, excellent depth of blackcurrant, plum and slightly minty flavours, French oak complexity and firm tannins.

(****) Alexander, Dusty Road Cabernet Franc

ATA RANGI VINEYARD

Puruatanga Road, Martinborough. Est 1980. Owners: Clive Paton, Phyllis Pattie, Oliver Masters and Alison Paton. Production: 6,750 cases.

Ata Rangi rivals Martinborough Vineyard for the title of New Zealand's most illustrious Pinot Noir producer. The Ata Rangi style is powerfully built and concentrated, while retaining a beguiling fragrance, suppleness and sweet-fruit appeal.

Clive Paton studied dairying and went sharemilking before he purchased his Puruatanga Road property in 1980. While working vintages at the now-defunct Abel and Co. and Delegat's in the early 1980s, he planted his own vineyard and grew vegetables to generate an initial cashflow until his first wine flowed in 1985. After building his own winery in time for the 1987 harvest, Paton doubled his winemaking team by marrying Phyllis ('Phyll') Pattie, formerly a Montana winemaker in Marlborough.

The winemaking team swelled to three in 1995 when Clive Paton and Phyll Pattie formed a partnership with Clive's sister, Alison, and her husband, Oliver Masters, who has a postgraduate diploma in viticulture and oenology from Lincoln University. Although partners in the wine company, the couples retain separate ownership of their vineyards.

Clive Paton and Phyll Pattie's 3-hectare vineyard is planted principally in Pinot Noir, Cabernet Sauvignon and Merlot, with smaller blocks of Syrah and Chardonnay and experimental plots of Sangiovese and Nebbiolo. Alison Paton's adjacent 2-hectare vineyard is established in Pinot Noir, Cabernet Sauvignon and Cabernet Franc, and the partners also buy grapes from Martinborough growers as well as from the Dalnagairn Vineyard in Hawke's Bay.

The wines are consistently top-flight. Dalnagairn Chardonnay is a buttery, intensely citrusy wine, delightful in its youth. Structured for the long haul, the locally grown Craighall Chardonnay is a powerful, beautifully balanced wine with an outstanding intensity of citrusy, mealy, biscuity flavour and a tight, savoury finish.

Full, fresh and vivacious, with delicate, strawberryish flavours, the Cabernet Sauvignon, Merlot and Syrah-based Summer Rosé can be irresistible. Célèbre, a distinctive Cabernet Sauvignon-based red with smaller proportions of Merlot and Syrah, is a robust, spicy, often slightly herbaceous red with deep colour, oak complexity and a rich, sustained flavour.

Early vintages of Ata Rangi's multiple gold medal and trophy-winning Pinot Noir were full of grace and charm, but lately the wine has acquired deeper, more complex flavour and a firmer underlay of tannin. Why is it so good? 'A great site, good clones and low yields,' says Paton, unhesitatingly. Perfumed and cherryish, full, rich and spicy, with new-oak complexity and a taut, lingering finish, it handsomely rewards cellaring for three to five years.

*****   Craighall Chardonnay, Pinot Noir
(*****½)   Summer Rosé
****   Célèbre, Dalnagairn Chardonnay

BENFIELD & DELAMARE VINEYARDS

Cambridge Road, Martinborough. Est 1987. Owners: Bill Benfield and Sue Delamare. Production: 450 cases. Winery sales by appointment.

Bill Benfield is surrounded by Pinot Noir producers, but he's not about to join them. A red-wine specialist, he's a leading proponent of growing Cabernet Sauvignon and Merlot in Martinborough. In Benfield's view, the district's 'rainfall distribution, length of season, heat summation and frost incidence are all positive pointers towards Cabernet and Merlot grape varieties'.

Benfield, an architect turned winemaker, and his partner, Sue Delamare, a former librarian, planted their first vines in 1987. Their densely planted, 2.5-hectare vineyard in shallow, gravelly soils is established principally in Cabernet Sauvignon and Merlot, with smaller plots of Cabernet Franc and Malbec. The vines are trained very low to the ground to enhance ripening from ground heat (at the cost of increasing the frost risk) and pruned severely (eight to ten buds per plant) to ensure low yields.

Benfield and Delamare's first 'commercial' vintage in 1991 yielded 42 cases and their total output has never reached 500 cases. A Song For Osiris, the second-tier label, is full of character and can be almost as fine as the top wine. Labelled Benfield & Delamare, this is a slightly leaner and less lush wine than the finest Hawke's Bay reds, but impressively concentrated, with bright, deep colour, a fragrant, cedary bouquet and rich blackcurrant/plum flavours, complex and taut.

****½ Benfield & Delamare
(****) A Song For Osiris

BLOOMFIELD VINEYARDS

119 Solway Crescent, Masterton. Est 1981. Owners: The Bloomfield family. Production: 4,500 cases.

Away from the Wairarapa's high profile cluster of wineries at Martinborough, David Bloomfield is quietly carrying on Masterton's tradition of winemaking established by William Beetham over a century ago.

Bloomfield, an affable, lively former architectural draughtsman, planted his first vines in 1981 and produced his first commercial wines in 1986. Other shareholders in the business are Bloomfield's wife, Janet Saunders, and David's parents, Eric and Pamela.

Solway, the boulder-strewn, 8-hectare estate vineyard, is planted in Cabernet Sauvignon, Merlot and Cabernet Franc, with smaller plots of Pinot Noir and Sauvignon Blanc. Janet Saunders' parents also own the 1.5-hectare Lyndor Vineyard in the hills east of the town, where Merlot, Cabernet Sauvignon and Cabernet Franc are cultivated.

The top wines are marketed as Bloomfield, with a second-tier red labelled Solway. The Sauvignon Blanc is plain, but the extremely rare Pinot Noir is characterful, with rich cherry and coffee-like flavours. The Cabernet Sauvignon-predominant Solway red is typically a chunky, slightly rustic wine with lots of spicy, green-edged flavour.

David Bloomfield's key achievement is Bloomfield Cabernet Sauvignon/Merlot/Cabernet Franc. French oak-aged for up to twenty months, this is a classy, generous wine with deep colour, mouthfilling body and excellent depth of firm, spicy, brambly flavour.

**** Cabernet Sauvignon/Merlot/Cabernet Franc
(***½) Pinot Noir
**½ Solway Cabernet Sauvignon/Merlot/Cabernet Franc
** Sauvignon Blanc

BLUE ROCK VINEYARD

Dry River Road, Martinborough. Est 1986. Owners: The Clark family. Production: 4,500 cases.

Out on a limb, 8 kilometres from the wineries huddled at Martinborough, Blue Rock Vineyard sits on a beautiful, exposed site with sweeping views over the south Wairarapa countryside. Pummelled by strong westerlies, the trees grow branches only on one side, but the fierce wind also helps to keep the vines' foliage dry and their fruit largely disease-free.

Nelson Clark, a lifelong sheep and cattle farmer who felt the need to diversify, planted his first vines in 1986. The first commercial wines in 1991 were made elsewhere, but prior to the 1993 vintage the company erected its own winery. Blue Rock is a family affair: Nelson's wife, Beverley, runs the vineyard and their daughter, Jenny, who has a post-graduate diploma in horticultural science, makes the wine.

A wide array of varieties have been established in the 6-hectare vineyard: Chardonnay, Sauvignon Blanc, Riesling, Pinot Noir, Cabernet Sauvignon, Cabernet Franc, Meunier and Syrah. The wines do not rank among the region's finest, but are typically sound, with freshly acidic flavours.

Blue Rock Sauvignon Blanc is ripely flavoured and racy. The Riesling has lacked ripeness and flavour intensity, but the fully barrel-fermented Chardonnay is a bold style with strong, steely, appley flavours wrapped in nutty oak. The rare Méthode Traditionnelle – based on the classic Champagne trio of Chardonnay, Pinot Noir and Meunier – is an austere, vigorous wine, lemony, limey and steely.

The Cabernet Sauvignon and Pinot Noir tend to be full-flavoured, although sometimes green-edged. Magenta, blended from the vineyard's five red-wine varieties, offers plenty of berry-ish, minty flavour.

*** Chardonnay, Sauvignon Blanc
**½ Cabernet Franc, Cabernet Sauvignon, Magenta,
Méthode Traditionnelle, Pinot Noir
** Riesling

CANADORO WINES

*c/- 16 Twomey Grove, Melrose, Wellington. Est 1993. Owners: Greg
and Lesley Robins. Production: 450 cases. No winery sales.*
Canadoro is a weekend affair for Wellingtonians Greg and Lesley
Robins, whose 1.2-hectare Cabernet Sauvignon and Chardonnay
vineyard in Martinborough, yielded its first crop in 1993.

The Chardonnay is a softly mouthfilling, oaky wine with
strong, peachy, creamy flavours in a very upfront style. The
Cabernet Sauvignon is more distinguished – impressively gutsy,
with deep colour, rich, ripe blackcurrant and spice flavours and
well-integrated French oak.

(****½) Cabernet Sauvignon
(***) Chardonnay

CHIFNEY WINES

*Huangarua Road, Martinborough. Est 1980. Owner: Rosemary
Chifney. Production: 1,500 cases.*
In the wine-lover's imagination, Martinborough is Pinot Noir
country. At the Chifney winery, however, the spotlight is firmly
on Cabernet Sauvignon.

Stan Chifney, who died in 1996, was a key pioneer of
Martinborough wine. An amiable, snowy-bearded Englishman,
he arrived in New Zealand in the early 1970s with a career background in vaccine production. As a 'retirement hobby', Chifney
started planting his vineyard in 1980. In his partly subterranean
winery, built before his first commercial vintage in 1984, Chifney
processed many of the early vintages of his neighbouring winemakers while they awaited the construction of their own wineries. Before he died, the popular Chifney won gold medals in New
Zealand for his 1986 and 1994 Cabernet Sauvignons. His wife,
Rosemary, now heads the small wine company, assisted by their
daughter, Sue.

The 4-hectare vineyard, in loamy surface soils over stony subsoils, is planted in Cabernet Sauvignon, Merlot, Cabernet Franc,
Chardonnay, Chenin Blanc and Gewürztraminer. Grapes have
also been bought from other Martinborough growers and
Hawke's Bay.

The American-oak aged Cabernet Sauvignon is typically
vibrantly fruity, crisp and fresh, with strong, berryish, slightly
herbal flavours. Its quality ranges more widely than the Cabernet
Sauvignons made further north, but top vintages can be wholly
satisfying.

Chifney's white wines, in the past mediocre, have made major advances in recent vintages. The Gewürztraminer, a robust style (often harbouring 14 percent alcohol) with a heady, musky fragrance and loads of very ripe, intensely varietal, soft flavour, is arguably Chifney's greatest wine. The Chenin Blanc (another unfashionable variety in the region championed by Stan Chifney) has varied in quality, but at its best is delightfully fresh and aromatic, with good depth of appley, lemony, appetisingly crisp flavour. The briefly oak-aged Chardonnay displays delicate citrusy, slightly buttery flavours, with lots of drink-young appeal.

**** Cabernet Sauvignon, Gewürztraminer
***½ Chardonnay, Chenin Blanc
(***) Rosé
**½ Chiffonnay, Enigma

DRY RIVER WINES

Puruatanga Road, Martinborough. Est 1979. Owners: Dr Neil and Dawn McCallum. Production: 3,750 cases. Winery sales by appointment.
A glance at the star ratings below shows why the little Dry River winery has built up a cult following in New Zealand. With prestigious varieties like Chardonnay and Pinot Noir, and less fashionable grapes like Gewürztraminer, Riesling and Pinot Gris, Dr Neil McCallum consistently produces some of New Zealand's most stylish, intensely flavoured and long-lived wines.

McCallum, a former scientist with a distinguished academic record which culminated in an Oxford doctorate in chemistry, planted his first vines in shallow loess over gravels in 1979. He was the first of the 'gang of four' (which by 1980 included Clive Paton of Ata Rangi, Stan Chifney and Derek Milne of Martinborough Vineyard) to pioneer the planting of commercial vineyards in Martinborough.

Today the 4-hectare estate vineyard is close-planted in Gewürztraminer, Sauvignon Blanc (being partly replaced with Viognier), Pinot Gris, Chardonnay and Pinot Noir. Riesling, Chardonnay and Pinot Noir are purchased from the nearby Craighall vineyard, and sometimes botrytised grapes from Marlborough.

Pursuing quality the Dry River way involves training the vines on the Scott-Henry system, which by dividing the canopy reduces fruit shading and disease; manual leaf-plucking around the ripening bunches in early summer; avoiding irrigation to encourage drought stress, which gives greater weight and concentration in the wine; and crop thinning at *veraison* to limit most yields to less than seven tonnes per hectare.

Dry River wines, McCallum underlines to his mail-order customers at every opportunity, are built to last. 'In our view an essential feature of fine wine is longevity and the qualities which are able to develop during the cellaring process. Our approach to winemaking is therefore to optimise the cellaring qualities of a given wine.' McCallum adopts a 'low-tech' approach to winemaking by, for instance, avoiding cold stabilisation and reducing filtration to a minimum.

The wines are immaculate. The Gewürztraminer is delicate yet concentrated and richly spiced; the Riesling springy and chock-full of lemon/lime flavour. The much acclaimed Pinot Gris is a mouthfilling wine with slow-building, intense, peachy, spicy flavours, needing several years to unfold its full splendour.

The French oak-fermented, lees-aged Chardonnay is robust, with searching grapefruit-like flavours, a savoury, mealy complexity and taut acidity. Only the ripe-flavoured Sauvignon Blanc, which retains a cool-climate freshness and zip, is slightly overshadowed by the wines of other producers.

From all five of the above white-wine varieties, McCallum has produced breathtakingly beautiful botrytised sweet wines, sometimes light and fragile, sometimes high in alcohol and very powerful. To underline his extraordinary versatility, he also makes a strikingly full-bodied, dark and spicy, densely flavoured and firm-structured Pinot Noir.

***** Chardonnay, Gewürztraminer, Pinot Gris, Pinot Noir, Riesling, Selection and Botrytis Selection sweet whites
**** Sauvignon Blanc

GLADSTONE VINEYARD

Gladstone Road, Gladstone. Est 1990. Owners: David and Christine Kernohan. Production: 2,000 cases.

Piercing Sauvignon Blancs and Rieslings, bursting with pure, delicate, mouth-wateringly crisp flavour, are the key attractions at this beautiful boutique winery in the Wairarapa countryside, midway between Masterton and Martinborough.

The founder, Australian Dennis Roberts, worked as a veterinarian before he planted 3 hectares of Sauvignon Blanc, Riesling, Pinot Gris, Cabernet Sauvignon, Merlot and Cabernet Franc in a former bed of the nearby Ruamahanga River. A year after the first 1990 vintage, a stylish, verandahed, two-storey winery rose. Gladstone Sauvignon Blanc, Riesling and the full, supple Cabernet Sauvignon/Merlot swiftly established a strong reputation, although the Chardonnay, based on Hawke's Bay grapes, proved less successful. (The 1996 vintage, markedly superior to its predecessors, was the last.)

After six vintages, Roberts returned to Wellington, selling Gladstone to Christine and David Kernohan. Christine, a Scottish MBA, runs the company; David is dean of the School of Architecture at Victoria University of Wellington.

The Sauvignon Blanc is clearly but not pungently herbaceous, with a beautifully scented bouquet, ripeness, flavour depth and vigour; the deftly oaked Fumé Blanc is equally lush and lovely. The Riesling, intensely floral and tangy, is one of the North Island's finest. Gladstone's other notable wine is the Cabernet Sauvignon/Merlot (not to be confused with the lower-tier Cabernet/Merlot), at its best a bold, rich-coloured wine with lush, sweet-tasting fruit and silky tannins.

****½   Sauvignon Blanc
(****½) Fumé Blanc
****   Riesling
***½   Cabernet Sauvignon/Merlot
**½   Cabernet/Merlot, Chardonnay

HAU ARIKI WINES

Regent Street, Martinborough. Est 1994. Owners: Hau Ariki Marae.
New Zealand's first marae (Maori meeting place) to produce wine on a commercial basis, Hau Ariki's interest was fired by Mike Eden, formerly of Mission Vineyards in Hawke's Bay, who retired to Martinborough. The 3-hectare vineyard, planted in the late 1980s, is tended by voluntary workers from the marae. The elders plan to invite tourists to stay on the marae, learn about Maori culture and enjoy Maori hospitality – including Hau Ariki wines.

The first vintage flowed in 1994. The wines to date have been of an uneven standard, with some lacking cleanness, but the oak-aged Sauvignon Blanc offers full, ripe gooseberry flavours wrapped in toasty oak.

(***)   Sauvignon Blanc
(**½) Cabernet Sauvignon
(**)   Pinot Noir
(*½)   Rosé

LINTZ ESTATE

Kitchener Street, Martinborough. Est 1989. Owners: The Lintz family. Production: 4,500 cases.
A fast-rising star of the Martinborough wine scene, Lintz Estate produces an increasingly impressive lineup of Rieslings, Sauvignon Blancs and Cabernet-based reds, backed up by such distinctive wines as the bottle-fermented Riesling Brut and the super-sweet, treacly Optima Noble Selection.

Chris Lintz, whose parents came to New Zealand from Germany after the Second World War, graduated in zoology from Victoria University in Wellington and later gained a diploma in viticulture and oenology from the famous Geisenheim Institute. After working in the Saar and at Montana and Brookfields, in 1989 he planted his first vines in Martinborough, and two years later made the first Lintz Estate wines.

A key source of fruit is the company's 8-hectare Moy Hall vineyard (between the Dry River and Te Kairanga wineries), planted in Merlot, Cabernet Franc, Cabernet Sauvignon, Pinot Noir, Meunier, Gewürztraminer, Sauvignon Blanc, Riesling, Chardonnay and Optima. Grapes are also drawn from local growers and the tiny, 0.5-hectare vineyard adjacent to the winery, planted in Riesling.

Lintz Estate initially earned a reputation for chunky, bold-flavoured reds, but recently the white wines have shown excellent form. The magnificently fragrant, concentrated and flavour-crammed Riesling Dry (especially) and slightly honeyish, medium-sweet Saint Anthony Riesling are both impressive; so is the immaculate, vibrantly fruity, richly flavoured Sauvignon Blanc.

The Cabernet/Merlot (almost as much Cabernet Franc as Cabernet Sauvignon-based) is a sturdy red with rich plum/raspberry flavours, oak complexity and firm, balanced tannins.

The Vitesse Cabernet Sauvignon is similarly bold, flavour-packed and tautly structured, while the powerful and tannic, but not especially refined, Pinot Noir has often been described as a Pinot Noir for Cabernet drinkers.

Chris Lintz's innovative streak comes to the fore in such distinctive wines as his fragrant, lemon and lime-flavoured, lightly yeasty and crisp bottle-fermented Riesling Brut, which makes an ideal aperitif. The Optima Noble Selection (lesser versions are labelled Optima Late Harvest) is an ultra-sweet, oily, rampantly botrytised wine, awash with honeyish, apricot-rich flavour.

(*****) **Riesling Dry**
****½ **Optima Noble Selection**
**** **Cabernet/Merlot, Sauvignon Blanc**
(****) **Saint Anthony Riesling**
***½ **Chardonnay, Riesling Brut, Spicy Traminer, Vitesse Cabernet Sauvignon**
(***½) **Optima Late Harvest**
*** **Cabernet Estate Cuvée, Pinot Noir**

MARGRAIN VINEYARD

Ponatahi Road, Martinborough. Est 1992. Owners: Graham and Daryl Margrain. Production: 500 cases.

After 25 years in the building industry, Wellingtonians Graham and Daryl Margrain felt like a change. The result: Margrain 'winery, accommodation and conference complex', featuring a 4.5-hectare vineyard planted in 1992 in Chardonnay, Pinot Gris, Merlot and Pinot Noir, a small winery built in 1996, and eight luxury accommodation villas.

The first 1994 vintage, based on bought-in grapes, was followed by the first estate-grown wines, made by Strat Canning. The mouthfilling, richly flavoured Martinborough Chardonnay 1995 shows every sign of sophisticated winemaking, and the Pinot Gris 1996 is powerful and intensely varietal, with a strong surge of peachy, slightly earthy, crisp, fractionally sweet flavour.

(****½) **Chardonnay**
(****)   **Pinot Gris**

MARTINBOROUGH VINEYARD

Princess Street, Martinborough. Est 1980. Owners: Derek and Duncan Milne, Claire Campbell, Russell and Sue Schultz, Larry McKenna. Production: 12,000 cases.

Martinborough Vineyard produces wines of scintillating quality. The notably refined and savoury Pinot Noir has been the most eye-catching success, but this is backed up by a delightful selection of white wines.

Larry McKenna, the winemaker and general manager, is a stocky Australian who spent six years at Delegat's before he joined Martinborough Vineyard as a partner in 1986. The founders were pharmacist Russell Schultz and his wife Sue; Duncan Milne and his wife, Claire Campbell; and Milne's brother, Derek, formerly a soil scientist and now a consultant, who in the late 1970s played a crucial role in unravelling Martinborough's viticultural potential.

The first vines were planted in 1980. Today the 10 hectares of vineyards encircling the winery are planted predominantly in Pinot Noir and Chardonnay, with some Sauvignon Blanc. The nearby Smith vineyard – 2 hectares of Pinot Noir and Riesling – was purchased in 1986. Martinborough Vineyard also buys fruit from local growers, and manages the Cleland and McCreanor vineyards, where 4 hectares of Pinot Noir, Chardonnay and Pinot Gris are cultivated.

Right from the start the Pinot Noir unfolded extraordinary quality. The debut 1984 vintage (only twelve cases were produced) was arrestingly rich in flavour, and until the end of the decade the wine's fullness, fragrance and richness was unmatched by any other New Zealand Pinot Noir. McKenna's recipe for quality Pinot Noir has three crucial ingredients: 'berry fruit flavours, with something more than strawberry ripeness, underpinned by quality oak and complexity – that earthy, mushroomy character that is almost indefinable'.

Produced from a range of clones – principally 10/5 for 'fruitiness' and Pommard for 'body, structure and tannin' – the famous Pinot Noir is a delicate, intensely varietal wine, fragrant and full, with sweet-tasting fruit and cherryish, slightly smoky, very persistent, velvety flavours. The 1991 to 1994 vintages all won gold medals at the Australia National Wine Show. In top vintages, a bolder, deeper-coloured, mouthfilling Pinot Noir Reserve appears, crammed with smoky, spicy, dark cherry flavours.

The Chardonnay is a very classy, finely balanced wine with great depth of rich, mealy, buttery, grapefruit-like flavours. The Sauvignon Blanc is lush and mouthfilling, its ripe melon and passionfruit-evoking flavours cut with fresh, lively acidity.

The Riesling Dry possesses piercing lemon/lime flavours, with a sliver of sweetness and tense acidity. The sweet, botrytised Riesling Late Harvest is full-bloomed, rich and honeyish, with good acid spine.

A notable newcomer from 1996 is the Pinot Gris, fermented and matured in seasoned oak barriques. This is a weighty dry wine with delicious depth of peachy, nutty flavour, rounded and long.

*****   Chardonnay, Pinot Noir, Reserve Pinot Noir
(*****) Pinot Gris, Riesling Late Harvest
****½   Riesling Dry
****   Sauvignon Blanc

MUIRLEA RISE

Princess Street, Martinborough. Est 1988. Owners: Willie and Lea Brown. Production: 825 cases.

Willie Brown is one of New Zealand's few members of the wine trade to have leapt into wine production. After a long career as a wine retailer and then wine distributor, in 1988 he and his wife, Lea, planted their first vines just across the road from Martinborough Vineyard. Brown is passionate about Pinot Noir: 'Years ago someone gave me a bottle of Chambolle-Musigny; it was pure sunshine and buttercups. I keep looking for that experience again.'

The 1.5-hectare clay and gravel vineyard is devoted principally to close-planted Pinot Noir, with smaller plots of Syrah and Cabernet Sauvignon, and next door Shaun Brown, Willie and Lea's son, is planting another hectare of Syrah and Cabernet Sauvignon. With its annual output of less than 1,000 cases, Muirlea Rise is one of Martinborough's smaller wineries.

The Pinot Noir is soft and 'feminine' (to borrow Brown's adjective), with a floral bouquet, medium-full body and subtle, cherryish, mushroomy flavours. Justa Red is a non-vintage, light, easy-drinking blend, made principally from barrels of Pinot Noir not chosen for the top label. The popular Après Wine Liqueur, basically a vintage-dated, briefly oak-aged ruby 'port', is a dark, delicious mouthful overflowing with blackcurrant and plum-like flavours, sweet and creamy-smooth.

****   Après Wine Liqueur
***½   Pinot Noir
**½   Justa Red

MURDOCH JAMES ESTATE

Cnr New York Street and Cambridge Road, Martinborough. Est 1986. Owners: Roger and Jill Fraser. Production: 250 cases. No winery sales.

Two of New Zealand's rarest reds flow from this 2.5-hectare vineyard,

named after Roger Fraser's late father. After buying a block of
bare land in 1986, Fraser and his wife, Jill, planted it in Pinot Noir
and Syrah vines, but three years later Fraser was transferred by
his employers to Australia. Most of the grapes have since been
sold, but each year since 1993 a few hundred cases of Murdoch
James wine have been made at Ata Rangi.

The Pinot Noir is fragrant, mouthfilling and full of rich, ripe,
plummy, complex flavour. The first 1995 Shiraz (only 50 cases
were produced) is a fleshy wine with strong black-pepper aromas, very good depth of plum and spice flavours and positive tannins – a serious red for cellaring.

(*****)Pinot Noir
(****) Shiraz

NGA WAKA VINEYARD

*Kitchener Street, Martinborough. Est 1988. Owners: Roger and Carol
Parkinson, Gordon and Margaret Parkinson. Production: 2,650 cases.*
In a region famed for its Pinot Noirs, Roger Parkinson is a white-
wine specialist. Nga Waka makes penetratingly flavoured, steely
whites designed for long-term cellaring.

Nga Waka is a family affair. Roger Parkinson, who controls the
production and marketing, holds a BA in history and French and
in 1988 graduated from Roseworthy College in Australia with a
graduate diploma in wine. His wife, Carol, an accountant, handles the finances and Roger's parents are also shareholders.

Nga Waka takes its name from the three nearby hills, Nga
Waka a Kupe (the canoes of Kupe), which lie like upturned
canoes not far from Martinborough. The 4-hectare, stony, silty
vineyard, established in 1988, is planted principally in Sauvignon
Blanc and Chardonnay, with 20 percent Riesling. The first vintage flowed in 1993.

Right from the start – when the debut 1993 Sauvignon Blanc
won a gold medal at the 1994 Air New Zealand Wine Awards –
the wines have looked distinctly classy. Richly scented, with
pure, lush fruit characters and great zip, the Sauvignon Blanc is
one of the region's – and New Zealand's – finest. The Riesling is
typically dry but perfumed and impressively concentrated, with
lively acidity and great aging potential. Barrel-fermented, the
Chardonnay is very tightly structured, with intense grapefruit,
nutty oak and mealy flavours and a crisp, flinty finish. These are
immaculate, slowly evolving wines that reward long keeping.

***** Sauvignon Blanc
****½ Chardonnay, Riesling

PALLISER ESTATE

Kitchener Street, Martinborough. Est 1988. Owner: Palliser Estate
Wines of Martinborough Limited. Production: 20,000 cases.

One of the largest and best wineries in the Wairarapa, Palliser
Estate is named after Cape Palliser, the southernmost tip of the
North Island. Its Chardonnay, Riesling and Sauvignon Blanc are
consistently outstanding.

Ownership of the company is spread over about 135 shareholders. Wyatt Creech (now an MP and Minister of Education)
planted the first vines in 1984. Four years later, Creech formed an
unlisted public company to take over his vineyard and erect
Palliser Estate's graceful colonial-style winery, but he remains a
shareholder. Today the key figures are managing director Richard
Riddiford, a member of one of the Wairarapa's wealthiest farming
families, and winemaker Allan Johnson, who during his child-
hood worked in Hawke's Bay vineyards, later graduated from
Roseworthy College and joined Palliser Estate in 1990.

The company's 30 hectares of vineyards are planted in
Chardonnay, Riesling, Sauvignon Blanc and Pinot Noir. Palliser
Estate also purchases grapes from growers in Martinborough and
further afield.

The wines are marketed under two labels. The flagship
Palliser Estate label is reserved for wines grown wholly or predominantly in Martinborough, while lower-tier Martinborough
wines or those grown in other regions are sold as Palliser Bay.

Palliser Bay Chardonnay, both tank and oak-fermented, is a
flavoursome, fruit-driven style, designed for early drinking.
Palliser Bay Oak Aged Sauvignon Blanc, grown in Hawke's Bay,
has varied in quality but in top form is impressively substantial,
rich and rounded. Palliser Bay Pinot Noir, based on young vines,
is clearly varietal in a light, savoury and forward style.

The trio of top whites under the Palliser Estate label compris-
es the excitingly rich-scented and lush Sauvignon Blanc, with its
very ripe, searching, sweet-fruit delights and racy acidity; the
intense and zingy, lemon-lime flavoured Riesling, made in a
slightly sweet, appetisingly crisp style; and the French oak-fermented, lees-aged Chardonnay, a mouthfilling and stylish wine
with excellent depth of citrusy, mealy, buttery flavour. The
Palliser Estate range also features a softly mouthfilling, coffee
and spice-flavoured Pinot Noir; a bright-pink, crisp, satisfyingly
dry Rosé of Pinot; and a rich, floral, honeyed botrytis Riesling, all
sweetness and delicacy.

***** Palliser Estate Chardonnay, Riesling, Sauvignon
        Blanc
****½ Palliser Estate Botrytis Riesling, Pinot Noir
(****) Palliser Bay Oak Aged Sauvignon Blanc
***½   Palliser Estate Rosé of Pinot
(***) Palliser Bay Chardonnay, Pinot Noir

TE KAIRANGA WINES

Martins Road, Martinborough. Est 1986. Owner: Te Kairanga Wines Limited. Production: 17,500 cases.

Te Kairanga ('the land where the soil is rich and the food plentiful') is one of the largest wineries in Martinborough. After a poor performance in the mid-to-late 1980s, the company has recently won respect with a stream of Pinot Noirs and Chardonnays.

The founders, Tom Draper and his wife, Robin, in 1983 bought a run-down vineyard planted five years earlier by publisher Alister Taylor. After the Drapers brought in partners, extensive vineyards fanned out across free-draining, stony terraces of the Huangarua River. For several years after the first 1986 vintage, the wines proved disappointing, but their standard rose following the 1989 arrival of full-time winemaker, Australian Chris Buring, who previously spent 23 years at Lindemans.

Tom Draper retired as manager in 1993, but the Drapers still own the largest stake among Te Kairanga's approximately 160 shareholders. In the Te Kairanga vineyard adjacent to the winery and the East Plain vineyard across the road (the cooler of the two sites), 30 hectares of Chardonnay, Sauvignon Blanc, Riesling, Pinot Gris, Pinot Noir, Cabernet Sauvignon and Merlot are planted. Grapes are also purchased from Gisborne and Hawke's Bay.

Of the two Sauvignon Blancs, the locally grown, intensely aromatic, ripely flavoured and subtle Sauvignon Blanc Barrel Aged is markedly superior to the plain, green-edged Gisborne/Martinborough model. In cooler vintages the Cabernet Sauvignon-based reds are light and leafy, but in warmer years they offer fresh, buoyant, red berry and plum flavours.

'Chardonnay and Pinot Noir are the two varieties we're absolutely committed to,' says general manager Andrew Shackleton. 'They're the best for this area, with the greatest future in terms of quality and demand.' Top vintages of the partly barrel-fermented Chardonnay are bold and creamy, with rich flavours and taut acidity. The Reserve Chardonnay, based on the ripest fruit, fully barrel-fermented and lees-aged, is even more powerful and searching, with a lovely depth of grapefruit, lime and oak flavours and authoritative acidity.

The Pinot Noir, matured in seasoned French oak casks, is an intensely varietal wine that places its accent on vibrant, plummy, sweet-tasting fruit flavours, deliciously fresh and supple. Its Reserve big brother, more new oak-influenced, is a markedly bolder, richer and more complex style, fragrant, full and spicy, with the ability to cellar well for several years. Only produced in top vintages, this is Te Kairanga's most distinguished wine.

***** Reserve Pinot Noir
****½ Reserve Chardonnay
(****) Sauvignon Blanc Barrel Aged
***½ Chardonnay, Pinot Noir

(***)   Cabernet Sauvignon/Merlot
**½   Cabernet Sauvignon
(**)   Gisborne/Martinborough Sauvignon Blanc
(*)   Castlepoint Cabernet Sauvignon

VOSS ESTATE

Puruatanga Road, Martinborough. Est 1988. Owners: Gary Voss and Annette Atkins. Production: 2,250 cases.

Voss Estate is tiny, and Gary Voss and his partner, Annette Atkins, are determined to keep it that way. 'Around 2,000 cases is where we want to stay,' says Voss. 'We can handle that ourselves [apart from hiring grape-pickers], even though we're knackered at vintage.'

In 1987 Voss and Atkins were so impressed by Ata Rangi's Pinot Noir and Cabernet-based red, Célèbre, they bought land almost next door. A year later, they planted their first vines. The first wine, based on Hawke's Bay grapes, flowed in 1991, followed in 1993 by the first Martinborough-grown release.

Voss, a BSc in zoology, studied oenology in Australia and worked vintages at Ata Rangi and De Redcliffe, before plunging into winemaking on his own account. Annette Atkins works as a 'cellar-rat' in the winery and tends the 2-hectare, low-cropping (average 5 tonnes per hectare) vineyard, planted in Pinot Noir, Chardonnay, Sauvignon Blanc, Cabernet Sauvignon, Merlot and Cabernet Franc.

The Sauvignon Blanc is a ripe, fleshy wine with melon and capsicum-like flavours. The Reserve Chardonnay, barrel-fermented and lees-aged, is fat, savoury and buttery, with loads of flavour.

The Waihenga Cabernet/Merlot/Franc (Waihenga is the Maori name for Martinborough) offers strong red berry-fruit and mint flavours, French oak complexity and taut tannins. I prefer the Pinot Noir, berryish and mouthfilling, with bold colour and very good depth of ripe, slightly peppery flavour.

**** Pinot Noir, Reserve Chardonnay
***½ Sauvignon Blanc, Waihenga Cabernet/Merlot/Franc

WALKER ESTATE

Puruatanga Road, Martinborough. Est 1988. Owners: Brendan and Elizabeth Walker. Production: 300 cases.

A mystery grape variety whose identity puzzles ampelographers and that even DNA testing has not been able to identify, forms the foundation of this tiny producer's top wine, Notre Vigne.

Brendan Walker and his wife, Elizabeth, an experienced viticulturist, first planted vines next to Ata Rangi in 1988. Today their 1-hectare vineyard is established in Riesling, Chardonnay and the unknown grape, initially believed to be Syrah.

At first the grapes were sold, but when the Walkers produced an experimental wine called Rooster's Blood, 'everyone liked it,' recalls Brendan Walker, 'so we thought we'd have a go at commercial winemaking'. The Walker Estate wines, first made in 1993, are produced by Brendan and Elizabeth's son, James, at a local winery.

The Riesling is a solid, floral and lemony wine with firm acidity and a distinct splash of sweetness. French oak-aged, the unique Notre Vigne is dark and chunky, brambly, plummy and smooth, in a very ripe, warm and powerful style. What could it be? The search continues ...

(****) Notre Vigne
(**½) Riesling

WALNUT RIDGE

Regent Street, Martinborough. Est 1988. Owners: Bill and Sally Brink. Production: 1,200 cases.

Tired of 'the public service and doing the *Dominion* crossword', Iowan Bill Brink headed for Martinborough and in 1988 began planting vines. Brink and his New Zealand-born wife, Sally, now own 2.5 hectares of Pinot Noir, Cabernet Sauvignon and Sauvignon Blanc.

The venture is named after a 1 to 2 metre rise (ridge is stretching it a bit far) that runs through the property. The Brinks sold their first few crops, but the first Walnut Ridge wine flowed in 1994.

The Pinot Noir is the early success – fragrant and smoky, with good body and depth of cherryish, subtle, well-rounded flavour. The Cabernet Sauvignon is typically fresh and flavoursome, but crisp and green-edged, lacking warmth. I have also tasted a promising, full-bodied, ripe, honey-sweet botrytised Sauvignon Blanc.

(***½) Botrytised Sauvignon Blanc, Pinot Noir
(**½) Cabernet Sauvignon

WINSLOW WINES

Princess Street, Martinborough. Est 1987. Owners: Steve and Jennifer Tarring. Production: 750 cases.

Some of the Wairarapa's richest claret-style reds flow from this tiny winery. 'I think we get enough sun and heat in Martinborough to ripen Cabernet Sauvignon,' says Steve Tarring. 'By New Zealand standards, even in poorer years we make an average Cabernet, and in good vintages we produce a very good wine.'

Winslow was founded by Tarring, a former marine biologist, and his wife, Jennifer. Ross Turner, Jennifer's father, has also been heavily involved from the start. The winemaker, employed on a part-time basis, is Strat Canning, a half-brother of Chris

Canning, the founder of De Redcliffe.

The first vines were planted in 1987 and the first wine was produced in 1991. The shingly, 2-hectare estate vineyard is planted in Cabernet Sauvignon (principally), Merlot and Cabernet Franc; grapes have also been purchased from growers in Hawke's Bay and Marlborough.

The Cabernet-based reds, especially the Reserve Cabernet Sauvignon/Cabernet Franc, are lush and concentrated, with deep, vibrant blackcurrant-like flavours and silky tannins. The Petra Cabernet Sauvignon is similarly bold and generous, but slightly less ripe-tasting, with a minty, herbal edge.

The Riesling is typically perfumed and zippy, with incisive lemon/lime flavours. The bright pink Rosetta Cabernet Rosé is one of New Zealand's top rosés – mouthfilling, delightfully fresh and delicate, with a lovely surge of strawberry/raspberry flavours, a splash of sweetness and finely balanced acidity.

Far out of the Martinborough mainstream, Winslow also produces a smooth, cinnamon and clove-flavoured William Ross Cabernet Liqueur. Fortified with French brandy, this deliciously sweet and spicy wine is irresistible on a cold winter's night in the Wairarapa.

(*****) **Rosetta Cabernet Rosé**
(****½) **Reserve Cabernet Sauvignon/Cabernet Franc**
(****)   **Riesling, William Ross Cabernet Liqueur**
(***½) **Petra Cabernet Sauvignon**

Nelson

The Nelson wine trail runs from the silty Waimea Plains southwest of the city of Nelson into the blue-green Upper Moutere hills, climbing into some of the most gorgeous wine country in New Zealand. This is a region characterised by small wineries, but the Seifried, Neudorf and Tasman Bay (Spencer Hill) labels have made their presence felt well beyond the region itself.

Today's Nelson winemakers are heirs to a long viticultural tradition. F.H.M. Ellis and Sons pioneered grape and fruit wine production near Takaka in the nineteenth century, and between 1967 and 1976 Viggo du Fresne produced gutsy hybrid reds on the Ruby Bay coast.

Nelson, however, is still a small wine-producing region. With the scarcity of properties suitable for large-scale viticulture and the province's distance from key transport routes, the major wine companies have not invested here. With 97 hectares of bearing vines in 1996, Nelson accounted for only 1.6 percent of the national producing vineyard area, although a flurry of recent planting is expected to increase the bearing area to 174 hectares (2.3 percent of the national total) by 1999.

With its warm summers and unusually long hours of sunshine, the region is climatically well suited to viticulture, although the average autumn rainfall is significantly heavier than in Marlborough. Chardonnay, Sauvignon Blanc, Pinot Noir and Riesling are the most commonly planted varieties (Cabernet Sauvignon struggles to consistently achieve full ripeness) and the consistently outstanding Neudorf Moutere Chardonnay has proved Nelson's ability to produce wine as striking as its vineyard settings.

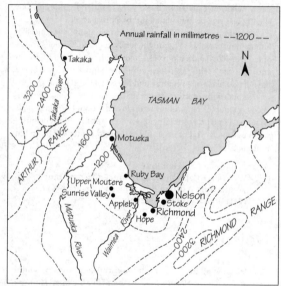

GLOVER'S VINEYARD

Gardner Valley Road, Upper Moutere. Est 1984. Owners: Dr David and Penny Glover. Production: 2,250 cases.

Renowned for his taut, grippy reds, Dr David Glover drives a car with the number plate TANNIN and wears a T-shirt vowing that his Cabernet Sauvignon is Merlot-free.

Glover planted his first vines in the Upper Moutere hills in 1984, after spending sixteen years in Australia, where he gained a PhD in algebra and worked in the Defence Department. Today the low-cropping, 3-hectare vineyard on a gentle north-facing clay slope is planted in Pinot Noir, Cabernet Sauvignon and Sauvignon Blanc. Grapes are also purchased from Nelson growers and occasionally further afield.

The estate-grown Pinot Noirs are typically very gutsy and full-flavoured, with the Front Block Pinot Noir slightly more floral and supple than the more tannic Back Block Pinot Noir. There is also a softer, charming Pinot Noir Cerise, based on bought-in grapes, that is designed for early drinking

The Moutere Cabernet Sauvignon, matured for a year in new and one-year-old French oak barriques, is typically sturdy, with rich colour, strong brambly fruit characters and a tight finish. In lesser vintages, a fresh, berryish, lightly oaked Mt Lodestone Cabernet is marketed. Hoary Head (named after a hill on the Upper Moutere skyline) is a chunky, flavoursome, oak-aged quaffer blended from Cabernet Sauvignon and Pinot Noir.

Glover's white wines were initially outshone by his reds, but the latest vintages have been fresher and more aromatic. The Richmond Riesling, which varies from bone-dry to medium-dry, is a slightly austere wine with penetrating lemon/lime flavours and bracing acidity; the medium-sweet Late Harvest model is pale and appley, with a Mosel-like lightness. There is also a flinty, dry, nettley Sauvignon Blanc that is very much a food style.

***½ Back Block Pinot Noir, Front Block Pinot Noir, Moutere Cabernet Sauvignon
***   Richmond Riesling
(***) Pinot Noir Cerise, Richmond Riesling Late Harvest
**½   Moutere Sauvignon Blanc
(**½) Hoary Head, Mt Lodestone Cabernet, Nelson Chardonnay

HOLMES BROTHERS DIRECT

McShanes Road, Richmond. Est 1991. Owners: The Holmes family. Production: 1,700 cases.

Under the Richmond Plains label, David Holmes and his two brothers produce wines sold largely through their own direct marketing operation in the UK. The wines are also sold locally at the Grape Escape, a sales and tasting venue shared with Te Mania Estate in a relocated, 130-year-old cottage in McShanes Road.

The 4-hectare vineyard near Richmond, planted in 1991, is run organically and has full Bio-Gro certification. The first 1995 wines, a Chardonnay and Sauvignon Blanc, have been followed by a Pinot Noir, Rosé and blended red.

The Sauvignon Blanc is very lightly oaked, with plenty of fresh, brisk, limey flavour. The Chardonnay, partly wood-fermented, is very crisp and appley in a distinctly cool-climate style.

(***) Richmond Plains Sauvignon Blanc
(**½) Richmond Plains Chardonnay

MOUTERE HILLS VINEYARD

Eggers Road, Sunrise Valley, Upper Moutere. Est 1993. Owners: Simon and Alison Thomas. Production: 650 cases.

In an old shearing shed turned winery in the Sunrise Valley in the Upper Moutere hills, ex-teachers Simon and Alison Thomas produce a trickle of wine, rarely seen beyond Nelson.

The couple purchased the property, originally a sheep farm, in 1993. A 1.5-hectare vineyard has been established in Chardonnay, Sauvignon Blanc, Cabernet Sauvignon, Merlot and Pinot Noir. While waiting for their vines to bear fruit, the couple have purchased grapes from the Waimea Plains, Marlborough and Hawke's Bay.

Even at full throttle, Moutere Hills Vineyard will produce only about 1,500 cases. The Nelson Riesling is pale and light, with good depth of citrusy, appley flavour and tense acidity. The Marlborough Sauvignon Blanc, partly barrel-fermented, is a very distinctive, easy-drinking style – crisp, slightly sweet, ripe and nutty. The Nelson Chardonnay is mouthfilling and crisp but assertively oaked, with citrusy, very toasty flavours.

Sunrise Valley Red, based on Pinot Noir, briefly oak-aged, is a light, simple quaffer. The Nelson Cabernet/Merlot lacks complexity but offers pleasant drinking, with berryish, green-edged flavours, fresh and smooth.

(***) **Marlborough Sauvignon Blanc, Nelson Riesling**
(**½) **Nelson Cabernet/Merlot, Nelson Chardonnay**
(**)   **Sunrise Valley Red**

NEUDORF VINEYARDS

Neudorf Road, Upper Moutere. Est 1981. Owners: Tim and Judy Finn. Production: 4,500 cases.

Many dream about cultivating a small block of vines in an idyllic setting and producing a rivulet of top-flight wine. In the rolling hills of the Upper Moutere, near the hamlet of the same name, Tim and Judy Finn have done exactly that.

Neudorf is the source of some of Nelson's finest wines and one of New Zealand's most illustrious Chardonnays. Tim Finn, a former dairying advisory officer, has impressive academic credentials and the distinctly rugged air of a man of the soil. Judy Finn has been heavily involved in the winery's sales and administration since the first vintage in 1981.

The 6-hectare vineyard is planted in Moutere clays, threaded with gravel. After many years of trials, the Burgundian grapes Chardonnay and Pinot Noir have emerged as the key varieties, backed up by Sauvignon Blanc and Riesling, and small plots of Sémillon and Cabernet Sauvignon. A small amount of fruit is bought in from Nelson and Marlborough.

In his handsome macrocarpa winery, with its roof pitched high to conceal the tanks within, Finn makes a tight range of stylish, immaculate, intensely flavoured wines. Produced from small crops of very ripe fruit, the Moutere Chardonnay is fermented in French oak barriques (50 percent new) and given extended lees contact. An arresting wine, gloriously fragrant and mouthfilling, with an exceptional depth of lush, creamy, nutty flavour and the ability to mature well for several years, it ranks among the greatest of all New Zealand Chardonnays and has won major awards in New Zealand, Australia and the UK.

Neudorf Riesling is also outstanding, with piercing lemon-lime aromas and a beautifully poised, slightly sweet, rich palate. The Sauvignon Blanc is a dry, full-bodied style with fresh passionfruit-lime aromas and ripe, lingering flavours. The Sémillon is typically full-bodied and zingy, with ripe, non-aggressive, gently herbaceous flavours.

Encouraged by his earlier success with a light, drink-young red made from Pinot Noir, Tim Finn is now pursuing a more serious and complex style, concentrated and tautly structured. With deep colour, rich cherry and spice flavours, quality French oak and a backbone of firm tannins, this is an impressive red.

***** Moutere Chardonnay, Moutere Riesling
****½ Moutere Pinot Noir
**** Sauvignon Blanc, Sémillon
(***) Village Chardonnay

PELORUS VINEYARD

Patons Road, Hope, Richmond. Est 1980. Owners: Andrew Greenhough and Jenny Wheeler. Production: 2,000 cases.

Flavour-packed, zesty Rieslings flow from this small winery at Hope, south of Nelson city. Not to be confused with the Cloudy Bay sparkling sold as Pelorus, the winery takes its name from the Pelorus River which rises in the nearby Richmond hills. Pelorus began life as Ranzau Wines, a part-time venture established by Trevor Lewis in 1980. Andrew Greenhough, an MA in art history, and his partner, Jenny Wheeler, who handles the administration and sales, bought the property in 1991. The 3-hectare estate vineyard, planted in clay loams, is established principally in Pinot Noir and Chardonnay, with smaller plots of Riesling and Merlot. Grapes are also purchased from local growers.

Despite his initial lack of winemaking experience (in 1990 he worked as a cellarhand at Villa Maria), Greenhough swiftly learned the ropes of winemaking and is now a rising star of the Nelson wine scene. At its best the Riesling is a strikingly perfumed and incisively flavoured wine, vibrantly fruity and tangy.

The Chardonnay, French oak-fermented, is savoury and citrusy, with good flavour depth and acidity. The Sauvignon Blanc is bitingly crisp, with strong, fresh, green capsicum-like aromas and flavours. The Pinot Noir is an attractive red with quite good concentration of ripe, sweet-fruit flavours and a subtle oak seasoning.

**** Riesling
***½ Chardonnay, Pinot Noir
*** Sauvignon Blanc

POMONA RIDGE VINEYARD

Pomona Road, Ruby Bay. Est 1979. Owners: Peter and Jeanette Hancock, John and Jenny Marchbanks. Production: 500 cases.

This tiny Pinot Noir specialist lies in the coastal hills above Ruby Bay. The 1.2-hectare vineyard, devoted wholly to Pinot Noir, was established on a north-facing clay slope by Andy du Fresne in 1979. The current owners – Peter and Jeanette Hancock, and John and Jenny Marchbanks – run the vineyard on a part-time basis and produced their first Pinot Noir in 1994.

French oak-matured, the Pinot Noir has been of uneven quality, but the strong, vibrant, sweet-fruit flavoured 1994 vintage showed the potential.

(**) **Pinot Noir**

RUBY BAY WINES

Korepo Road, Ruby Bay. Est 1976. Owners: David and Christine Moore. Production: 1,800 cases.

This low profile winery sits on a stunning site overlooking the broad sweep of Tasman Bay. The wines, not widely seen beyond Nelson, include a rich, peachy, buttery-soft Reserve Chardonnay.

Founded as Korepo Wines in 1976 by Craig Gass, the company produced solid but unmemorable wines, and in 1989 the vineyard and winery were purchased by David and Christine Moore. Moore, previously a biochemistry lecturer at Christchurch Polytechnic, later gained a graduate diploma in wine from Roseworthy College in South Australia before he moved into full-time winemaking at Ruby Bay.

Pinot Noir, Sauvignon Blanc, Riesling and Chardonnay are the principal varieties in the pretty 3-hectare terraced vineyard, which Moore describes as a warm, relatively early-ripening site. Grapes are also purchased from Nelson growers and further afield.

Ruby Bay's range includes a fleshy, savoury and creamy barrique-fermented Reserve Chardonnay; a full-bodied, citrusy, appetisingly crisp Riesling Medium; a fragrant, spicy, silky Pinot Noir and a chunky Cabernet/Merlot with good depth of slightly herbaceous, blackcurrant and plum flavours.

(***½) **Cabernet/Merlot, Pinot Noir, Reserve Chardonnay**
(**½) **Riesling Medium**

SAXTON ESTATE

774 Main Road, Stoke. Est 1967. Owners: Wayne and Lynne Laurie. Production: 750 cases.

Nelson's oldest winery is Saxton Estate, a pocket-sized vineyard on the main road south at Stoke, near Nelson city. Irish-born Rod Neill, who named the venture Victory in remembrance of Lord

Nelson's ship, made his first trial plantings in 1967 and began hobbyist winemaking in 1972.

The 1-hectare vineyard is planted principally in Pinot Noir, with smaller plots of Chasselas, Breidecker, Reichensteiner and Cabernet Sauvignon. Grapes are also bought from several Nelson growers.

During the 1980s, silver medals were won by the pale, light Gamay Beaujolais and slightly richer Seibel 5455. Wayne and Lynne Laurie bought the property in 1995, changed the name to Saxton Estate and upgraded the winery and grounds, but the wines, from 1997 produced with the assistance of Saralinda McMillan, formerly of Seifried Estate, are rarely seen beyond Nelson.

SEIFRIED ESTATE

Redwood Road, Appleby. Est 1974. Owners: Hermann and Agnes Seifried. Production: 55,000 cases.

Seifried Estate is by far the largest winery in Nelson. It plays a valuable role in the New Zealand wine industry, producing good wines at affordable prices, and for decades has been a standard-bearer for Riesling.

Hermann and Agnes Seifried planted their first vines in the Upper Moutere's clays in 1974. Austrian-born Seifried graduated in wine technology in Germany, and later produced wine in Europe and South Africa, before he came to New Zealand in 1971 as winemaker for the Apple and Pear Board's unsuccessful venture into apple wine production. The burly, indefatigable Seifried and his wife, Agnes, who handles the company's administration, exports and public relations, for many years called their winery Weingut Seifried.

The original winery was sited near the village of Upper Moutere, where the Seifrieds still own a 12-hectare block of Chardonnay, Riesling, Sylvaner and Pinot Noir. The nearby, 22-hectare Redwood Valley vineyard is planted in Sauvignon Blanc, Riesling and Gewürztraminer.

In 1993 the Seifrieds opened a handsome vineyard restaurant at Appleby, closer to the city of Nelson, followed in 1996 by the erection of a new winery there and the closure of the old winery. A 34-hectare vineyard has also been developed at Appleby, planted in Chardonnay, Sauvignon Blanc, Pinot Noir and Cabernet Sauvignon. Grapes are also bought from growers in Nelson and Marlborough.

Riesling and Gewürztraminer, for many years the twin focal points of the Seifried range, have recently been supplemented by a growing output of Chardonnay and Sauvignon Blanc. The wines, reliable and often impressive, are mostly branded as Seifried Estate, with an alternative selection of well-priced wines marketed under the Old Coach Road label.

The Riesling Dry is a more austere style than most New Zealand Rieslings, but in top vintages is highly fragrant, with pure, fresh, intense lemon/lime flavours and a long, rich, steely finish. The Riesling is a medium-dry style with fullness of body and strong, ripe flavours.

The Gewürztraminer is floral and well-spiced in a medium-dry, easy-drinking style. Also based on Gewürztraminer, the freeze-concentrated Ice Wine is richly perfumed and mouthfilling, with strong, citrusy, spicy, honey-sweet flavours.

Ripely aromatic, with an abundance of fresh, gooseberry and melon-like flavours and a zingy finish, the Sauvignon Blanc is consistently excellent and sharply priced. Its stablemate under the Old Coach Road label is almost as good and offers similarly outstanding value.

The three-tier Chardonnay range includes the strongly wooded, firmly structured Barrel Fermented Chardonnay, a fleshy, rich and nutty wine which takes three years to break into full stride; the deliciously ripe and fruity Nelson Chardonnay, which is both tank and barrel-fermented but entirely oak-aged; and the briefly oak-aged, less complex but attractively lemony and lively Old Coach Road Chardonnay.

The reds are less impressive. The Pinot Noir is typically a light, raspberryish style, simple, fresh and soft. The Cabernet Sauvignon tends to lack weight and flavour intensity, with distinct leafy characters.

**** **Riesling Dry, Sauvignon Blanc**
***½ **Barrel Fermented Chardonnay, Ice Wine, Riesling**
*** **Nelson Chardonnay, Gewürztraminer, Old Coach Road Chardonnay, Old Coach Road Sauvignon Blanc**
½ **Cabernet Sauvignon, Pinot Noir

SPENCER HILL ESTATE

Best Road, Upper Moutere. Est 1990. Owners: Philip and Sheryl Jones. Production: 9,000 cases.

American Phil Jones is no advocate of single-vineyard varietal wines: 'I'm a real blender,' he says. 'New Zealand, with its cool climate, is marginal for grape-growing, so we've got to blend regions and varieties to achieve consistency of quality.' From the first 1994 vintage, Jones' astutely crafted, fat and well-rounded Chardonnays have enjoyed eye-catching success on the show circuit.

The winery was named after Philip and Sheryl Jones' son, Spencer. A Californian with degrees in viticulture and pest management who also studied winemaking at Fresno State University, Jones later got 'side-tracked', spending 18 years running a large agricultural consultancy. After visiting New Zealand to 'get away', he decided to emigrate permanently, and planted his first vines off Gardner Valley Road, between Glover's and Neudorf, in 1990.

On low-fertility clay slopes, 12.5 hectares of principally Chardonnay, Sauvignon Blanc and Pinot Noir vines have been established, supplemented by smaller plots of Sémillon, Pinot Gris, Merlot, Cabernet Franc, Pinotage and Cabernet Sauvignon. Grapes are also purchased from several regions in the South and North Islands, even Gisborne.

The majority of the production is marketed under the Tasman Bay brand. The top Spencer Hill label ('reserved for the wines I truly like,' says Jones), is a more vineyard-designated, oak-influenced range.

The two Tasman Bay Chardonnays (reserve and non-reserve) are adroitly structured, harmonious wines based principally on Marlborough fruit, with rich, citrusy, slightly mealy and buttery flavours and enormous drinkability. A full malolactic fermentation imparts a seductive softness, without subduing their intense fruit flavours. The reserve model is barrel-aged longer, with a higher percentage of French rather than American oak.

Tasman Bay Reserve Fumé is a barrel-fermented blend of Sauvignon Blanc and Sémillon with ripe, melon-like, non-aggressive flavours, oak/lees complexity and a well-rounded finish. For sheer drinkability, it rivals the Chardonnays.

The red wine range includes a light but elegant and supple, very easy drinking Tasman Bay Pinot Noir; a chunky, ripe Tasman Bay Merlot/Cabernet/Franc, matured in French and American oak barriques, with warm chocolate and spice flavours, some complexity and moderate tannins; and a fragrant, robust Spencer Hill Merlot/Franc/Cabernet with excellent concentration and length.

(****½) Tasman Bay Marlborough Chardonnay, Tasman Bay Reserve Chardonnay
(****)   Spencer Hill Merlot/Franc/Cabernet, Tasman Bay Reserve Fumé
(***½) Tasman Bay Merlot/Cabernet/Franc
(***)   Tasman Bay Pinot Noir

TE MANIA ESTATE

Pughs Road, Richmond. Est 1990. Owners: Jon and Cheryl Harrey. Production: 2,300 cases.

Te Mania ('The Plains') was established in 1990 by Jon and Cheryl Harrey, who planted their Home Block vineyard in Riesling, Chardonnay and Sauvignon Blanc. The Bartlett Block, planted in 1995, features the same three varieties plus Sémillon, Merlot, Cabernet Franc, Malbec and Pinot Noir. The Harreys now own 8 hectares of vines on the Waimea Plains.

After initially selling their Riesling grapes to other local companies, whose wines won several awards, Jon and Cheryl produced ther first Te Mania wines in 1995. The wines are produced at a local winery by a consultant winemaker, and a sales/tasting area in McShanes Road is shared with Holmes Brothers Direct.

The Riesling is scented and floral, with good depth of citrusy, limey, crisp, slightly sweet flavour. The Sauvignon Blanc offers incisive, herbaceous flavours, fresh and lively. The barrique-fermented Chardonnay is robust, complex, creamy and bursting with flavour, and red wines will also join the range.

(****) Chardonnay
(***) Riesling, Sauvignon Blanc

Marlborough

Think Marlborough, and it's hard not to think Sauvignon Blanc. During the past decade, the explosively flavoured and zesty Sauvignon Blancs of Marlborough have taken the world by storm.

Marlborough is by far New Zealand's largest wine region, with almost 40 percent of the total national vineyard. The region's rise has been spectacularly swift. Montana planted the first commercial vineyards in 1973, produced its first Marlborough Müller-Thurgau and Cabernet Sauvignon in 1976, and in 1979 bottled its first Sauvignon Blanc. Those pungent early Sauvignon Blancs, bursting with green-edged aromas and flavours, were without parallel anywhere else in the wine world, even in the Loire; Marlborough was on its way to international stardom.

The aristocracy of the Marlborough wine scene includes some of the biggest names in New Zealand wine – Montana, Corbans, Cloudy Bay, Hunter's. In the past two or three years, relative newcomers such as Lawson's Dry Hills, Saint Clair and Fromm have also carved out strong reputations. The community of Marlborough-based wine producers is growing swiftly: 20 in 1993, 44 in 1997.

Overseas investment is streaming into the region. Australian winemakers have been active in Marlborough since 1985, when David Hohnen of Cape Mentelle set up Cloudy Bay to supply the Australian market. Corbans Marlborough Winery, now wholly Corbans-owned, was originally funded by Corbans and Wolf Blass. Domaine Chandon of Victoria produces a brilliant bottle-fermented Marlborough Brut.

European winemakers are also scattered around the region. Almuth Lorenz, raised in the Rheinhessen, is winemaker and part-owner of Merlen; Edel Everling, the co-founder of Johanneshof Cellars, was born at Rudesheim. The Fromm winery, specialising in red wines, was set up by Swiss immigrants, Georg and Ruth Fromm.

Most conspicious of all are the mounting links between Marlborough and the great houses of Champagne. Deutz Marlborough Cuvée is produced by Montana under the technical

guidance of Deutz and Geldermann. The two largest shareholders in Highfield, which recently launched its first bottle-fermented bubbly, are Asians with a connection to the Champagne house
of Drappier. Veuve Clicquot is now the majority shareholder in
Cloudy Bay. Moet & Chandon, owner of Domaine Chandon, is
involved in masterminding the production of Domaine Chandon
Marlborough Brut. Sauvignon Blanc is currently the star
of the Marlborough wine scene, but long-term, the region's
greatest gift to the wine world may be its classy bottle-fermented
sparklings.

For a wine region with such a big reputation, Marlborough (or
at least the Wairau Valley, where most of the vines are concentrated), is remarkably small. Rugged mountains up to almost
3,000 metres straddle most of Marlborough. The Wairau Valley,
14 kilometres wide at its eastern extremity, where it meets the
sea at Cloudy Bay (so named because after heavy rain, its waters
turn cloudy with silt from the Wairau River), runs 26 kilometres
inland. From the Wither Hills to the south to the towering
Richmond Ranges on the valley's northern flanks is only about 10
kilometres.

The warmest of the South Island's winelands, Marlborough is
also significantly cooler than Hawke's Bay. Grapes ripen slowly
in the region's warm, sunny days and cool nights, with a relatively low autumn rainfall enabling the fruit to be left late on the
vines for an extended ripening period. The soil types are variable, even within individual vineyards, with free-draining, shingly sites the most sought after.

To counter the dehydrating effects on the vines of the hot, dry
nor-wester, Wairau Valley winemakers draw irrigation water from
an extensive aquifer within the valley's alluvial gravels.
Vineyards are also now spreading into the slightly higher
Waihopai Valley, where the frost risk is greater but land is
cheaper. The Awatere Valley, east and over the Wither Hills
from the Wairau Valley, was pioneered by Vavasour in the
mid-to-late 1980s, but the lack of an aquifer has slowed vineyard
development.

To call Marlborough Sauvignon Blanc country is an oversim-
plification. Over two-thirds of New Zealand's Sauvignon Blanc is
planted in Marlborough, and Sauvignon Blanc and Chardonnay
together account for 63 percent of all the region's vines. But the
province's almost 3,000 hectares of vineyards in 1996 included
substantial areas of Riesling, Cabernet Sauvignon, Pinot Noir,
Sémillon, Müller-Thurgau and Merlot. Despite the generally disappointing performance of Cabernet Sauvignon in Marlborough,
high hopes are held for the earlier-ripening Pinot Noir and Merlot
varieties.

There is a growing awareness that exactly where in the
Wairau Valley vines are planted can have a significant effect on
wine styles, reflecting local variations in soil and climate. In the

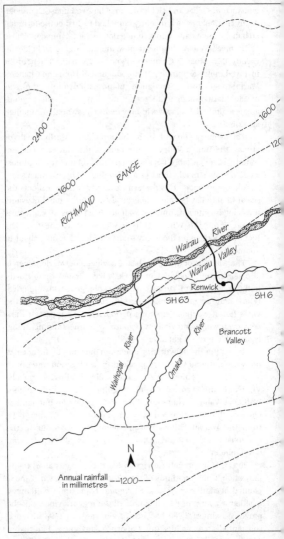

Annual rainfall
in millimetres ---1200---

stony soils on the north side of the valley, Sauvignon Blanc
grapes ripen earlier than those on the less gravelly south side. 'If
you want to make a very herbaceous, greener style of Sauvignon
Blanc,' says John Belsham of Rapaura Vintners and Foxes Island,
'you choose a site with medium-high fertility and good soil moisture retention. For a lusher, less aggressive Sauvignon Blanc, you

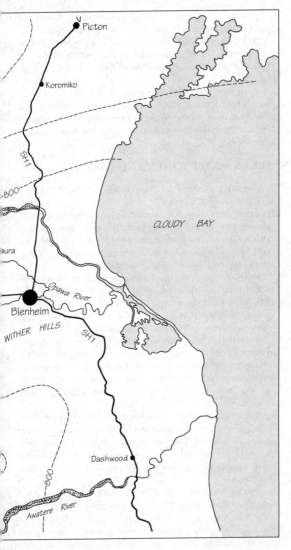

choose a stony site which matures its fruit two to three weeks earlier.'

Phylloxera is widespread in Marlborough, reducing crops and retarding ripening. In 1994, only 27 percent of the producing vines were grafted onto phylloxera-resistant rootstocks, although after massive replanting 75 percent will be by 1999.

A stream of 'grower labels' has recently flowed in Marlborough. The term 'grower label' is used when a former specialist grape-grower keeps back part or all of his or her crop, has the wine made at a local winery, and then controls the marketing of the new brand. Notable examples are Jackson Estate and Saint Clair.

Apart from the many wineries with a physical presence there, a host of North Island and South Island companies also draw fruit from Marlborough, recognising the international appeal of its mouth-wateringly fresh, crisp and flavour-packed white wines.

ALLAN SCOTT WINES AND ESTATES

Jacksons Road, Blenheim. Est 1990. Owners: Allan and Catherine Scott. Production: 26,500 cases.

For many years, Allan Scott worked for large wineries as a viticulturist. Now he and his wife, Catherine, own extensive vineyards in the Jacksons Road area near Cloudy Bay and produce a small range of white wines that are pure Marlborough – fresh, appetisingly crisp and awash with flavour.

Raised in North Canterbury, Scott arrived in Marlborough in 1973 as a vineyard labourer for Montana. After joining Corbans in 1980, he set up the Stoneleigh Vineyard and was the company's national vineyards manager from 1982 to 1989. The first wines under the Allan Scott label flowed in 1990.

From 1993 to 1994, Allan Scott Wines and Estates formed part of Appellation Vineyards (with Cellier Le Brun and Morton Estate), but the Scotts subsequently withdrew from the venture and regained ownership of the winery they founded. The couple are also now part-owners of Chancellor Wines in North Canterbury.

The 22 hectares of vineyards encircling the winery are planted in Sauvignon Blanc, Riesling and Chardonnay. Grapes are also purchased from Marlborough growers. The early wines were made at the local Vintech contract winemaking facility (now called Rapaura Vintners) but since 1996 the wines have been produced on-site.

The top wines carry the Allan Scott label, with a second tier selection called Mount Riley. The Sauvignon Blanc (like the French, Scott simply calls it Sauvignon) is often the best wine in the range, with fresh, strong, gooseberry and lime aromas and flavours and zingy acidity. The medium-dry Riesling has varied in quality, but top vintages show great fragrance and vigour.

The Chardonnay, half barrel-fermented, is a mouthfilling style that places its accent on fresh, vibrant, citrusy fruit flavours. Also under the Allan Scott label is a honey-sweet, botrytis-affected Autumn Riesling that in favourable vintages is exceptionally oily and treacly. Of the modestly priced wines labelled as Mount

Riley, the pick of the bunch to date is the Sauvignon, which in top vintages shows much of the intensity and vivacity of its Allan Scott stablemate.

****½ Allan Scott Sauvignon
**** Allan Scott Autumn Riesling
***½ Allan Scott Chardonnay, Allan Scott Riesling
(***½) Mount Riley Sauvignon
(**) Mount Riley Chardonnay
(*) Mount Riley Merlot

CAIRNBRAE WINES

Jacksons Road, Blenheim. Est 1980. Owners: Murray and Daphne Brown. Production: 10,500 cases.

Over the fence from Cloudy Bay, Murray and Daphne Brown run a cosy, unpretentious vineyard restaurant and produce a rock-solid lineup of Marlborough white wines.

Previously Southland farmers, the Browns came to Marlborough intending to buy a stock property, but instead signed up in 1980 to supply grapes to Corbans. The couple still sell part of their crop to other companies, but since 1992 have produced a swelling volume of wine under their own label.

The 18-hectare vineyard is planted in Sauvignon Blanc, Sémillon, Riesling, Chardonnay and Cabernet Franc. The wines are made at a local winery; there are no production facilities on-site.

The medium-dry Riesling is a typical Marlborough style: perfumed and tangy, with incisive lemon-lime flavours. The Sauvignon Blanc, full and fresh, with good depth of lively, limey flavours, is partnered by a flavoursome, green-edged and spicy Oak Aged Sauvignon Blanc, matured in American oak barriques.

The Chardonnay, partly fermented in American oak, is a drink-young style, fresh, vibrantly fruity and crisp. This has recently been joined by a slightly richer, more complex Reserve Chardonnay, fermented and matured in new American oak casks, in which well-ripened melon and passionfruit-evoking flavours hold sway, with restrained wood influence and a crisp, tight finish.

***½ Oak Aged Sauvignon Blanc, Riesling
(***½) Reserve Chardonnay
*** Chardonnay, Sauvignon Blanc

CELLIER LE BRUN

Terrace Road, Renwick. Est 1980. Owner: Resene Paints Limited. Production: 26,000 cases.

'I'm a fan of Bollinger rather than Taittinger,' says Daniel Le Brun, revealing his personal preference for bold, rich-flavoured, 'gutsy' sparkling wines. Le Brun pioneered sparkling wine production in Marlborough and built up a glowing track record of show successes, but in 1996 his involvement with the company that bears his name ended.

Le Brun was born near Epernay into a family which has produced Champagne since the seventeenth century. Frustrated by restrictions placed on the expansion of individual landholdings in Champagne, he visited New Zealand in 1975 and became excited by Marlborough's potential for sparkling wine production. By 1980 Le Brun and his New Zealand wife, Adele, had planted their first vines near Renwick.

The 16-hectare, densely spaced vineyard was established in the traditional grape varieties of Champagne: Chardonnay, Pinot Noir and Meunier. To duplicate the constant coolness of the chalk cellars of Champagne, Le Brun's bottle-fermented sparklings were aged in steel-lined caves under several metres of earth.

Regal Salmon Limited gained a controlling interest in Cellier Le Brun in 1987, but Daniel and Adele Le Brun retained a minority stake and their respective roles in production and sales. In 1993 the owners of Cellier Le Brun sold their shares to Appellation Vineyards (a company that briefly merged Cellier Le Brun, Morton Estate and Allan Scott) in exchange for shares in Appellation. A year later, when the Appellation venture unravelled, Resene Paints Limited took control of Cellier Le Brun, but again the Le Bruns stayed in a working role and with a minority shareholding. In 1996, however, the couple's involvement in the company was abruptly terminated.

Lowering some prices and the appointment of a new winemaker, Allan McWilliams, were among the company's first major moves in the post-Daniel Le Brun era. 'We want to retain the traditional Le Brun style but improve the quality control,' says McWilliams, who previously worked for Negociants New Zealand, where he was heavily involved in the production of Nautilus Cuvée Marlborough. 'The wines will still be bold and richly flavoured, but less broad, less oxidative.'

Some of the sparkling wines now available were made by Daniel Le Brun but disgorged and liqueured by McWilliams. Lighter in colour and fresher than the Le Brun style of the past, with greater finesse, they represent a step up in quality and should enhance the prestige of the brand.

The non-vintage Daniel Le Brun Méthode Traditionnelle (which accounts for about 70 percent of the company's total sales) is a blend of 60 percent Pinot Noir, 30 percent Chardonnay and 10 percent Meunier. Held on its yeast lees for two-and-a-half years, it is impressively lively, crisp, yeasty and full-flavoured. It's more restrained than in the past, but none the worse for that, with a steady 'bead' and fragrant, strawberryish aromas.

The onion skin-coloured Brut Taché is a non-vintage style with a full, yeasty, raspberryish, slightly earthy and creamy flavour. Soft and slightly sweet, it is *taché* (stained) with the colour of Pinot Noir grapes, on which it is wholly based.

All Chardonnay-based, the Blanc de Blancs is strikingly rich, with exceptional depth of toasty, nutty, yeasty flavour, tightly structured and lingering. The Vintage Méthode Traditionnelle, blended from Pinot Noir and Chardonnay and matured longer on its yeast lees than the non-vintage, is an enticingly fragrant, rich and complex, firmly structured wine that in several vintages has risen to great heights.

The stylish Cuvée Adele, which matures splendidly, was designed by Daniel Le Brun as a 'feminine' wine, dedicated to his wife. A blend of 80 percent Chardonnay and 20 percent Meunier, aged on its yeast lees for three-and-a-half years, it is a very refined wine, tight, nutty and vigorous, with greater delicacy than most of the Le Brun range.

Under its Terrace Road label, Cellier Le Brun also produces a trio of mid-priced still table wines. Terrace Road Sauvignon Blanc has ripe passionfruit-like aromas, with moderate flavour depth. Terrace Road Pinot Noir is cherryish and spicy, but lacks the warmth and roundness of fully ripe fruit. The pick of the three is the partly barrel-fermented Terrace Road Chardonnay, a broad, savoury, buttery-soft wine, very forward in its appeal.

*****	Daniel Le Brun Blanc de Blancs, Daniel Le Brun Vintage Méthode Traditionnelle
(****½)	Daniel Le Brun Cuvée Adele
****	Daniel Le Brun Brut Taché, Daniel Le Brun Méthode Traditionnelle NV
(***½)	Terrace Road Chardonnay
(**½)	Terrace Road Pinot Noir, Terrace Road Sauvignon Blanc

CLOUDY BAY VINEYARDS

Jacksons Road, Blenheim. Est 1985. Owner: Cape Mentelle (NZ). Production: 90,000 cases.

A striking wine that overflows with fresh, ripely herbaceous and zingy flavour, in the glass Cloudy Bay Sauvignon Blanc fully lives up to its international reputation. Cloudy Bay is one of the country's most prestigious wineries and its classic Sauvignon Blanc is a key ambassador for New Zealand wine in world markets.

David Hohnen, part-owner of Cape Mentelle, a leading Western Australian winery, is the driving-force behind Cloudy Bay. Hohnen's interest in New Zealand wine was aroused when a group of Kiwi winemakers visited him in 1983. 'I had my '82 Sémillon/Sauvignon Blanc in barrels and said: "Get a load of this." They said: "If you think that's herbaceous, see what we've got in the car." Penfolds 1983 Sauvignon Blanc from Marlborough just blew me away. It was a bit sweet, but it had fruit characters that we would never get in Australia.'

When Hohnen moved to establish a new winery in Marlborough, New Zealand was on the verge of the glut-induced price war of 1985–86. 'It was a terrific gamble,' he recalls. 'I just had this gut feeling that told me it was the right thing to do. New Zealand Sauvignon Blanc simply hadn't been discovered and seemed to me to have a great future.'

Construction of the stylish, concrete-slab winery in Jacksons Road began in 1985 under the direction of Australian winemaker Kevin Judd, a Roseworthy College graduate fresh from a successful spell at Selaks. Today Judd still controls the day-to-day running of Cloudy Bay, with Hohnen visiting several times each year to assist with crucial blending decisions. Corbans supplied the grapes for Cloudy Bay's early vintages, in return for the right to crush their own Marlborough fruit at the Cloudy Bay winery.

From the beginning, Hohnen planned to sell much of Cloudy Bay's output in Australia, but New Zealand wines were not highly regarded there. So Hohnen sent key Australian wine retailers a pack containing a bottle, a glass and a jar of New Zealand mussels, carrying the message: 'Before you open this box, get a corkscrew and some fresh crusty bread.' Bottles were broached and almost overnight Cloudy Bay was a smash hit.

Cloudy Bay's spare and evocative label attracted nearly as much praise as the wine itself. Again Hohnen deserves the credit. 'Looking out the window of an Air New Zealand Friendship as we were landing in Blenheim, I saw the three-tiered silhouette of the mountains in the distance and got an instant vision of the Cloudy Bay label.'

The global expansion of Cloudy Bay was enhanced in 1990 by Veuve Clicquot Ponsardin's purchase of a controlling interest in Cape Mentelle – and thus Cloudy Bay. David Hohnen has retained a 20 percent shareholding. According to Kevin Judd, the tie with Veuve Clicquot has brought two key benefits: 'Financial stability and greater access to overseas markets.' Today Cloudy Bay wines are exported to about 25 countries, principally Australia and the UK.

On flat, shingly soils adjacent to the winery, 60 hectares of vines are established, principally Sauvignon Blanc, Chardonnay and Sémillon, with smaller plots of Pinot Noir, Merlot and Malbec. Cloudy Bay is gradually developing two other large vineyards at Renwick and in the Brancott Valley, and grapes are also purchased from growers on long-term contracts.

If you ask Kevin Judd for the key to the irresistibly zesty, rich-flavoured style of Cloudy Bay Sauvignon Blanc, he points to 'the fruit flavours that are in the grapes when they arrive at the winery'. The blend typically includes 5 to 10 percent Sémillon, and 10 percent barrel fermentation adds 'a subliminal dimension, something extra, but it's hard to taste oak in the wine'. Mouthfilling, with an arresting intensity of gooseberry and green capsicum-like flavour, a touch of complexity and a rich, trailing finish, it softens and mellows with age but remains a pleasure to drink for at least a decade.

Although living in the shadow of the exceptional Sauvignon Blanc, the Cloudy Bay range also includes a strapping, mealy, barrel-fermented Chardonnay that achieves great heights at about four years old. Pelorus, made from Pinot Noir and Chardonnay matured on its yeast lees for three years, is a powerful, creamy, nutty, magnificently full-flavoured sparkling. Occasionally an exquisitely perfumed, succulent and steely Late Harvest Riesling also appears.

Cloudy Bay's red-wine emphasis is moving away from Cabernet-based reds to Pinot Noir. The Cabernet/Merlot is a stylish, complex wine with plummy, spicy flavours, but it tends to lack the ripeness and richness of more northern Cabernets (let alone those of Cape Mentelle). By contrast, the early trial vintages and first commercial release of Pinot Noir from 1994 have been highly satisfying reds – generous, with concentrated dark cherry and spice flavours, complexity and a long, supple finish.

*****   Chardonnay, Pelorus, Sauvignon Blanc
(*****)   Late Harvest Riesling
(****½) Pinot Noir
***½   Cabernet/Merlot

CONDERS BEND WINES AND ESTATES

Est 1991. Owner: Delegat's Wine Estate. Production: 6,750 cases.
This small Marlborough company was recently purchased by Delegat's from its founder, Craig Gass, who formerly owned the Korepo (now Ruby Bay) winery in Nelson. After selling Korepo, Gass established the Conders Bend label by purchasing grapes from Marlborough growers and processing them at the Rapaura Vintners (formerly Vintech) contract winemaking facility.

Conders Bend wines have been consistently good – the Sauvignon Blanc mouthfilling, with rich, lush tropical-fruit flavours; the barrel-fermented Chardonnay robust, citrusy and buttery-soft; the Riesling fresh, lively and flavour-packed.

Delegat's purchase has given them the Conders Bend brand, and stocks of the established wines and an unreleased sparkling.

**** Sauvignon Blanc
***½ Chardonnay, Riesling

DOMAINE CHANDON (NZ)

Est 1990. Owner: Moet & Chandon. Production: 3,400 cases.
What better way for Moet & Chandon, the great Champagne house, to celebrate its 250th anniversary in 1993 than by launching the first 1990 vintage of its Domaine Chandon Marlborough Brut?

Domaine Chandon (NZ) is a wholly-owned subsidiary of Moet & Chandon and a sister company of the Yarra Valley winery, Domaine Chandon (Australia). Moet's stated objective with its Marlborough wine is 'to produce a wine that reflects Marlborough *terroir* in its aroma and flavour but at the same time, by careful blending of the base wines, produce a flavoursome, rich, long palate structure with a dry, yet soft finish which is in the Moet house style'.

The wine is a blend of Marlborough Pinot Noir, Chardonnay and Meunier, produced at the Hunter's winery by Dr Tony Jordan, managing director of Domaine Chandon (Australia), and Richard Geoffery, a Champagne-based senior winemaker for Moet & Chandon. Production is small, climbing from 700 cases in 1990 to 3,400 cases in 1996.

The style has evolved since the first 1990 release, reflecting a growing proportion of Pinot Noir (the 1993 vintage is 54 percent Pinot Noir, 32 percent Chardonnay and 14 percent Meunier) and increased use of malolactic fermentation. The 1992 and 1993 vintages are among the most scintillating sparkling wines ever made in New Zealand, with extremely intense, intricate, yeasty, tight-knit, smooth flavour.

***** **Domaine Chandon Marlborough Brut**

FORREST ESTATE

Blicks Road, Renwick. Est 1989. Owners: Dr John and Brigid Forrest. Production: 4,000 cases.

Pure, fresh, very ripe Marlborough fruit flavours, uncluttered by oak, are the hallmark of Dr John Forrest's white wines. This small Renwick winery has a big reputation for its Sauvignon Blanc, Riesling and Chardonnay.

Forrest, born in Marlborough, graduated with a PhD in biochemistry and then worked as a government research scientist before he and his wife, Brigid, planted their first vines in 1989. After gaining winemaking experience as a cellarhand at local wineries, Forrest made his first wine in 1990 – and scooped the trophy for champion rosé at that year's Air New Zealand Wine Awards.

The 16-hectare estate vineyard is planted mainly in Sémillon, Sauvignon Blanc, Chardonnay, Merlot, Cabernet Franc and Cabernet Sauvignon. Fruit is also purchased from local growers. Forrest is also part-owner (with Australian viticulturist Bob Newton) of the 16-hectare Cornerstone Vineyard in Gimblett Road, Hawke's Bay, source of the perfumed, ripe and smooth Cornerstone Vineyard Cabernet/Merlot, a French and American oak-aged red with impressively concentrated flavour.

The early wines were made at the Vintech (now Rapaura Vintners) contract winemaking facility, but Forrest's own winery rose prior to the 1996 vintage. The Sauvignon Blanc is scented, mouthfilling and abounds with crisp, ripely herbaceous flavour. The Sémillon Oak Aged is full-bodied, rich-flavoured and rounded, with wood handling and malolactic fermentation toning down its herbaceousness.

Forrest Estate Riesling is a tangy, slightly sweet style, very fragrant and flavourful. The Chardonnay, given very limited exposure to oak but matured on its yeast lees to add character, is a vibrant, fruit-driven wine, delightful in its youth.

Gibson's Creek is a mid-priced, American oak-aged blend of Cabernet Sauvignon, Merlot and Cabernet Franc, soft, berryish and slightly green-edged. Bright pink, with fresh, floral aromas, the Cabernet Rosé is a dryish wine with a lovely depth of crisp, delicate, raspberryish flavours – one of New Zealand's finest rosés.

****½ Sauvignon Blanc
****   Cabernet Rosé, Chardonnay, Cornerstone Vineyard
        Cabernet/Merlot, Riesling
***½   Sémillon Oak Aged
***   Gibson's Creek

FOXES ISLAND WINES

Est 1988. Owners: John Belsham and Anne Graham. Production: 1,400 cases.
When the swollen Wairau and Opawa rivers burst their banks in the past, an island would be created of slightly elevated land at the western end of Rapaura Road, where Rapaura Vintners now stands. John Belsham, manager and part-owner of Rapaura Vintners, calls his personal range of wines after the site where the wines are made – Foxes Island.

Belsham established a strong reputation as winemaker for Matua Valley and then Hunter's prior to his involvement with Rapaura Vintners (formerly Vintech). He and his wife, Anne Graham, own a 4.5-hectare vineyard in Giffords Road, planted in Chardonnay and Pinot Noir, and buy fruit from other Marlborough growers. Their first vines were planted in 1988 and the first Foxes Island wine flowed in 1992.

The rarely seen Pinot Noir is weighty, full-flavoured and supple. The Chardonnay, partly barrel-fermented, is a robust, high-flavoured, generous wine, peachy, biscuity and soft.

****   Chardonnay
(***) Pinot Noir

FRAMINGHAM VINEYARD

Conders Bend Road, Renwick. Est 1981. Owners: Rex and Paula Brooke-Taylor. Production: 6,000 cases. No winery sales.
Exceptional Rieslings spring from Rex and Paula Brooke-Taylor's stony, free-draining Framingham Vineyard on the outskirts of Renwick.

The Brooke-Taylors planted their first vines in 1981, and have supplied the grapes for many top Rieslings made by Corbans, Dry River and Grove Mill. The couple were co-founders of the Grove Mill winery, but sold their shares in 1990 and four years later produced the first wine under their own Framingham Vineyard label.

The 16-hectare vineyard, grown in an old bed of the Opawa River, is planted principally in Riesling, with smaller plots of Sauvignon Blanc, Cabernet Sauvignon, Merlot, Cabernet Franc, Syrah and Malbec.

The Chardonnay is delicate and lemony, with a touch of oak and well-rounded finish. Both the Riesling Classic Dry and Riesling Medium are richly fragrant wines with fresh, concentrated, slightly honeyish flavours. Framingham's outstanding achievement is the gorgeously perfumed Selection Riesling, a medium style with steely acidity and very searching, delicate, citrusy, honeyish flavours.

(*****) **Selection Riesling**
(****) **Riesling Classic Dry, Riesling Medium**
(***)   **Chardonnay**

FROMM WINERY

Godfrey Road, Blenheim. Est 1992. Owners: Georg and Ruth Fromm. Production: 5,250 cases.

Fromm is a red-wine specialist. 'Everybody makes white wines here,' says Georg Fromm. 'We thought: if Chardonnay and Sauvignon Blanc thrive in Marlborough, so should reds.' Deliciously ripe, concentrated and supple, Fromm La Strada Pinot Noir is one of the region's leading reds.

Georg and Ruth Fromm come from Switzerland, where Georg's family has made wine for four generations and he still owns a small vineyard, planted mainly in Pinot Noir. Swiss winemaker Hatsch Kalberer, who previously worked at Matawhero for nine years, has been heavily involved in the project from the start. The Fromms plan to export up to half of their output to Switzerland, where Georg is confident his Pinot Noir 'will compete well with Burgundy'.

The 6-hectare estate vineyard, where planting began in 1992, is devoted wholly to red-wine varieties – Pinot Noir, Merlot, Syrah, Malbec, Cabernet Franc, Cabernet Sauvignon and Sangiovese. The vines are close-planted (at more than double the average density in New Zealand) and most tasks are performed manually, including leaf-plucking and harvesting. Grapes are also purchased from local growers.

The first wines flowed in 1992, based on bought-in fruit. Single-vineyard wines have been marketed, but most are blended from different sites and sold under the brand name La Strada ('The Road').

The Pinot Noirs have been an instant success story, with greater depth and authority than has hitherto been the norm in Marlborough. Mouthfilling and concentrated, they are generous, warm and ripe-tasting, with a seductive fragrance and suppleness. La Strada Reserve Pinot Noir is especially dark and characterful, but the standard model is full of drink-young charm. The Cabernet Sauvignon is slightly green-edged, but possesses satisfying body and flavour depth. The blended Vino Rosso is a very decent quaffer, fuller-flavoured than most of Marlborough's reds.

Although placing its accent on reds, Fromm also produces a weighty, ripe, well-rounded Chardonnay and a bold, barrique-fermented Reserve Chardonnay with loads of peachy-ripe, complex, creamy flavour.

(★★★★½) Reserve Pinot Noir
(★★★★)   Pinot Noir, Reserve Chardonnay
(★★★)   Cabernet Sauvignon, Chardonnay, Vino Rosso
(★★½)   Rosé

GILLAN ESTATE WINES

Rapaura Road, Renwick. Est 1994. Owners: Gillan and Young Company Limited. Production: 9,000 cases.

A forthcoming, ripely scented and flavourful Sauvignon Blanc and stylish bottle-fermented sparkling are the key achievements of this young company in Rapaura Road, between Corbans and Merlen.

The husband and wife team of Terry and Toni Gillan first crossed paths in London when Toni, a New Zealander, rented one of Terry's flats. After coming to Marlborough in 1987, the couple invested extensively in Blenheim property, including the Grove Mill winery.

After withdrawing from Grove Mill when their bid to purchase a controlling share proved unsuccessful, the Gillans formed a new company with grapegrowers Hamish and Anne Young, who own the 9-hectare Eastfields vineyard, planted in Sauvignon Blanc and Chardonnay. 'It's a pooling of talents,' says Toni Gillan. 'Hamish is the grapegrower, Terry is the manager and I'm the marketer.'

The Mediterranean-style winery, which has tasting facilities and a barrel hall, is also used for temperature-controlled storage of the sparkling wine during its lengthy maturation on yeast lees. Much of the other processing, by consultant winemaker Sam Weaver, is handled away from the site.

The Eastfields Sauvignon Blanc caused a big splash when the first 1994 vintage won the trophy for champion Sauvignon Blanc at that year's Air New Zealand Wine Awards. Fresh and delicate, with strong, citrusy, limey aromas and flavours in a deliciously easy-drinking style, the Sauvignon Blanc is an attractively ripe wine, yet retains its cool-climate vigour and impact.

Eastfields Chardonnay, about one-third oak-aged, is a fruit-driven style with fresh, ripe, rounded flavours. The Marlborough Merlot is a medium-bodied wine with pleasant, slightly leafy,

plum/berry flavours. The Brut Reserve, a 70/30 blend of
Chardonnay and Pinot Noir, lees-aged for two years, is full and
lively, with excellent depth of buttery, citrusy, yeasty flavour and
a creamy finish.

**** **Brut Reserve, Eastfields Sauvignon Blanc**
***½ **Eastfields Chardonnay**
½ **Marlborough Merlot

GROVE MILL WINE COMPANY

Waihopai Valley Road, Renwick. Est 1988. Owners: Private share-
holders. Production: 55,000 cases.

Like many Marlborough wineries, Grove Mill produces impressive Rieslings, Sauvignon Blancs and Chardonnays. Less pre-
dictably, the company is also playing a major role in exploring
the region's potential for less fashionable varieties like Pinot Gris
and Gewürztraminer.

Grove Mill was founded in 1988 by 23 shareholders, many of
them grapegrowers. Terry Gillan and his wife, Toni, driving forces
in the early years, have since departed to set up their own winery. Still there, however, is the original winemaker, David Pearce,
who held the senior post of winemaker at Corbans' Gisborne
Winery before he came south to set up Grove Mill.

The winery was originally sited near the heart of Blenheim in
a brick-walled remnant of the 139-year-old former Wairau
Brewery. This small, richly atmospheric building, however, could
only accommodate an output of about 10,000 cases. Rising production forced a shift in 1994 to a larger winery in the Waihopai
Valley, near the township of Renwick.

The first 17 hectares of vineyards surrounding the winery were
planted in Sauvignon Blanc and Chardonnay, but Gewürztraminer,
Pinot Gris and Pinot Noir are also being established. Growers in
the Wairau Valley supply most of the winery's grapes.

Grove Mill Riesling is an immaculate, beautifully perfumed
wine with incisive lemon/lime flavours interwoven with abundant sweetness and fresh, lively acidity. The Sauvignon Blanc is
mouthfilling, with rich gooseberry and green capsicum-like
flavours and lovely balance and vigour.

Several Chardonnays are produced. The flagship Lansdowne
Chardonnay, named after the local rugby ground, has varied in
style, but the latest vintages are tightly structured, lemony, nutty
and crisp, unfolding well over several years. The mid-priced
Marlborough Chardonnay is more attractive in its youth, with
subtle oak/lees characters filling out the soft, ripe, intense, citrusy fruit flavours. The Winemaker's Reserve Chardonnay, based
wholly or partly on Gisborne fruit, is an upfront style, deliciously
lush, ripe, savoury and soft.

The Gewürztraminer is a big, well-ripened, musky wine,
medium-dry, fruity and smooth. The Pinot Gris is weighty, with

well-concentrated, peachy flavours. Both wines have a distinct splash of sweetness.

The reds are typically dark, gutsy and full-flavoured, but also sometimes herbaceous and slightly astringent. The Cabernet Sauvignon, French oak-aged for eighteen months, is weighty and rich, although slightly leafy. The Winemaker's Reserve Merlot lacks a bit of fragrance and charm but is densely coloured, chunky, chewy and powerful.

*****   Riesling Sauvignon Blanc
****   Gewürztraminer, Lansdowne Chardonnay,
           Marlborough Chardonnay, Winemaker's Reserve
           Chardonnay
***½   Pinot Gris
(***½)Cabernet Sauvignon, Winemaker's Reserve Merlot

HAWKESBRIDGE WINES AND ESTATES

Hawkesbury Road, Renwick. Est 1994. Owners: Michael and Judy Veal. Production: 1,700 cases. Winery sales by appointment.

'The wine is safe until the last guard is shot,' reported the Russian security firm providing protection for a consignment of Hawkesbridge wine sent by train from London to Moscow.

Michael and Judy Veal switched from running a public relations agency in Wellington to growing grapes and making wine near Renwick, alongside the bridge in Hawkesbury Road. The land was once owned by Montana, who uprooted their vines, and later planted in Müller-Thurgau before the Veals began planting Sauvignon Blanc in 1990.

Today the 13-hectare vineyard is planted principally in Sauvignon Blanc, Chardonnay and Müller-Thurgau, with much of the crop still sold to other wine companies (one of which makes the Hawkesbridge wine). Production is planned to grow to around 5,000 cases.

The Sauvignon Blanc is mouthfilling, lively and incisively flavoured, with a good balance of ripe tropical-fruit and herbaceous characters. Sophie's Vineyard Chardonnay is a celebration of lush, ripe fruit flavours, with 'minimal' oak contact but lovely freshness, fragrance and depth.

(****)   Sophie's Vineyard Chardonnay
(***½) Sauvignon Blanc

HIGHFIELD ESTATE

Brookby Road, Blenheim. Est 1989. Owners: Shin Yokoi, Tom Tenuwera and Neil Buchanan. Production: 15,000 cases.

After a hesitant start, Highfield is making consistently good wines. On a rise overlooking the Omaka Valley, its soaring, Tuscan-inspired observation tower is visible from all over the south side of the Wairau.

Bill Walsh, a grapegrower since the mid-1970s, and his sons, Philip and Gerald, founded the company in 1989. However, the early wines were mediocre and marketed poorly; within two years Highfield was in receivership. Shin Yokoi, an Osaka-based manufacturer of fire-fighting apparatus, is now the major shareholder, in partnership with another Japanese investor, UK-based Tom Tenuwera, and Wellington businessman Neil Buchanan, who is also Highfield's general manager.

The 1.5-hectare estate vineyard is planted in Chardonnay, Sauvignon Blanc and Merlot. Highfield also owns a 10-hectare block in the heart of the Wairau Valley, planted in Sauvignon Blanc and Chardonnay, and purchases fruit from local growers. Tony Hooper, an Australian graduate of Roseworthy College, has made the wine since 1991.

The top range, labelled Elstree, features a powerful, fleshy, oak-matured Sauvignon Blanc with rich, ripe, non-herbaceous flavours; the bold, lush, biscuity, soft Elstree Chardonnay; and the very fresh and lively, delicately flavoured, moderately complex Elstree Cuvée, based on Pinot Noir and Chardonnay. Highfield has also produced several superb honey-sweet dessert wines, initially from Müller-Thurgau but most recently from botrytis-infected Riesling.

The Sauvignon Blanc is fresh and smooth in an easy-drinking style with quite good depth of melon- and lime-like flavours; the Dry Riesling is scented and full, with ripe, delicate flavours. The Chardonnay is typically fat, with lots of savoury, buttery, well-rounded flavour. The Merlot, French oak-matured, shows marked vintage variation – light and leafy in cool years, in warmer vintages it is chewy, with quite good depth of plummy, spicy flavour.

****½ Botrytised Riesling
(****) Elstree Chardonnay, Elstree Sauvignon Blanc
***½ Chardonnay, Dry Riesling, Sauvignon Blanc
(***½) Elstree Cuvée
*** Merlot

HUNTER'S WINES

Rapaura Road, Blenheim. Est 1982. Owner: Jane Hunter. Production: 45,000 cases.

Jane Hunter, awarded an OBE in 1993 and an honorary DSc in 1997 for her contributions to the wine industry, produces two of Marlborough's classic Sauvignon Blancs and a Chardonnay of notable delicacy and finesse.

Ernie Hunter, an extroverted entrepreneurial Irishman, founded Hunter's in 1982. With Almuth Lorenz, now at Merlen, as winemaker, the fledgling winery made an eye-catching debut at the 1982 National Wine Competition by entering six wines and collecting six medals. However, beset by financial problems, in

1984 Ernie Hunter turned to export, establishing footholds in the UK and US and twice winning the popular vote at the *Sunday Times* Wine Club Festival in London. A man of formidable energy and charisma, one of the pioneers of New Zealand wine exports, he died in a motor accident in 1987, aged 38. His wife, Jane, then stepped in as the managing director.

Born into a South Australian grapegrowing family, Jane Hunter studied agricultural science, majoring in viticulture and plant pathology, before coming to Marlborough in 1983 as Montana's chief viticulturist. Following her husband's premature death, she thought about leaving the region. 'But then I thought, what's the point? We worked so hard to build it up. It would have been a waste if I'd walked away.'

Since Jane Hunter took the helm, the company's output has more than doubled and the wines are now shipped to a dozen countries in Europe as well as the US, Asia, Australia and the Pacific.

Chardonnay, Sauvignon Blanc, Gewürztraminer, Pinot Noir and Cabernet Sauvignon are the key varieties in the 18-hectare estate vineyard, planted in silty loams overlying riverstones. Fruit is also purchased from contract growers in the Wairau and Awatere valleys.

'Australians can only dream of the intensity of fruit and natural acidity in Marlborough,' says winemaker Gary Duke, himself an Australian, who joined Hunter's in 1991. Another Australian, eminent oenologist Dr Tony Jordan, has been a consultant for more than a decade.

Hunter's Sauvignon Blanc bursts with lush, pure, ripe gooseberry and green capsicum-like flavours, enlivened by fresh, mouth-watering acidity. For the unwooded Sauvignon Blanc, Duke is after 'lifted fruit characters and a powerful, round, long palate'. The Sauvignon Blanc Oak Aged is a 'riper and less herbaceous' style, with only a subtle twist of oak. Both wines are consistently outstanding, amongst the region's most distinguished Sauvignon Blancs.

The Chardonnay, matured in French oak barriques, typically one-third new, is a classy, immaculate wine with searching, citrusy, mealy flavours, subtle wood influence and good acid spine. The Riesling and Gewürztraminer, both produced in a medium-dry style, are fresh, fragrant and flavoursome, but in most vintages slightly overshadowed by their Sauvignon Blanc and Chardonnay stablemates.

The Pinot Noir is light, fresh and supple; the Cabernet/Merlot richer in flavour but typically green-edged. Hunter's Brut is the winery's best-kept secret. Based on half Chardonnay, half Pinot Noir and Meunier, matured on its yeast lees for two-and-a-half years, this is a full and vigorous sparkling with strong, yeasty, complex flavours, crisp, slightly creamy and long.

*****	Chardonnay, Sauvignon Blanc, Sauvignon Blanc Oak Aged
****½	Brut
***½	Gewürztraminer, Riesling
***	Cabernet/Merlot, Pinot Noir, Spring Creek Vineyard Sauvignon Blanc/Chardonnay

ISABEL ESTATE VINEYARDS

Hawkesbury Road, Renwick. Est 1994. Owners: Michael and Robyn Tiller. Production: 5,750 cases.

The bulk of the grapes from Michael and Robyn Tiller's 52-hectare vineyard just south of Renwick are sold to other wine companies. In 1994, the couple 'threw a bit of Pinot Noir grape juice into a barrel to see what would happen' – and won a gold medal with the first Isabel Estate Pinot Noir.

The vineyard, established in 1982 in free-draining gravels over a clay sub-soil, is densely planted in Sauvignon Blanc, Chardonnay and Pinot Noir. The wines, not produced on-site, are made by consultant winemaker Sam Weaver.

If the standard of the debut 1994 vintage can be repeated, Isabel Estate could have a great future. Although the wine saw no new oak, it is superbly fragrant, rich-flavoured, plummy and supple.

(*****) Pinot Noir

JACKSON ESTATE

Jacksons Road, Blenheim. Est 1988. Owner: John Stichbury. Production: 27,000 cases. No winery sales.

Searching for an edge, John Stichbury keys into American satellites for long-range weather forecasts. Such enterprise pays off – his Sauvignon Blanc, Reserve Chardonnay, bottle-fermented sparkling and sweet white wines are all superb.

Jackson Estate was originally a partnership between John, who lives in Marlborough and runs the vineyard, and his brother, Warwick, a Wellington-based businessman. On the family property in Jacksons Road, settled in the 1840s by their great-great-grandfather, Adam Jackson (after whom the road is named), the brothers planted their first vines in 1988. The first wine flowed in 1991. However, in 1997 John Stichbury bought his brother's shareholding: 'The only change is the box number,' he jokes.

Pruned for low yields and not irrigated, the 40-hectare vineyard is planted in Sauvignon Blanc, Chardonnay, Riesling and Pinot Noir. Since no grapes are purchased from other growers, the wines all have single-vineyard status. However, another 6-hectare block nearby with lighter soils has been leased, and is being planted in Sauvignon Blanc and Chardonnay.

Jackson Estate is a vineyard, not a winery. The wines are all made by Australian Martin Shaw at Rapaura Vintners, the local contract winemaking facility.

The Sauvignon Blanc is a notably ripe-flavoured style, richly fragrant, vibrantly fruity and zingy, with lovely concentration and vigour. Jackson Estate's 'standard' range of white wines also features a full-bodied, flavoursome and soft Chardonnay, fermented in French oak barriques, and a consistently attractive, ripely scented, tropical fruit-flavoured Marlborough Dry, labelled as such to attract buyers who normally avoid Riesling.

The Pinot Noir is pleasant, with strawberryish, slightly smoky flavours, but lacks real depth. Few vintages have been seen of the intensely perfumed, tight-knit and complex Jackson Vintage, a bottle-fermented sparkling based on Chardonnay and Pinot Noir; powerful, fat and savoury Reserve Chardonnay; and super-ripe, deliciously treacly, botrytised Riesling and Chardonnay, but all have been of arresting quality.

*****	Sauvignon Blanc
(*****)	Botrytis Chardonnay, Botrytis Riesling, Jackson Vintage, Reserve Chardonnay
****	Marlborough Dry
***½	Chardonnay
(**½)	Pinot Noir

JOHANNESHOF CELLARS

State Highway One, Koromiko. Est 1991. Owners: Warwick Foley and Edel Everling. Production: 2,250 cases.

'*Klein aber fein,*' a German saying meaning 'small but fine', appeals to Warwick Foley. Johanneshof Cellars only makes a couple of thousand cases per year, but this is a memorable winery to visit.

Johanneshof Cellars lies near Koromiko, alongside the highway running from Blenheim to the Cook Strait ferry at Picton. Foley grew up in Marlborough, and after working vintages at several New Zealand wineries, spent five years making wine in Germany. His partner, Edel Everling, was born at Rudesheim and has a Geisenheim degree in viticulture and oenology. The name Johanneshof ('John's courtyard') is a tribute to her father, who once owned a vineyard in the Rheingau.

The first vines in the tiny estate vineyard, established in Pinot Noir, were planted in 1977, but the first wine flowed in 1991 and the winery was built in 1993. Most of the grapes are bought from Marlborough growers. The major attraction for visitors is a candle-lit tunnel plunging 45 metres into the hillside, lined with barrels of brandy and riddling racks full of sparkling wine.

The wood-aged Sauvignon Blancs are full and flavoursome, with some complexity and the ability to develop well for several years. The Chardonnay is lean, appley and steely, but the Gewürztraminer is strongly varietal, with very good flavour depth. Emmi Brut, a bottle-fermented blend of Chardonnay and Pinot Noir, is a gutsy wine, toasty and lively.

(****) **Reserve Fumé Blanc**
(***½) **Gewürztraminer**
(***½) **Emmi Brut, Fumé Blanc, Sauvignon Blanc**
(**½) **Chardonnay, Pinot Noir**

LAKE CHALICE WINES

Vintage Lane, Renwick. Est 1989. Owners: Phil Binnie, Chris Gambitsis and Ron Wichman. Production: 4,500 cases. Winery sales by appointment.

The imagery conjured up by the name is appealing, but Lake Chalice's extremely gravelly vineyard lies next to a quarry, not a lake. 'You could run the irrigation system here 24 hours a day and it wouldn't flood the vines,' says part-owner Phil Binnie.

Named after a lake in the nearby Richmond Range, the vineyard is on the north side of the Wairau Valley, near the Merlen winery. The founders, Lower Hutt restaurateurs Chris Gambitsis and Ron Wichman, were joined in 1991 by viticulturist Phil Binnie, a former policeman. The first vintage was 1992.

The low-vigour Falcon Vineyard, purchased in a run-down state in 1989, has since been replanted in 9 hectares of Sauvignon Blanc, Riesling, Chardonnay, Sémillon, Cabernet Franc, Cabernet Sauvignon and Merlot. Grapes are also bought from Marlborough growers. The partners in Lake Chalice own winemaking equipment but have not yet erected a winery; Gambitsis makes the wine elsewhere.

The Chardonnay, French oak-fermented, is a mouthfilling wine with strong, ripe flavours and lively acidity. The Sémillon, French and American oak-matured, is a moderately herbaceous style, with the wood adding richness and roundness.

The Sauvignon Blanc and Riesling can be rewarding, but are typically solid rather than memorable. Full, fresh, spicy and supple, the Cabernet/Merlot/Franc is a pleasant drink-young style.

(***½) **Chardonnay**
(***) **Sémillon**
(**½) **Cabernet/Merlot/Franc, Riesling, Sauvignon Blanc**

LAWSON'S DRY HILLS

Alabama Road, Blenheim. Est 1992. Owners: Ross and Barbara Lawson, and other shareholders. Production: 12,000 cases.

One of the most successful small wineries to emerge in Marlborough in the past five years, Lawson's Dry Hills produces a tight array of weighty, richly flavoured, intensely varietal white wines.

The winery lies on the outskirts of Blenheim, near the sun-baked Wither Hills from which the company takes its name. Ross

Lawson (a former sheep musterer and shearer, possum hunter, trade union organiser and swimming pool builder) planted his first vines in 1981, but sold his crop to other wineries before the first Lawson's Dry Hills wines flowed in 1992.

Gewürztraminer is the sole variety cultivated in the 4-hectare estate vineyard, planted in moderately fertile clay soils. Most of the winery's grapes are purchased from local growers. Claire and Mike Allan, who produced most of the early wines, recently departed and the winemaker is now Mike Just, a New Zealander who studied and made wine in Germany, and later worked at the Merlen winery, before joining Lawson's Dry Hills prior to the 1997 vintage.

The wines are consistently rewarding, with very impressive fullness of body and richness of flavour. The Gewürztraminer is weighty yet delicate, with deep, positively spicy, citrusy flavour and power right through the palate. The Riesling, a medium style, exhibits finely balanced acidity and a lovely spread of lemon-lime flavours, penetrating and long.

A powerful, ripe-flavoured wine, the Chardonnay is two-thirds fermented and matured in French oak casks. Mouthfilling, rich, complex, toasty and firmly structured, it drinks well in its youth but also rewards cellaring. The Sauvignon Blanc (5 percent fermented in French oak barriques) is deeply scented, very intense and zingy, with gooseberry, melon and green capsicum-evoking flavours, authoritative acidity and a sustained finish.

***** Sauvignon Blanc
****½ Chardonnay
**** Gewürztraminer, Riesling
*** Pinot Noir

MERLEN WINES

Vintage Lane, Renwick. Est 1987. Owner: Merlen Wines Limited. Production: 8,000 cases.

Almuth Lorenz, a white-wine specialist and the driving-force behind the Merlen winery, is a tall, extroverted Geisenheim Institute graduate. As a child, she worked in her parents' vineyard and winery in the Rheinhessen. After arriving in New Zealand in 1981, Lorenz made the first five vintages of Hunter's wines, and is quick to admit one of the advantages of her German birth: 'Here I've got novelty value.'

Lorenz's plans to establish her own winery were given impetus by Jeremy Cooper, a university lecturer in management (and Lorenz's partner), who organised a group of principally local investors to back her. In the absence of a winery, the first Merlen wine, the acclaimed 1987 Chardonnay, was barrel-fermented in a rented refrigerated container. In late 1988, however, the small Merlen winery opened in Vintage Lane, off Rapaura Road. Its name, says Lorenz, is 'derived from the ancient name for

Marlborough in England. The area was originally called Merlborough from the legend that Merlin the magician practised his arts there.'

The shingly, sandy, 5-hectare estate vineyard is planted in Chardonnay, Gewürztraminer, Sauvignon Blanc, Sémillon and Morio-Muskat. Grapes are also purchased from local growers.

Lorenz makes no reds: 'Wines should make themselves – like Riesling, Sauvignon Blanc and Chardonnay do here. In Marlborough, reds need a lot of work.' However, she does produce fruit brandies under the Spirit of Marlborough brand. In the past, the white wines were of a variable standard, but recent vintages have shown a steady rise in quality.

Aromatic varieties like Riesling, Gewürztraminer and Sauvignon Blanc feature strongly in the Merlen range. Riesling, naturally, is a favourite. Lorenz aims for 'the equivalent of a *kabinett halbtrocken*: light, with a touch of botrytis, and closer in style to a Rheingau than Mosel'. Strong, ripe, citrusy flavours hold sway in this characterful wine, produced in a distinctly medium style supported by racy acidity.

The Gewürztraminer is full-bodied and ripe-tasting, with a crisp, spicy, slightly sweet finish. The Müller-Thurgau is light and floral, with citrusy, limey flavours and a slightly sweet, freshly acidic finish. The Morio-Muskat ('made for average people looking for a five o'clock drink') is similar to the Müller-Thurgau, but slightly sweeter and softer. The Sauvignon Blanc is fleshy and ripe in favourable vintages, with rich tropical-fruit characters. The Chardonnay, too, is bold and mouthfilling, with ripe, peachy, toasty, well-rounded flavours.

**** Chardonnay
***½ Gewürztraminer, Müller-Thurgau, Riesling, Sauvignon Blanc
*** Morio-Muskat

MOUNT LINTON WINES

Est 1994. Owner: The MacFarlane family. Production: 1,500 cases. No winery sales.

A low-profile label worth getting to know, Mount Linton wines are grown in the MacFarlane family's 20-hectare vineyard in the Rapaura area of the Wairau Valley. Most of the grapes are sold to other companies, but the family's own wines, named after Mount Linton Station in Southland and first made in commercial volumes in 1994, are of a consistently high standard. The Chardonnay is freshly scented, with deliciously strong, citrusy flavours and deftly balanced oak. The Sauvignon Blanc is full, ripe, lively and richly flavoured.

(****) Chardonnay
(***½) Sauvignon Blanc

NAUTILUS ESTATE

Blicks Road, Renwick. Est 1985. Owner: Negociants New Zealand.
Production: 35,000 cases.

Wine judges often disagree, but the judges at the 1994 Australia
National Wine Show in Canberra, 1994 Royal Hobart Wine Show,
1994 Air New Zealand Wine Awards, 1995 Sydney International
Wine Competition, 1995 International Wine Challenge in
London, and 1995 International Wine and Spirit Competition in
London were unanimous on one point: Nautilus Marlborough
Sauvignon Blanc 1994 deserved a gold medal. No other New
Zealand Sauvignon Blanc has enjoyed such striking success on
the international show circuit.

Nautilus wines have been produced since 1985 by one of New
Zealand's best-known wine distributors, Negociants New
Zealand, itself controlled by S. Smith & Son, owner of the
Yalumba winery in the Barossa Valley. The winemaking team of
Matt Harrop and Helena Lindberg is supervised by Alan Hoey, a
senior winemaker at Yalumba who visits New Zealand frequently.
Most of the wines are made at Rapaura Vintners (formerly
Vintech) in Marlborough, in which Negociants has a 25 percent
stake.

The 11-hectare Nautilus Estate vineyard at Renwick, where
there is also a sales outlet, is planted principally in Chardonnay
and Pinot Noir. Grapes are also purchased from growers in
Marlborough and Hawke's Bay.

Apart from the Nautilus range, based almost entirely on
Marlborough fruit, Negociants also produces Hawke's Bay wines
under the Half Moon Bay label, and 'affordable, fruit-driven
wines for everyday drinking' from vineyards around the country,
sold as Twin Islands.

Nautilus Marlborough Sauvignon Blanc is a classy, richly fragrant wine with mouthfilling body and a strong surge of ripe, passionfruit and lime-like flavours, enlivened by fresh acidity. The
fragrant, refined, non-vintage Nautilus Cuvée Marlborough, a 3:1
blend of Pinot Noir and Chardonnay, displays rich, subtle, yeasty
flavours, very crisp, firm and sustained.

Only produced in top vintages, Nautilus Estate Reserve
Chardonnay is a distinguished wine with excellent depth of ripe,
citrusy fruit, integrated oak and a firm finish. Nautilus
Marlborough Chardonnay is an elegant wine showcasing fresh,
ripe fruit, with subtle oak/lees-aging characters, a slightly
creamy texture and lots of drink-young appeal.

Nautilus Cabernet Sauvignon/Merlot/Cabernet Franc is a
firm, slightly leafy Marlborough red with strong, red berry and
mint flavours wrapped in sweet American oak.

The Twin Islands and Half Moon Bay selections offer consistently well made wines, with the lightly wooded, tropical fruit-
flavoured Half Moon Bay Sauvignon Blanc and smooth,

full-bodied, cherry and spice-flavoured Twin Islands Marlborough Pinot Noir offering especially good value.

*****	Nautilus Marlborough Sauvignon Blanc
(****½)	Nautilus Estate Reserve Chardonnay
****	Nautilus Cuvée Marlborough, Nautilus Marlborough Chardonnay
***½	Nautilus Cabernet Sauvignon/Merlot/Cabernet Franc
(***½)	Half Moon Bay Sauvignon Blanc, Twin Islands Marlborough Pinot Noir
***	Twin Islands Brut, Twin Islands Sauvignon Blanc
(**½)	Twin Islands Hawke's Bay Chenin Blanc, Twin Islands Merlot/Cabernet Sauvignon, Twin Islands Marlborough Unwooded Chardonnay

OMAKA SPRINGS ESTATE

Kennedys Road, Omaka Valley. Est 1992. Owners: Geoffrey and Robina Jensen. Production: 10,500 cases.

After 33 years as a pilot for the Royal Navy and British Airways, Nelson-born Geoffrey Jensen settled in the Omaka Valley to grow grapes and make wine. His first release, 1994 Omaka Springs Sauvignon Blanc, promptly won a gold medal at the 1995 Liquorland Royal Easter Wine Show.

Jensen and his wife, Robina, own 40 hectares of vines in the Omaka Valley, south of Renwick. The Jensens purchased their land in 1992, naming the winery after three spring-fed ponds on the property. Some of their grape crop is sold to other wine companies. Chris Young, a Roseworthy College graduate, makes the wine with the assistance of consultant Tony Bish.

The wines are typically fresh and clean, but sometimes lack flavour concentration. The Sauvignon Blanc is grassy, with a sliver of sweetness and lively acidity. The Chardonnay is a lightly wooded style, appley and flinty; the Riesling slightly sweet and crisp, with moderate depth of apple and lemon flavours.

The Cabernet/Merlot is fresh and fruity in a crisp, slightly herbaceous style. The Merlot is not complex but attractively ripe and buoyant, with smooth, blackcurrant, spice and plum-like flavours.

***	Merlot, Sauvignon Blanc
**½	Cabernet/Merlot, Chardonnay, Riesling
**	Sémillon

PONDER ESTATE

New Renwick Road, Renwick. Est 1994. Owners: Michael and Diane Ponder. Production: 4,750 cases.

A full-time artist and large-scale olive-grower, Michael Ponder couldn't resist also getting involved in 'the biggest thing that's ever hit the area'. In 1987 he and his wife, Diane, bought a bare block of land at the mouth of the Brancott Valley and started planting grapevines.

Today 20-hectares of Sauvignon Blanc, Chardonnay, Riesling and Pinot Noir are cultivated in the Ponders' silty, gravelly soils. Most of the crop is sold to another wine company. Ponder Estate's own wines, not made on-site, were launched from the 1994 vintage. The Sauvignon Blanc is typically scented and ripe, although not intense. The Chardonnay, French and American oak-aged, is fresh and soft in an easy-drinking style.

*** Sauvignon Blanc
**½ Chardonnay

SAINT CLAIR ESTATE WINES

New Renwick Road, Blenheim. Est 1994. Owners: Neal and Judy Ibbotson, Charles and Sandy Wiffen. Production: 25,000 cases. No winery sales.

Of the fast-growing band of grape-growers turned winemakers in Marlborough, Neal Ibbotson is producing some of the most impressive results.

The company is based on the edge of Blenheim, on a property once owned by the town's founder, James Sinclair. Ibbotson came to the region as a farm adviser, but gradually specialised in viticulture, and has supplied grapes to other wine companies since 1978. He and his wife, Judy, own 38 hectares of vineyards in the Wairau, Omaka and Awatere valleys, with Sauvignon Blanc, Chardonnay, Riesling and Pinot Noir the key varieties.

The winemaking venture is a partnership between the Ibbotsons (the majority shareholders) and Charles and Sandy Wiffen. The wines, not produced on-site, are made by consultant winemaker Kim Crawford.

Since the first 1994 vintage, the wines have been of a consistently high standard. Tropical fruit characters abound in the delightful Sauvignon Blanc, a very easy-drinking style which displays lush, ripe fruit and a rich, well-rounded finish. The Riesling is also delicious – packed with rich, ripe, passionfruit-lemon flavours in an intense, zesty style harbouring an abundance of sweetness. The Chardonnay is a fruit-driven style, full, vibrantly fruity and crisp, with a restrained American oak influence.

The Merlot is lightly oaked and buoyantly fruity, with good depth of fresh, supple blackcurrant-plum flavours. The Single Vineyard Merlot, launched from the 1996 vintage, is a dark wine with mouthfilling body, sweet oak characters and impressively ripe, concentrated, brambly flavour.

****½ Sauvignon Blanc
**** Riesling
(****) Single Vineyard Merlot
*** Chardonnay, Merlot

SERESIN ESTATE

Bedford Road (off Highway 63), Renwick. Est 1992. Owner: Michael Seresin. Production: 2,000 cases.

With a trio of startlingly good wines from the 1996 vintage, Seresin Estate announced its arrival as a major new force on the Marlborough wine scene.

Michael Seresin, who left New Zealand in 1966, aged 23, now owns a film company in London and a holiday home in Tuscany. In 1992 he began planting a large vineyard and olive grove on 67 hectares of river terraces in Bedford Road, 3 kilometres west of Renwick.

The first stage of the winery was built prior to the 1997 vintage. By the year 2000, the winery and olive pressing complex, with underground barrel hall, tasting room, and four-storey apartment tower, will be complete. Winemaker Brian Bicknell previously worked at Babich, Selaks and Coopers Creek in New Zealand, and gained extensive international experience in Bordeaux, Hungary and as chief winemaker for Errazuriz, one of Chile's leading producers.

The wines are all estate-grown. Production is expected to climb swiftly from 2,000 cases in 1996 to 30,000 cases by 2000, focusing on Sauvignon Blanc, Chardonnay, Pinot Gris, Riesling, a botrytised Riesling, a bottle-fermented sparkling, Pinot Noir and a Merlot-predominant blend.

The '96 Seresin Estate Sauvignon Blanc is a stylish and immaculate wine. Fermentation with indigenous yeasts, a touch of barrel fermentation, partial malolactic fermentation, and maturation on yeast lees have added complexity, while retaining the wine's intense, piercing fruit flavours and racy acidity.

The '96 Chardonnay Reserve is an equally memorable debut. Hand picked from 'prime' terraces, fermented in all-new French oak barriques and held on its yeast lees for almost a year, this is a very intense, fragrant and mouthfilling wine with rich, citrusy, nutty, mealy flavours and firm acid spine. The 1996 Chardonnay is similar in style to the Reserve, slightly less concentrated but still classy.

(*****) **Chardonnay Reserve, Sauvignon Blanc**
(****) **Chardonnay**

TE WHARE RA WINES

Anglesea Street, Renwick. Est 1979. Owners: Allen and Joyce Hogan. Production: 2,500 cases.

Te Whare Ra (House in the Sun) is a tiny winery with an extremely limited presence in retail outlets. However, the mail-order customers who attend Allen Hogan's tastings in cities around New Zealand are able to purchase some of the most thrillingly botrytised sweet white wines in the country.

Hogan, a rugged individualist, was the first to follow in Montana's footsteps and establish a winery in Marlborough, although on a dramatically different scale. After working at a small winery in Western Australia, followed by two vintages at Montana's Marlborough winery and another at Te Kauwhata research station, in 1979 Hogan and his wife, Joyce, planted their first vines in gravelly, loamy soils at Renwick.

The estate vineyard now covers 6 hectares of Gewürztraminer, Chardonnay, Riesling, Sémillon, Cabernet Sauvignon, Merlot and Cabernet Franc. Hogan also buys fruit from local growers.

In his earth-brick winery, Hogan fashions bold, richly alcoholic dry and medium-dry wines produced from late-harvested fruit with high sugar levels. The Duke of Marlborough Chardonnay, fermented in barrels and tanks but fully wood-aged, reveals peachy, ripe fruit, buttery oak and strapping body. The Boots 'N' All Chardonnay, estate-grown, fully barrel-fermented and lees-aged for a year, is an even burlier wine, savoury, tautly structured and chock-full of body and flavour.

The heady Duke of Marlborough Gewürztraminer is crammed with spice, alcohol and fruit. The Duke of Marlborough Riesling, a medium style, is typically powerful, weighty, and ripely flavoured, rich and slightly raisiny. Blended from Sauvignon Blanc and Sémillon, the Fumé Blanc is a robust wine with strong, herbal, nutty flavours.

QDR (Quaffing Dry Red) is just what it says: a light, Cabernet-based, green-edged red for no-fuss drinking. The top red is Sarah Jennings Cabernet Sauvignon/Merlot/Cabernet Franc, a fresh, vibrant, supple wine with plenty of berryish, slightly leafy flavour.

The stars of Te Whare Ra range, however, are the rampantly botrytised sweet whites, made from several varieties, notably Riesling. The Botrytis Bunch Selection Riesling, based on grapes with less than 60 percent botrytis infection, is poised and honeyish, with a lovely harmony of alcohol, sweetness and acidity. Made from heavily raisined bunches with 60 to 90 percent botrytis infection, the markedly sweeter Botrytis Berry Selection Riesling is a perfumed and nectarous beauty, oily and opulent.

***** Botrytis Bunch/Berry Selection sweet whites
**** Duke of Marlborough Gewürztraminer, Duke of Marlborough Riesling
(****) Boots 'N' All Chardonnay
***½ Duke of Marlborough Chardonnay, Fumé Blanc, Sarah Jennings Cabernet Sauvignon/Merlot/Cabernet Franc
(***) Rosé
(**) QDR

VAVASOUR WINES

Redwood Pass Road, Dashwood. Est 1986. Owner: Vavasour Wines Limited and Company. Production: 26,000 cases.

The pioneer of winemaking in the Awatere Valley, Vavasour sits on the terraced banks of the Awatere River, 4 kilometres from the sea, with the 2,900-metre Mt Tapuaenuku rearing to the south. The immaculate, penetratingly flavoured Sauvignon Blancs and Chardonnays are consistently top-flight.

Peter Vavasour's family has farmed in the Awatere, east and over the hills from the larger Wairau Valley, for a century. In 1986, convinced of the Awatere's winemaking potential, Vavasour formed a partnership with carefully selected shareholders, including wine merchants, bankers and accountants. Viticulturist Richard Bowling, who departed from the company in 1996, was also a prime mover.

At first, the plan was for Vavasour to be a small winery. However, the company suffered a financial crisis in 1990, which led the directors to conclude that the company was undercapitalised and that an annual production level of 7,000 cases was not viable. A major expansion programme was embarked upon – involving the planting of substantial new vineyards higher up the Awatere Valley and winery extensions – designed to gradually boost the winery's output to 40,000 cases.

Glenn Thomas, a Roseworthy College graduate who worked at several Australian wineries and then as winemaker at Corbans' Gisborne Winery from 1986 to 1988, has been the winemaker since the first 1989 vintage. Since the recent phasing out of the Vavasour reserve label, the wines are marketed in a three-tiered range, with Vavasour Single Vineyard at the top, followed by Vavasour and Dashwood.

The widely available Dashwood Sauvignon Blanc, blended from several Awatere Valley vineyards, is a zesty, aromatic wine with thrusting tropical fruit and green capsicum flavours and a freshly acidic finish. The classy Awatere Valley Sauvignon Blanc, largely tank-fermented, with a small percentage barrel-fermented and lees-aged, is a memorable mouthful of piercing, ripely herbaceous flavour, with subtle oak, tangy acidity and a rich, trailing finish. The Single Vineyard Awatere Valley Sauvignon Blanc is a rounder style, full-bodied, complex and richly flavoured, needing a couple of years to break into full stride.

Dashwood Chardonnay offers incisive lemon/melon flavours, a touch of oak/lees-aging complexity and good acid spine. The Awatere Valley Chardonnay, entirely French oak-fermented, is weighty, very refined and tight, with impressively concentrated and complex, vibrantly fruity, nutty flavours. The Single Vineyard Awatere Valley Chardonnay is an even more powerful wine crammed with sweet, ripe fruit, high alcohol and savoury, mealy, rounded flavour.

Although Vavasour's dark, mouthfilling, richly flavoured and minty Cabernet Sauvignon Reserve has ranked among Marlborough's top reds, the grape does not ripen consistently in the Awatere Valley. Richly fragrant, with searching, cherryish, mushroomy flavours, the rare but classy Pinot Noir Reserve is a clear signpost to Vavasour's red-wine future.

(*****)   Awatere Valley Sauvignon Blanc, Single Vineyard
               Awatere Valley Chardonnay

(****½)   Awatere Valley Chardonnay, Pinot Noir Reserve,
               Single Vineyard Awatere Valley Sauvignon Blanc

****   Cabernet Sauvignon Reserve, Dashwood Sauvignon
               Blanc

***½   Dashwood Cabernet/Merlot, Dashwood
               Chardonnay, Dashwood Pinot Noir

WAIRAU RIVER WINES

Cnr Rapaura Road and State Highway 6. Est 1991. Owners: Phil and Chris Rose. Production: 33,000 cases.

The back label of Wairau River Sauvignon Blanc promises 'elegance and power' – and delivers the goods. Mouthfilling and lively, with an exciting rush of fresh, pure flavour, it couples lush, rich fruit with piercing nettley characters. This is one of Marlborough's champion Sauvignon Blancs.

Phil and Chris Rose pioneered grapegrowing on the north side of the Wairau Valley in 1977. After attracting 56 objections from local farmers concerned that their own hormone sprays would damage vineyards, the Roses took the issue to the Court of Appeal and 'basically won hands down'.

Today the Roses own over 100 hectares of vines, with much of the crop sold to other wineries. The 60-hectare Giffords Road vineyard, alongside the Wairau River, is planted principally in Sauvignon Blanc, Chardonnay and Pinot Noir. In Rapaura Road, a further 40 hectares of Chardonnay, Sauvignon Blanc, Riesling, Pinot Noir, Pinot Blanc and Meunier has been established. Another 3 hectares of Sauvignon Blanc vines surround the company's graceful headquarters on the corner of Rapaura Road and the main Blenheim–Nelson highway.

When Wairau River's first Sauvignon Blanc from the 1991 vintage won a gold medal and trophy at that year's Air New Zealand Wine Awards, the label instantly gained a high profile. The wines are made directly across the road at Rapaura Vintners, in which the Roses own a 25 percent stake.

The top wines are labelled as Wairau River, with lower-priced wines sold as Wairau River Richmond Ridge. The Richmond Ridge Sauvignon Blanc is a pungent style with a strong attack of grassy, freshly acidic flavour. Richmond Ridge Chardonnay is fresh and crisp, with minimal oak but plenty of lemony, slightly limey flavour.

Wairau River Chardonnay, one-third oak-matured, is fat and buttery-soft, with lush fruit flavours. It is overshadowed, however, by its Sauvignon Blanc stablemate, which marries ripe, tropical fruit and rapier-like herbaceous characters in a mouthfilling, tangy, arrestingly full-flavoured style.

***** **Sauvignon Blanc**
***½ **Chardonnay**
*** **Richmond Ridge Chardonnay, Richmond Ridge Sauvignon Blanc**

WHITEHAVEN WINE COMPANY

1 Dodson Street, Blenheim. Est 1994. Owners: Greg and Sue White, John Reid, Hugh Molloy, Simon Waghorn and Jane Forrest. Production: 10,000 cases.

The winemakers of several small Marlborough wineries previously held senior production posts at Corbans. Simon Waghorn resigned from the top job at Corbans' Gisborne winery because he wanted to be a shareholder, 'and instead of overseeing the winemaking process, I wanted to get my hands back on the barrels and pumps'.

Whitehaven produced its first wines in 1994 in the former Grove Mill winery, which the company leases, in downtown Blenheim. The six owners are Waghorn and his wife, Jane Forrest (no relation to winemaker John Forrest); Auckland-based John Reid and Hugh Molloy; and the major shareholders, Greg White (a former merchant banker) and his wife, Sue.

Whitehaven does not own vineyards or a winery – only winemaking equipment. The grapes are grown on contract at several Marlborough vineyards – Bladen, de Gyffarde, Le Grys and Wairau Peaks – with whose owners Whitehaven has close links; some of the vineyard owners market small batches of their own wines, also made at Whitehaven.

Waghorn produces consistently impressive wines, priced right. The Riesling is freshly scented, with ripe, delicate lemon-lime flavours to the fore, a sliver of sweetness, finely balanced acid and a long finish. The Sauvignon Blanc, matured on its yeast lees to add a touch of complexity, is a deliciously full, penetrating wine with very good depth of ripe, gently herbaceous flavour. The Barrel Fermented Sauvignon Blanc is a truly stylish wine revealing an excellent depth of lively, nettley, and spicy flavour.

The Chardonnay, very lightly oaked but given extended lees-aging, is delicious in its youth – full and fruity, with fresh, appley flavours and a soft finish. The French and American oak-fermented Mendoza Chardonnay is a firm, crisp style with taut, limey flavours, toasty oak and good flavour depth.

****½ Riesling
**** Sauvignon Blanc
(****) Barrel Fermented Sauvignon Blanc
(***½) Marlborough Chardonnay, Mendoza Chardonnay

WITHER HILLS VINEYARDS

Est 1992. Owner: Brent Marris. Production: 750 cases. No winery sales.

With twelve New Zealand, Australian and UK gold medals for his first six releases, there's no doubting the quality of Brent Marris's wines. Still best known as Delegat's winemaker since 1986, Marris produced the first wine under his own Wither Hills label in 1992.

The son of John Marris, a prominent Marlborough grape-grower, Brent Marris named his venture after the ranges that form the southern flanks of the Wairau Valley. A winery will eventually be built on the corner of St Leonard's and Middle Renwick Roads, where 6 hectares of Chardonnay and Sauvignon Blanc have been planted. West of Renwick, a second, 12-hectare vineyard has been established in Sauvignon Blanc, Chardonnay, Riesling and Pinot Noir.

The Sauvignon Blanc is striking, with a voluminous fragrance, mouthfilling body, very rich, sweet-tasting fruit, subtly integrated oak and a long finish. Barrel-fermented and lees-aged, it is an astutely assembled wine, yet still a celebration of Marlborough fruit flavours and hugely drinkable. The Chardonnay is equally classy and very full-bodied, with lush, concentrated fruit flavours, a mealy, biscuity complexity derived from cask fermentation and lees-aging, and a rich, creamy finish. The first Pinot Noir flowed in 1997, and will be followed by a Riesling.

***** Chardonnay, Sauvignon Blanc

Canterbury

Vineyards are spreading like wildfire in Canterbury. With 270 hectares of vines bearing by 1999 – up from 35 hectares planted in 1986 – Canterbury ranks as New Zealand's fourth-largest wine region, ahead of the Wairarapa, Auckland and Otago. Over 10 percent of the wine producers are based there.

Chardonnay, Riesling and Pinot Noir are the major successes to date in this relatively cool southern region. Warm summer days alternating with cool nights and long, dry autumns produce grapes high in 'extract' (stuffing) and acidity, although in some years (more than the winemakers expected during the early-to-mid-1990s) the fruit struggles to achieve full ripeness.

Canterbury's wineries are clustered in two main areas: the flat countryside surrounding Christchurch, and an hour's drive north, in undulating terrain at Waipara. Hot, dry nor-westers buffet vineyards in both areas, but the North Canterbury vineyards are protected from the province's cooling coastal breezes by the Teviotdale Hills to the east. You can taste the difference in ripening conditions: the wines from the south are typically leaner and more racy; those from Waipara are more robust and rounder.

The richly flavoured Corbans Private Bin Amberley Riesling, the honey-sweet Giesen Botrytised Riesling and the powerful, stylish Pegasus Bay Chardonnay are the three classics of Canterbury wine, but the region's youthful wine industry still has many years ahead of sorting out the best combinations of meso (local) climates, soils and grape varieties. Canterbury's finest wines are yet to come.

Waipara

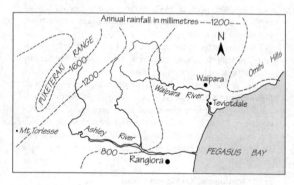

Finding enough water to irrigate the vines can be a struggle and frosts are a danger, but there's a major wine district emerging in North Canterbury. With over 200 hectares of vines planted, ten producers up and running and more on the horizon, Waipara is fast emerging as Canterbury's most successful wine region.

This is Chardonnay, Pinot Noir and Riesling country. The vineyards are draped over flat to gently sloping terrain in soils ranging from lighter gravels south of the Waipara River to clay and limestone to the north. John McCaskey of Glenmark – who pioneered viticulture in North Canterbury in the early 1980s – stresses that the hot, dry nor-westers dictate Waipara's weather: 'The trees, even the power poles, lean with the winds.'

The major concentration of vineyards lies 4 kilometres north of the township of Waipara, straddling the Christchurch-Picton highway. Here, tightly clustered, are the vineyards of Waipara

Springs, Mark Rattray, John Corbett (who grows the grapes for the famous but inaccurately labelled Corbans Private Bin Amberley Riesling), Mountford Vineyard (which offers luxury accommodation, dinner and breakfast at $NZ230 per night), and several other growers. Alan McCorkindale, until recently winemaker at Corbans Marlborough Winery, has also purchased a block here.

American Michael Reid has electrified the local wine community by planting 40 hectares of vines between the established Pegasus Bay and Chancellor vineyards, with most of the output earmarked for the US market.

CHANCELLOR WINES

133 Mt Cass Road, Waipara. Est 1995. Owners: Tony and Helen Willy, Allan and Catherine Scott. Production: 4,500 cases. No winery sales.

One of Canterbury's top Sauvignon Blancs flows from Tony and Helen Willy's vineyard in Mt Cass Road, Waipara.

The Willys, grape-growers since the early 1980s, formed the Waipara Estates partnership to produce wine under the Chancellor label with prominent Marlborough winemakers Allan and Catherine Scott. The 11-hectare vineyard is planted in Sauvignon Blanc (principally) and Cabernet Sauvignon; future plantings will concentrate on Chardonnay, Riesling and Pinot Noir.

The Chancellor range, launched in 1995, is now produced at the Allan Scott winery in Marlborough and includes Marlborough white wines. Chancellor Waipara Sauvignon Blanc is freshly aromatic, with subtle oak adding a touch of complexity and plenty of appetisingly crisp, green capsicum and lime-like flavour.

(***½) Sauvignon Blanc

DANIEL SCHUSTER WINES

Reeces Road, Waipara. Est 1986. Owners: Danny and Mari Schuster, Brian and Shelley McCauley, Don Petrie. Production: 4,500 cases. Winery sales by appointment.

Danny Schuster has been a guru of the Canterbury wine scene ever since he made the gold medal-winning St Helena Pinot Noirs from 1982 and 1984, which electrified the local wine community.

Born in Germany, Schuster worked in Europe, South Africa and Australia before joining St Helena from 1980 to 1985. The partners in the Daniel Schuster company (previously called Omihi Hills) are Danny and Mari Schuster, Brian and Shelley McCauley, and (since 1996) Don Petrie, who also owns 6.5 hectares of Chardonnay and Pinot Noir vines at Rakaia, near Ashburton, far to the south of most of the established Canterbury vineyards.

First planted in 1986, the 6-hectare, close-planted, non-irrigated Omihi Hills vineyard in the hills east of the state highway at Waipara is devoted principally to Pinot Noir, with a smaller plot of Pinot Blanc. Grapes have also been bought from growers in Canterbury, Marlborough and Hawke's Bay.

Schuster's wines have so far been characterful rather than consistently distinguished. The Barrel Fermented Chenin Blanc, grown in Hawke's Bay, is a moderately complex, rather Chardonnay-like wine with toasty, nutty, buttery flavours and tense acidity.

In the past, the Canterbury Pinot Noir has been light and sometimes unripe, with savoury, cherryish flavours of moderate depth. Now expressly designed as a drink-young style, since 1996 the wine has been a blend of Rakaia fruit and grapes grown on the cooler, east-facing slopes of the Omihi Hills vineyard. Matured in seasoned oak casks, the 1996 vintage is the best yet, with enjoyably fresh and smooth, cherryish flavours and some savoury complexity.

The flagship Omihi Vineyard Pinot Noir (previously labelled Reserve Waipara) has tended to be light to medium-bodied, mellow and supple, with pleasant cherryish flavours but also a lack of stuffing. The 1995, however, is a bigger wine with some richness and complexity, worth cellaring.

*** **Barrel Fermented Chenin Blanc, Omihi Vineyard Pinot Noir**
½ **Canterbury Pinot Noir, Marlborough Chardonnay

GLENMARK WINES

McKenzies Road, Waipara. Est 1981. Owner: John McCaskey. Production: 1,600 cases.

Steely, scented Rieslings in styles to suit most palates – dry and medium – are the flagship wines from Glenmark. Founded at Waipara in 1981, the winery is owned by John McCaskey, a down-to-earth, entrepreneurial character who is the pioneer of North Canterbury wine. McCaskey still farms part of the old Glenmark sheep station, whose magnificent former homestead ('where peacocks roamed free and swans drifted on the man-made lake') is the centrepiece of the Glenmark labels.

In light silts over free-draining gravels, McCaskey has planted principally Riesling vines, with smaller plots of Müller-Thurgau, Gewürztraminer, Chardonnay, Pinot Noir and Cabernet Sauvignon. Another 4-hectare vineyard is being developed in Chardonnay, Sauvignon Blanc, Cabernet Sauvignon, Merlot and Cabernet Franc.

The winemaker since 1991 has been Australian Kym Rayner, who previously worked at Penfolds (Gisborne) and Montana (Blenheim) before he acquired a stake in Torlesse Wines. Since 1992, when Torlesse purchased a half share in Glenmark's winery building on the state highway at Waipara, Glenmark and Torlesse have shared a production facility and winemaker.

The Dry Riesling is scented, honeyed and steely, and ages gracefully for several years; the greater sweetness of the Medium Riesling gives it more drink-young appeal. Both wines display a rather Germanic fragility and raciness.

The Gewürztraminer varies in intensity, but top vintages are weighty, with rich gingerbread and black pepper flavours, ripe and rounded. The barrique-fermented, lees-matured Weka Plains Chardonnay is toasty and buttery, citrusy and mealy, with lots of character and a crisp, lingering finish.

The rare ('one row, one barrique,' says McCaskey of the 1996 vintage) barrel-fermented Weka Plains Sauvignon Blanc mingles tropical fruit and herbaceous flavours in a crisp, full-flavoured style with some complexity. Triple Peaks and Triple Peaks Dry, low-priced blends of Riesling and Müller-Thurgau, are pleasant everyday-drinking wines – light and floral, citrusy and tangy.

The Pinot Noir is light in colour and body, with crisp, simple, raspberryish flavours. The much better-known Waipara Red, blended from Cabernet Sauvignon, Pinot Noir and Merlot, is a green-edged wine of varying flavour depth but always a smooth tannin structure.

***½   Dry Riesling, Weka Plains Chardonnay
***   Gewürztraminer, Medium Riesling
(***) Triple Peaks Dry, Weka Plains Sauvignon Blanc
**½   Pinot Noir, Waipara Red
(**½) Triple Peaks
(**)   Red

MARK RATTRAY VINEYARDS

418 Omihi Road, Waipara. Est 1992. Owners: Mark and Michelle Rattray. Production: 4,000 cases. Winery sales by appointment.

Mark Rattray is widely seen as a Pinot Noir and Chardonnay specialist, yet his Sauvignon Blancs, grown in Waipara and Marlborough, can be even finer.

Born in Christchurch, Rattray returned to Canterbury in 1985 after a long absence. After studying for two years at the famous Geisenheim Institute in the Rheingau, he spent five years with Montana and six years with Penfolds in Auckland, before St Helena lured him south again. A partner in the Waipara Springs winery between 1990 and 1993, he has since acted as a consultant to several other Canterbury producers while simultaneously developing his own Mark Rattray Vineyards label.

The 4-hectare estate vineyard, established in silty loams across the road from Waipara Springs, is planted mainly in Pinot Noir and Chardonnay, with smaller plots of Sauvignon Blanc and Scheurebe (for a late harvest style). Rattray has also leased the

French Farm vineyard on Banks Peninsula, and purchases grapes from growers in Waipara and Marlborough.

The Waipara Chardonnay is full, buttery and soft in an elegant, moderately concentrated style. The Waipara Sauvignon Blanc is less assertive than its Marlborough stablemate, but mouthfilling and lively, flavoursome, limey and zesty. The Marlborough Sauvignon Blanc is ripely scented, full-bodied and dry, with incisive, steely melon and capsicum flavours.

The Aquilon ('north wind') Pinot Noir, expressly designed for early consumption, offers pleasing depth of plummy, slightly spicy flavour, a touch of complexity from maturation in seasoned French oak casks and moderate tannins. The Waipara Pinot Noir is an elegant middleweight, with fresh, buoyant raspberry and spice flavours wrapped in quality oak and reasonably firm tannins.

****	**Waipara Sauvignon Blanc**
(****)	**Marlborough Sauvignon Blanc**
***½	**Waipara Chardonnay, Waipara Pinot Noir**
***	**Aquilon Pinot Noir**

PEGASUS BAY

Stockgrove Road, Waipara. Est 1986. Owners: Ivan and Christine Donaldson. Production: 16,000 cases.

Pegasus Bay (named after the sweeping North Canterbury bay over the hills to the east) is the second-biggest winery in the province and Waipara's largest. More importantly, Pegasus Bay is setting new standards for Canterbury wine.

Ivan Donaldson, an associate-professor of neurology, wine judge and wine columnist for *The Press*, is the driving force behind Pegasus Bay. In Donaldson's eyes, 'New Zealand wines typically have no weakness of flavour, but often lack weight, texture, length and longevity'. Pegasus Bay wines are robust, rich-flavoured and rounded, in a vivid style contrast to the lightness, leanness and sharpness typical of many Canterbury wines.

The stony, 23-hectare estate vineyard, lying in an old glacier bed, is a few kilometres east of the main highway, just south of the Waipara River. Planting began in 1986 in this very low-cropping (below 5 tonnes per hectare) vineyard, where the principal varieties are Riesling, Chardonnay, Sauvignon Blanc, Sémillon, Pinot Noir, Cabernet Sauvignon, Merlot and Cabernet Franc.

Several Donaldsons run Pegasus Bay. Ivan's wife, Chris, is the business manager and their son, Edward, is the marketing manager. Another son, Roseworthy College graduate Matthew, makes the wine with Lynnette Hudson, who holds a post-graduate diploma in viticulture and oenology from Lincoln University and has been 'part of the family' since 1993.

First produced in 1991 but showing exciting quality advances since 1994, Pegasus Bay wines are consistently impressive and sometimes brilliant. The Chardonnay is a voluptuous wine, muscular and rich, with a seamless array of citrusy, biscuity, complex flavours and superb concentration and length. This wine takes its place among the few Canterbury classics.

The Sauvignon/Sémillon is full-bodied, with intense, ripe, exotic fruit flavours overlaid with subtle oak and lees-aging characters, finishing crisp and long. The Riesling is packed with lemony, limey, tangy, slightly honeyish flavour; the late-picked, sweeter Riesling, labelled Aria, is strikingly poised, rich and luscious.

Pegasus Bay's red wines reveal much greater stuffing, ripeness and flavour richness than most Canterbury reds. The Cabernet/Merlot is sturdy and dark, with deep, slightly minty flavours. Maestro, the top claret-style red, based on older vines and matured in a higher percentage of new oak, is a dark, generous wine with concentrated, brambly, spicy, minty flavours and ripe, rounded tannins. The Pinot Noir is mouthfilling, with strong raspberry and spice flavours, oak complexity and a rich, silky texture.

*****	**Chardonnay**
(*****)	**Aria**
****½	**Riesling, Sauvignon/Sémillon**
(****½)	**Maestro**
****	**Pinot Noir**
(****)	**Noble Sémillon/Sauvignon**
***½	**Cabernet/Merlot**

TORLESSE WINES

Ferguson Avenue, Waipara. Est 1987. Owners: Andrew Tomlin, Kym Rayner, Michael and Hazel Blowers, Dick and Vivian Pharis, Gary and Ann Fabris. Production: 4,750 cases. Winery sales by appointment.

After a disastrous start, Torlesse has rebounded with a stream of good wines, reflecting the skills of winemaker Kym Rayner. The company takes its name from Mount Torlesse and the Torlesse Range, inland from Christchurch.

Twenty shareholders, half of them grower-suppliers, founded Torlesse at West Melton in 1987. Production rather than marketing-orientated, within three years the winery was in receivership. Today the restructured company is owned by accountant Andrew Tomlin, winemaker Kym Rayner, Michael and Hazel Blowers of Christchurch, and two Canadian couples.

Rayner, an Australian, came to New Zealand in 1983 to run Penfolds' winery at Gisborne, and later worked at Montana's Blenheim winery before he joined Torlesse for the 1990 vintage. In 1992, the company purchased a half-share in the Glenmark winery building, and is now based at Waipara. Grapes are drawn from Andrew Tomlin's and Kym Rayner's own vineyards at Waipara, and purchased from growers in Canterbury and Marlborough.

The Marlborough white wines, grown in the Stoneview Vineyard, are consistently classy. The Marlborough Sauvignon Blanc is fresh, fragrant, vibrantly fruity and zesty, with punchy melon/capsicum flavours. The Marlborough Chardonnay is peachy, savoury, penetrating and soft, with great drinkability.

Torlesse's rock-solid range of Waipara wines features an impressively perfumed, peppery, rich and rounded Reserve Waipara Gewürztraminer; a floral, lean, delicately flavoured Waipara Riesling; and a peachy, toasty, mealy, buttery-soft Waipara Reserve Chardonnay. The Pinot Gris, grown at Yaldhurst, is a very satisfying, subtle wine with good weight and spicy, quince-like flavours.

Plummy, fresh and buoyantly fruity, the Marlborough Cabernet Sauvignon invites early drinking. Pinot Noir is also starting to come on stream – initially the fresh, crisp and raspberryish South Island Pinot Noir, a blend of Marlborough and Canterbury fruit, followed in 1996 by the first Waipara Pinot Noir.

****	Marlborough Chardonnay, Marlborough Sauvignon Blanc
(****)	Reserve Waipara Gewürztraminer
***½	Waipara Riesling
(***½)	Pinot Gris, Waipara Reserve Chardonnay
***	Müller-Thurgau
(***)	Marlborough Gewürztraminer, South Island Pinot Noir
**½	Marlborough Cabernet Sauvignon

WAIPARA DOWNS

Bains Road, Waipara. Est 1987. Owners: Keith and Ruth Berry. Production: 650 cases.

A fresh, savoury and flinty, rather Chablis-like Chardonnay is the key attraction at Ruth and Keith Berry's 'farm with a vineyard' in Bains Road, off the North Canterbury-to-Nelson highway.

When the Berrys, both former schoolteachers, bought the 319-hectare property, once part of Glenmark Station, in 1986, the first vines were already established. Wanting to diversify 'into something that wouldn't eat grass', a year later they started adding their own vines. Today the 4-hectare vineyard is planted principally in Chardonnay, with smaller plots of Riesling, Pinot Noir and Cabernet Sauvignon.

Consultant winemaker Mark Rattray has produced the wine since the first 1991 vintage. In 1995, the Berrys erected a concrete, tilt-slab winery. The Pinot Noir has varied in style, but at its best shows a Beaujolais-like simplicity, suppleness and charm. The Cabernet Sauvignon is typically chunky, flavoursome, green-edged and smooth. My favourite is the French and American oak-fermented Chardonnay, which offers plenty of fresh, appley, nutty flavour.

*** Chardonnay
**½ Cabernet Sauvignon, Pinot Noir

WAIPARA SPRINGS WINE COMPANY

State Highway 1, Waipara. Est 1987. Owners: The Moore and Grant families. Production: 10,500 cases.
One of Waipara's largest producers, selling its wines on-site, in Christchurch and the UK, Waipara Springs produces consistently attractive Rieslings, Chardonnays and Sauvignon Blancs.

Bruce and Jill Moore, the original owners of the property, planted a 4-hectare block of Chardonnay to supply Corbans in 1982. Five years later, when the Moores formed the Waipara Springs partnership with Andrew Grant and his mother, Beverley, the vineyard was expanded. A year after the first vintage flowed in 1989, the winery was built. Winemaker Mark Rattray and his wife, Michelle, became shareholders in 1990 but withdrew in 1993.

Today, Bruce Moore runs the 20-hectare Hutt Creek vineyard behind the winery, planted in Chardonnay, Riesling, Sauvignon Blanc, Cabernet Sauvignon and Pinot Noir, while Andrew Grant, who reports he is 'also a good shoveller at harvest', oversees the administration. The wines are made by Kym Rayner, who is also part-owner of Torlesse.

The Sauvignon Blanc is fresh and zingy, with strong redcurrant and green capsicum flavours. The Chardonnay is fleshy and firm, with tight, elegant flavours and a slightly creamy texture. The Riesling is fresh-scented, with a sliver of sweetness and good depth of tangy, lemon-lime-juice flavours.

The Pinot Noir and Cabernet Sauvignon are solid but green-edged, slightly lacking ripeness and roundness. The Cabernet Blush, with a faint touch of sweetness, can also be herbal, but top vintages are seductively pink, strawberryish and buoyant.

***½ Chardonnay
(***½) Sauvignon Blanc
*** Cabernet Blush, Riesling
**½ Cabernet Sauvignon, Pinot Noir

WAIPARA WEST

Ram Paddock Road, Waipara. Est 1991. Owners: Paul Tutton and family. Production: 4,500 cases. Winery sales by appointment.
Expatriate New Zealander Paul Tutton, who owns Waterloo Wine Co., a London-based wine importing and distribution business, is the driving force behind the Waipara West winery at the head of the Waipara gorge, 6 kilometres west of the main north-south highway.

In partnership with his sister, Vic, and her husband, Lindsay Hill, Tutton has planted 16 hectares of Sauvignon Blanc, Chardonnay, Riesling, Cabernet Sauvignon, Merlot, Cabernet Franc and Pinot Noir. The first commercial vintage flowed in 1996. The wines are produced on-site by Peter Evans, winemaker at St Helena from 1991 until mid-1997.

The Riesling is clean, crisp, appley and tight. A decidedly cool-climate style, the Sauvignon Blanc displays firm, lively acidity and searching herbaceous flavours, concentrated and lingering.

(***½) **Sauvignon Blanc**
(***)   **Riesling**

Christchurch

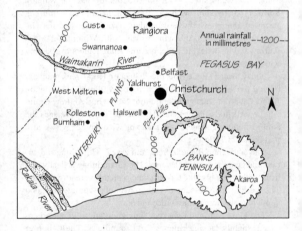

Over a dozen wine producers are based close to the city of Christchurch. Although great excitement currently surrounds the Waipara district in the north, in 1996 wines grown in the Christchurch area matched their northern rivals at the province's first Showtime Canterbury Wine Competition.

French peasants at Akaroa, on Banks Peninsula south-east of Christchurch, made the first Canterbury wines for their domestic tables in the mid-nineteenth century. Dr David Jackson and his fellow researchers at Lincoln University triggered the current revival of interest in Canterbury winemaking in 1973, by embarking on grape trials designed to pinpoint the most suitable varieties for the region's cool, dry climate.

Robin and Norman Mundy planted Canterbury's first commercial vineyard, St Helena, near Belfast, just north of Christchurch, in 1978. The three Giesen brothers – Theo, Alex and Marcel – have since built their winery at Burnham, south-west of the city, into Canterbury's largest.

The wineries on the pancake-flat Canterbury Plains are more exposed to the province's cooling easterly breezes than those in the north, although more sheltered vineyard sites can be found on Banks Peninsula. If you ask Waipara winemakers about the average difference in temperatures between North Canterbury and Christchurch, they reply: 'There's a jersey in it.'

The handsome French Farm winery/restaurant was established by John Ullrich and John Hibbard on Banks Peninsula, east of Christchurch, in 1991. The first 1991 wines were based on bought-in Canterbury and Marlborough grapes, but in 1994 the attached 3-hectare vineyard yielded its first Chardonnay and Pinot Noir. However, in 1994 production ceased; the vineyard and winemaking equipment were leased to Waipara winemaker Mark Rattray, and the popular restaurant was leased to Peter and Jayne Thornley. The wines sold at French Farm are now bought from other Canterbury winemakers.

DARJON VINEYARDS

North Eyre Road, Swannanoa. Est 1989. Owners: John and Michelle Baker. Production: 550 cases.

Only a rivulet of wine flows at Darjon, consumed largely in the stylish vineyard restaurant at Swannanoa, north-west of Christchurch.

For John Baker, an English engineer and hobbyist fruit winemaker who came to New Zealand in 1967, and his wife, Michelle, Darjon is a labour of love – both hold down full-time jobs elsewhere. The Bakers purchased their stony, wind-swept property in 1986, planted two hectares of Pinot Noir and Riesling in 1989, but not until 1995 did they harvest their first commercial crop. The wines are not made on-site.

The first wines, from 1992, were based entirely on Marlborough grapes, but Darjon's most distinctive wines are the estate-grown Pinot Noir and Riesling. The Pinot Noir is a light-bodied style with strawberryish, rounded flavours. The Riesling offers a fresh, floral bouquet, lightness of body and an enjoyable mouthful of crisp, citrusy flavour, slightly sweet and honeyed.

(***) **Riesling**
(**½) **Pinot Noir**

GATEHOUSE WINES

Jowers Road, West Melton. Est 1989. Owners: The Gatehouse family. Production: 1500 cases.

Gatehouse, a small winery at West Melton, is truly a family affair. Peter Gatehouse, who also works at Lincoln University and as a viticultural consultant, makes the wine. Carol, his wife, works in the vineyard. Peter's parents, Desmond and Esma, help with the administration and weekend sales, and Peter's brothers, Phillip and Stephen, are also shareholders.

The Gatehouses planted their first vines in fine, loamy soils in 1982 and in 1989 produced their first commercial wines. Four hectares of Riesling, Gewürztraminer, Chardonnay, Pinot Noir, Cabernet Sauvignon, Merlot and Malbec are now cultivated, and grapes are also purchased from another West Melton grower.

In his spacious winery (once belonging to Torlesse), Peter Gatehouse produces solid although rarely memorable wines, always sensibly priced. Top vintages of the Gewürztraminer can be impressive, with a pungent, peppery, slightly earthy fragrance and a weighty, full-flavoured palate.

The reds are typically light and herbaceous, but the American oak-aged Chardonnay offers pleasing depth of peachy, citrusy, crisp and lively flavour. The Riesling can lack delicacy, but develops well with age, building up strong, citrusy, steely flavours.

(***½) Gewürztraminer
(***)   Chardonnay
(**½) Estate Wine, Müller-Thurgau, Pinot Noir, Riesling
(**)   Cabernet/Merlot/Malbec

GIESEN WINE ESTATE

Burnham School Road, Burnham. Est 1981. Owners: Theo, Alex and Marcel Giesen. Production: 35,000 cases.

Brothers Theo, Alex and Marcel Giesen run Canterbury's largest winery. Until recently the Giesens sourced a high proportion of their grapes from Marlborough, but they now rely heavily on Canterbury fruit, producing a thrillingly intense, estate-grown Reserve Botrytised Riesling.

Born in the Rheinpfalz, where the family was engaged in stone quarrying and construction, but also made wine for its private consumption, the brothers emigrated to New Zealand in 1979 with their parents and were soon struck by two things: the lack of New Zealand-made dry Rieslings and the near-total absence of vineyards catering for the Christchurch market. By 1981 the first vines had been planted at their silty, stony property at Burnham, south-west of the city.

Today Theo and Alex concentrate on the company's administration and marketing, while Marcel oversees production. In the 20-hectare Burnham School Road vineyard encircling the winery, the key varieties are Riesling, Chardonnay, Müller-Thurgau, Ehrenfelser and Pinot Noir. The nearby Two Chain Road vineyard is planted in 6 hectares of Müller-Thurgau and Pinot Gris. Giesen also has a stake in an 8-hectare Sauvignon Blanc vineyard in Marlborough and buys grapes from Canterbury and Marlborough growers.

Since 1996, Giesen's wines have all been Canterbury-grown,

with the exception of the full, rich, tropical fruit-flavoured Marlborough Sauvignon Blanc, which recently leapt in quality following the launch of the second-tier Selwyn River label. Giesen's top wine is clearly the stunningly perfumed, honeyish and steely Reserve Botrytised Riesling, one of New Zealand's most brilliant sweet whites. The Botrytised Late Harvest Riesling is a less voluptuous wine with soft, delicate, pear and honey flavours.

Giesen's 'commercial' range of Canterbury wines features a citrusy, toasty Chardonnay with firm acidity; a slightly off-dry, smooth, flavourful Pinot Gris; a fairly light Pinot Noir with spicy, toasty aromas, oak complexity and smooth, ripe cherry/raspberry flavours; and a middleweight Merlot with pleasant, although not intense, plum/spice flavours and firm tannins.

The Canterbury Riesling, a slightly honeyish wine with quite good depth of crisp, lemony flavour in a distinctly medium style, is partnered by a Riesling Extra Dry with austere, searching flavours and razor-sharp acidity. The Reserve Burnham School Road Chardonnay is built for the long haul, with strong, peachy, citrusy, mealy flavours, wood/lees-aging richness and a flinty, long finish. Giesen's champion red is the estate-grown Reserve Canterbury Pinot Noir, a sturdy wine with intense, cherryish, complex flavours and a long, tight finish.

*****	Reserve Botrytised Riesling
(****½)	Reserve Canterbury Pinot Noir
****	Marlborough Sauvignon Blanc, Reserve Burnham School Road Chardonnay
***½	Riesling Extra Dry
(***½)	Botrytised Late Harvest Riesling, Canterbury Riesling, Voyage Méthode Traditionnelle
(***)	Canterbury Chardonnay, Canterbury Merlot, Canterbury Pinot Gris, Canterbury Pinot Noir
(**½)	Selwyn River Marlborough Chardonnay, Selwyn River Marlborough Sauvignon Blanc

KAITUNA VALLEY

1/4 Douglas Street, Lincoln. Est 1993. Owners: Dr Grant and Dr Helen Whelan. Production: 150 cases. No winery sales.

One of Canterbury's rarest and most distinguished Pinot Noirs is produced by Dr Grant Whelan, winemaker at Rossendale, and his wife, Helen, under their own Kaituna Valley label.

Whelan, formerly a tutor in wine science and viticulture at Lincoln University, draws the grapes from a north-facing, unirrigated, low-cropping vineyard, planted in 1979 by Graeme Stean in the Kaituna Valley on Banks Peninsula. When the first 1993 Kaituna Valley Pinot Noir won a gold medal and trophy at the 1995 Liquorland Royal Easter Wine Show, it broke a decade-long gold medal drought for the Canterbury region's Pinot Noirs since the 1984 St Helena.

Matured in French oak barriques, Kaituna Valley Pinot Noir is a mouthfilling, concentrated wine with sweet-fruit characters and savoury, smoky, cherryish flavours, impressively complex, supple and rich.

(****½) Pinot Noir

LANGDALE WINE ESTATE

Langdales Road, West Melton. Est 1989. Owners: Lew Stribling and shareholders. Production: 1,600 cases.

Much of this small producer's output is consumed in the attractive Langdale Café and Wine Garden at West Melton.

Owned by a large group of shareholders, including manager Lew Stribling, the vineyard was first planted in 1989 and produced its first commercial wines in 1994. Today 4.5 hectares are established in Pinot Noir, Riesling and Chardonnay, with smaller plots of Breidecker, Pinot Gris, Merlot and Cabernet Sauvignon. Langdale also buys grapes from Canterbury and Marlborough growers.

The wines, not made on-site, have been of variable quality, with a tendency to lack flavour depth. The estate-grown Riesling is light, fresh, delicate and crisp, but the best offering to date has been the Estate Chardonnay, a crisp, appley wine with engaging freshness and vigour.

(***) Estate Chardonnay
(**) Pinot Noir, Riesling
(*)   Breidecker Dry, Breidecker Medium, Marlborough
       Chardonnay

LARCOMB VINEYARD

Larcombs Road, Rolleston. Est 1980. Owners: Warren and Michelle Barnes. Production: 1600 cases.

Most of the wine produced at this small winery at Rolleston, south-west of Christchurch, is consumed in the cosy vineyard bar, at lunch or private functions. Larcomb was one of the pioneers of Canterbury wine.

The founder, John Thom, and his wife, Julie, planted the first vines in 1980 and produced their first wine in 1984. After releasing a stream of attractive Gewürztraminers, Rieslings, Pinot Gris and Pinot Noirs, in 1995 the Thoms sold Larcomb to Michelle Barnes, who runs the winery, and her husband, Warren, a hotel manager.

The 5-hectare vineyard is planted in Riesling, Pinot Gris, Chardonnay, Sauvignon Blanc (a rare variety this far south), Gewürztraminer, Breidecker and Pinot Noir. Only estate-grown grapes are used. Tony Coakley, of Sandihurst, makes the wine.

The Riesling stands out in the range: fragrant, with tense acidity and piercing lemon-lime flavours. Since the change of ownership, I have also tasted a pale, mild, slightly sweet Breidecker; a solid, fresh and tangy Sauvignon Blanc; and a crisp, light Pinot Noir.

(****) Riesling
(**½) Breidecker, Pinot Noir, Sauvignon Blanc

MELNESS WINES

1816 Cust Road, Cust. Est 1990. Owners: Colin and Norma Marshall. Production: 1,500 cases.

The gold medal-winning 1995 Pinot Noir first swung the spotlight on this small producer at Cust, inland from Rangiora, 35 minutes' drive north of Christchurch. Colin and Norma Marshall, former high school teachers, named the vineyard after the coastal village in Scotland where Norma's great-grandfather was born.

After cultivating grapes in suburban Christchurch to make wine on an amateur basis, the Marshalls planted their first vines at Cust in 1990. The 0.5-hectare, north-facing vineyard is established in Pinot Noir, Chardonnay and Gewürztraminer, and grapes are also purchased from Canterbury growers.

Since the first 1993 vintage, the wines have been made at Pegasus Bay by Matthew Donaldson and Lynnette Hudson, but the Marshalls plan to erect their own winery. The highlights of the range are the full-flavoured, slightly sweet and honeyed Floral (a Gewürztraminer, Morio-Muskat and Riesling blend); a barrel-fermented Chardonnay that in top vintages is subtle, mealy and rich, with power right through the palate; a very solid oak-aged Cabernet Sauvignon with plenty of colour and ripe blackcurrant- spice flavour; and the richly coloured Pinot Noir, a fleshy wine with smooth, concentrated cherry-plum flavours.

(****) Pinot Noir
(***½) Cabernet Sauvignon, Floral
(***) Chardonnay
(**½) Riesling, Rosé
(**) Middleton Cabernet Sauvignon

ROSEBANK ESTATE

Cnr Johns Road and Groynes Drive, Harewood, Belfast. Est 1993. Owners: The Shackel family. Production: 4,300 cases.

Consistently good, sometimes distinguished, wines flow from Rosebank, named after the 500 roses in its gardens. On Sundays up to 400 diners crowd its vineyard restaurant, where much of the wine is consumed.

The company, based near Belfast, north of Christchurch, was established by Brian and Margaret Shackel, who previously ran a South Island meat distribution business. Their first wine flowed in 1993. The manicured estate vineyard is tiny: a half-hectare of Chardonnay, Pinot Noir and Bacchus. Most of the grapes are drawn from growers in Canterbury and Marlborough (and wine is even shipped from South Australia for blending).

The Chardonnays are impressive. Rosebank Marlborough Chardonnay is full-bodied and lively, with good depth of citrusy/oaky flavour. The Canterbury Chardonnay is appley, nutty and slightly creamy; the Canterbury Reserve Chardonnay is tightly structured, delicate and intensely flavoured.

The Canterbury Pinot Noir is instantly attractive, with rich, ripe fruit and warm, supple, complex flavours. The Cabernet/Shiraz, a unique blend of Marlborough Cabernet Sauvignon and South Australian Shiraz, tones down the herbaceousness typical of Marlborough reds by adding soft, spicy Shiraz, creating a dark, more robust and flavoursome style than most New Zealand reds.

(****½) **Canterbury Reserve Chardonnay**
(****)   **Canterbury Pinot Noir**
(***½) **Canterbury Chardonnay, Marlborough Riesling**
***   **Cabernet/Shiraz, Marlborough Chardonnay**
(***)   **Sauvignon Blanc**

ROSSENDALE WINES

150 Old Tai Tapu Road, Halswell, Christchurch. Est 1987. Owners: Brent, Haydn and Grant Rawstron. Production: 4,000 cases.

The closest winery to the centre of Christchurch, Rossendale lies on the edge of the suburb of Halswell, sheltered by the Port Hills from cooling easterly winds. Diners in the 122-year-old restaurant – once a gardener's lodge at the homestead of Edward Stafford, premier of New Zealand for eight years during the 1850s and 1860s – drink much of Rossendale's classy wine.

Rossendale, a 166-hectare property complete with farm, vineyard, winery and restaurant, is owned by the Rawstron brothers, Brent, Haydn and Grant. From crop-farming in the 1970s, a decade later the Rawstrons turned to beef farming, and in 1987 they diversified again into grapes. Brent Rawstron, the manager, holds a post-graduate diploma in viticulture and oenology from Lincoln University.

In Rossendale's silty, sandy soils, 5 hectares of Pinot Noir and Chardonnay have been established. Grapes are also purchased from Marlborough. The wines, first produced in 1993, are made on-site by Grant Whelan, who also releases wine under his own Kaituna Valley label.

The Chardonnay, a very lightly wooded blend of Canterbury and Marlborough fruit, is fresh, fragrant and lively, with good flavour depth. Estate-grown, the Barrel Selection Chardonnay is a very stylish cool-climate style, mouthfilling, savoury, buttery and richly flavoured.

The French oak-matured Pinot Noir offers good depth of raspberry and cherry flavours. The Barrel Selection Pinot Noir is attractively scented and supple, with a rich, savoury palate. These are well-crafted, immaculate wines.

****   Barrel Selection Chardonnay
***½ Chardonnay, Barrel Selection Pinot Noir
***   Pinot Noir

ST HELENA WINE ESTATE

Coutts Island Road, Belfast. Est 1978. Owners: Robin and Bernice Mundy. Production: 15,000 cases.

Thread-like worms played a crucial role in the foundation of commercial winemaking in Canterbury. In 1978, after nematodes had ruined their potato farm's profitability, Robin and Norman Mundy planted the first vines on their Coutts Island property near Belfast, twenty minutes' drive north of Christchurch. Five years later, astounding winemakers and consumers alike, St Helena scored a gold medal with its dark-hued and velvety 1982 Pinot Noir.

Although still known principally for its Pinot Noir, St Helena is primarily a white-wine producer. In the 20-hectare estate vineyard, a wide range of grapes is planted – mainly Chardonnay, Pinot Noir, Pinot Blanc, Pinot Gris, Riesling, Müller-Thurgau and Bacchus. Bounded by branches of the Waimakariri River, with a high water table, this is a fertile vineyard site, needing no irrigation.

The glamour horse of the Canterbury wine scene a decade ago, St Helena has since been passed in terms of volume by Giesen and surpassed in quality by Pegasus Bay and others. Norman Mundy withdrew from the company in 1994, leaving his brother, Robin, and his wife, Bernice, in control of St Helena.

The premium wines are entirely estate-grown, although grapes are sometimes purchased for the bottom-tier range. Through a series of difficult vintages, Petter Evans, winemaker from 1991 to mid-1997, produced a stream of well made, enjoyable wines.

The Pinot Noir is an attractive middleweight, ruby-hued, with fresh, lifted strawberryish aromas, a buoyant, spicy palate and a well-rounded finish. The Reserve Pinot Noir, launched from the 1995 vintage, is fuller and richer, with sweet-fruit characters and considerable complexity.

At its best, the Chardonnay is robust, savoury and long-lived, although recent vintages have not shone. The Riesling is light and appley, with high acidity. More consistently rewarding are the sturdy, flinty, bargain-priced Pinot Blanc, a sort of poor man's Chardonnay; and the peachy, earthy, full-flavoured, strongly varietal Pinot Gris.

(****) Reserve Pinot Noir
***   Müller-Thurgau, Pinot Blanc, Pinot Gris, Pinot Noir
**½   Chardonnay, Riesling, Southern Alps Dry White
**   Port Hills Dry Red

SANDIHURST WINES

Main West Coast Road, West Melton. Est 1988. Owners: John and Joan Brough. Production: 8,500 cases.

Mouthfilling, perfumed and peppery, the flavour-crammed Gewürztraminer Reserve is the most eye-catching wine at this fast-growing West Melton winery. Sandihurst is named after the sandy knolls (hursts) found in the district.

After 33 years in the local fishing industry, in 1987 John Brough looked around for new fish to fry. 'There was a fair bit of hype in the papers about the success of Canterbury vineyards,' he recalls. A year later, Brough and his wife, Joan, planted the first vines on their wind-swept site, 25 kilometres inland from Christchurch.

The 16-hectare vineyard is planted predominantly in Chardonnay, Pinot Gris, Riesling and Pinot Noir, together with smaller plots of Gewürztraminer and Breidecker. Since the first 1992 all vintage, all the wines have been made on-site by Tony Coakley.

The Gewürztraminer Reserve is robust, rich-flavoured and dry in a serious, satisfying style. The standard Gewürztraminer is less concentrated and slightly sweeter, but clearly varietal, with good weight and depth of citrusy, spicy flavour.

The estate-grown, lightly oaked Canterbury Chardonnay is crisp, lemony and slightly buttery, with a touch of complexity from lengthy maturation on its yeast lees. Partly barrel-fermented, the Pinot Gris Reserve is mouthfilling, earthy and spicy, with greater depth than the slightly sweeter, non-reserve Pinot Gris.

The Pinot Noir Reserve is crisp and flavoursome, with firm, slightly austere, dark cherry and spice flavours. Not oak-aged, the standard Pinot Noir is produced in a buoyant Beaujolais style, fruity and soft.

(****) Gewürztraminer Reserve
*** Gewürztraminer
(***) Canterbury Chardonnay, Pinot Gris Reserve, Pinot Noir Reserve
(**½) Chardonnay, Patio Red, Pinot Gris, Pinot Noir, Riesling

SHERWOOD ESTATE WINES

Weedons Ross Road, West Melton. Est 1986. Owners: Dayne and Jill Sherwood. Production: 9,250 cases.

With its light, low-priced, widely available Pinot Noir and the robust, full-flavoured and firm reserve model, this West Melton winery is widely seen as a Pinot Noir specialist. However, its estate-grown Reserve Chardonnay is also distinguished.

Dayne and Jill Sherwood planted the first vines in their free-draining silt loams in 1986. Jill oversees the company's administration and restaurant. Dayne, who holds a BA, later added a post-graduate diploma in viticulture and oenology from Lincoln University before he plunged into full-time winemaking in 1990.

Chardonnay and Pinot Noir are the key varieties in the 6-hectare estate vineyard, supplemented by Riesling and Müller-Thurgau. Grapes are also purchased from Canterbury and Marlborough growers.

The Pinot Noir, based on estate-grown and other West Melton fruit, is a lightly oaked red, fresh, light, raspberryish and crisp, in a simple, no-fuss style. Dayne Sherwood sees it as offering 'a glimpse of what Pinot Noir can be'. The Reserve Pinot Noir, blended from Canterbury and Marlborough grapes and matured in new French oak barriques, is concentrated, oaky and tannic, with impressive flavour depth and complexity.

The Cabernet Franc, grown in Marlborough and not oak-aged, is a bolder, more tannic style than most New Zealand Cabernet Francs, with strong blackcurrant and red berry flavours. The Riesling is fresh, light, appley and steely.

Sherwood's estate-grown Unoaked Chardonnay is fresh, lemony and crisp in a pleasant, drink-young style. The Reserve Chardonnay, also estate-grown is a completely different beast. Fermented in new French oak casks, it reveals a fragrant, mealy, toasty bouquet, good body and strong, citrusy, slightly buttery and creamy flavours, with a crisp, long finish.

****   Reserve Chardonnay, Reserve Pinot Noir
(***) Cabernet Franc
**½   Pinot Noir, Riesling
(**½) Unoaked Chardonnay

Otago

At the southern frontier of New Zealand wine, Central Otago's vines grow in comparable latitudes to Bordeaux and Burgundy. However, ripening conditions are much cooler, reflecting New Zealand's temperate climate and the high-altitude location of the region's vineyards.

Pinot Noir has been the early success in Central Otago's majestic inland valleys – fragrant, vibrantly fruity red wine with rich, cherryish, spicy flavour and an easy-drinking, velvety texture. Pinot Noir and Chardonnay – both early-ripening varieties – account for two-thirds of the total vine plantings. The Chardonnays range in style from Rippon Vineyard's steely, green appley, distinctly Chablis-like wines grown on the shores of Lake Wanaka, to the rich, toasty and mealy reserve Chardonnays of Chard Farm and Gibbston Valley, near Queenstown.

'Site selection' is a buzz word in Central Otago wine circles. Some of the country's highest and lowest temperatures have

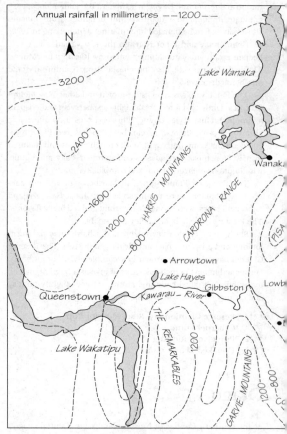

Annual rainfall in millimetres ‐‐1200‐‐

N

Lake Wanaka

3200

2400

1600

1200

800

HARRIS MOUNTAINS

CARDRONA RANGE

Wanak

(PISA

Arrowtown

Lake Hayes

Gibbston

Lowb

Queenstown

Kawarau – River

Lake Wakatipu

THE REMARKABLES

1200

GARVIE MOUNTAINS

1200

800

Co

been recorded in the province. Summers are hot, with cool nights, autumns extremely dry (ideal for hanging the grapes late on the vines) and winters icy. The hazardously low amount of heat in many parts of the province during the grapes' ripening period makes it essential that winemakers select a north-facing site with maximum exposure to the sun. Planting on slopes reduces the high frost risk by encouraging the drainage of cold air.

The youthfulness of this craggy region's vineyards (only 40 percent of the vines planted in 1996 were of bearing age) is striking. Yet Otago was the source of some of New Zealand's earliest wines. The first wine tasted by Romeo Bragato (later appointed Government Viticulturist) during his 1895 tour of New Zealand was at Arrowtown, near Queenstown, and 'although made after the most primitive fashion, it reflected great credit on the

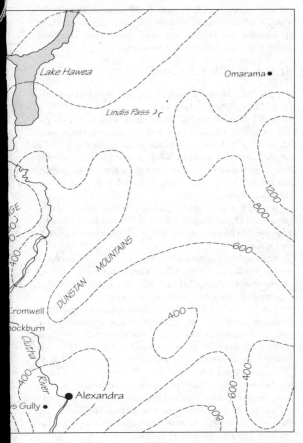

producer'. Noting also the flourishing condition of grapevines cultivated by gold-miners, Bragato enthused that Central Otago was 'pre-eminently suitable' for wine production.

The modern stirring of interest in viticulture followed trials by R.V. Kinnaird at Earnscleugh, who proved that Müller-Thurgau and Chasselas would ripen in Central Otago. Even more exciting were trials conducted by the DSIR (a Government research body) in the 1970s, which yielded fully ripe Gewürztraminer and Pinot Noir.

The initial centres of Central Otago wine were the Kawarau Gorge near Queenstown, Lake Wanaka and Alexandra. Now, vines are sprouting in the hot Bannockburn area near Cromwell and have started to spread beyond 'Central' to Omarama in North Otago. Between 1996 and 1999, the total area of bearing vines is expected to soar from 92 hectares to 221 hectares. Much of the region's output is still consumed in the tourist mecca of Queenstown, but Otago's perfumed, supple Pinot Noirs and freshly acidic white wines will soon be more widely seen.

BLACK RIDGE VINEYARD

Conroy's Road, Alexandra. Est 1981. Owners: Verdun Burgess and Sue Edwards. Production: 3,000 cases.

Dubbed a 'hero's vineyard' by a visiting wine merchant, the world's southernmost winery lies in Conroy's Gully, near Alexandra. In a dramatic landscape where bulldozers carved a vineyard site out of the black, wildly shaped schist, and the post holes were blasted by gelignite, Verdun Burgess and his partner, Sue Edwards, make a dark, fleshy Pinot Noir with a rush of soft, cherryish, plummy flavour.

A rugged extrovert with a pipe or gun (for shooting rabbits) constantly in hand, Burgess first came to Alexandra as a builder. After planting his first vines in 1981, in 1989 he plunged into full-time winemaking.

The 7-hectare vineyard, with a subsoil of hard, almost impenetrable rocks, is planted in Riesling, Gewürztraminer, Chardonnay, Breidecker and Pinot Noir. Winemaker Mike Wolter, appointed in 1992, died in a winemaking accident in mid-1997.

The Pinot Noir is deliciously fresh, buoyant and supple, with moderate complexity but oodles of flavour and drink-young appeal. The Cabernet Sauvignon is buoyantly fruity, fresh and flavoursome, but lacks real warmth and complexity. The Select Chardonnay is appley, oaky and slightly creamy, with good weight and flavour depth.

Earnscleugh Rise, based principally on Breidecker, is a slightly sweet quaffer, floral, light and mild. The Riesling is green appley and mouth-wateringly crisp, with a Mosel-like fragility, but the earlier-ripening Gewürztraminer is a mouthfilling, high alcohol wine with strongly peppery flavours.

****   **Pinot Noir**
***½   **Select Chardonnay**
***   **Gewürztraminer, Riesling**
½   **Earnscleugh Rise
(**½) **Cabernet Sauvignon**

CHARD FARM VINEYARD

Chard Road, Gibbston. Est 1987. Owners: Rob and Greg Hay. Production: 10,750 cases.

One of New Zealand's most stunning vineyards lies on a north-facing ledge 20 kilometres from Queenstown, with a glorious view across the Kawarau River to the snow-draped Cardrona Range. Chard Farm is one of Central Otago's largest wineries.

On land originally worked by Richard Chard in the 1870s as a market garden, supplying food to gold-miners, the Hay brothers planted their first vines in 1987. Greg, a marketing graduate, oversees the vineyard. Rob, a BSc who worked for three years in Baden and Wurttemberg, and later at Babich and Ruby Bay, oversees the winemaking and administration.

Two-thirds of the moderately fertile, silty 12-hectare estate vineyard is devoted to Pinot Noir and Chardonnay, with smaller plots of Riesling, Gewürztraminer, Pinot Gris and Sauvignon Blanc. The brothers also have a stake in another vineyard at nearby Lake Hayes, and since 1994 have purchased grapes from Bannockburn.

The lively, tangy white wines can be light and sharp in cool seasons, but in favourable vintages they are highly impressive, with intense aromas and flavours. The stylish Closeburn Chardonnay is a tightly structured wine, crisp, citrusy and savoury. The flagship Judge and Jury Chardonnay, like the Closeburn blended from estate-grown and Bannockburn grapes, is a more oak-influenced style with very good depth of crisp, peachy, toasty flavour.

At their best, the Riesling and Riesling Dry are packed with fresh, zingy lemon-lime aromas and flavours in a copybook cool-climate style. The Sauvignon Blanc, partly oak-aged, offers plenty of crisp, limey flavour. Very few vintages of the barrel-fermented, lees-aged Pinot Gris have been seen, but the deliciously weighty and richly flavoured '95 is an auspicious sign.

The 'standard' Pinot Noir possesses strong, ripe, almost sweet-tasting, cherryish flavours and subtle oak in a smooth-flowing style that can be amazingly enjoyable in its youth. The rare Reserve Bragato Pinot Noir is a bigger, more oaky wine with mouthfilling body, a beguiling silky texture and warm, rich, spicy fruit.

****	**Bragato Reserve Pinot Noir**
***½	**Closeburn Chardonnay, Judge and Jury**
	Chardonnay, Pinot Noir, Riesling, Riesling Dry
(***½)	**Pinot Gris**
***	**Sauvignon Blanc**
**½	**Gewürztraminer**

GIBBSTON VALLEY WINES

Queenstown-Cromwell Highway, Gibbston. Est 1981. Owners: Alan Brady and shareholders. Production: 13,000 cases.

When Alan Brady planted his first vines in the craggy Kawarau Gorge, 25 kilometres from Queenstown, in 1981, he wanted to 'make good wine and prove the doubters wrong at the same time'. Today the winery he founded produces an exceptional Pinot Noir and ranks among Central Otago's major tourist assets, attracting 50,000 visitors each year.

Irish-born, Brady is a former journalist and television producer. In 1990, six years after bottling his first experimental wine, he took in partners and moved into winemaking on a full-time basis. On a north-facing schist ledge, the 3-hectare estate vineyard is closely planted in Pinot Noir, Riesling, Pinot Gris and Sauvignon Blanc. Winery shareholders supply grapes from their nearby vineyards, and Gibbston Valley buys fruit from other growers in Otago and Marlborough.

Winemaker Grant Taylor, raised in North Otago, was chief winemaker at Domaine Napa for six years before he joined Gibbston Valley in 1993. 'Pinot Noir gets winemakers excited,' says Taylor. 'It's a love affair that lasts.' Gibbston Valley's dimly lit, 76-metre long underground cellars, carved into a bluff behind the winery in 1995, provide a stable, cool environment for maturing wine in bottles and casks – and a romantic setting for wine tastings and concerts.

The Pinot Noir is full and supple, with a touch of gamey complexity and excellent depth of plum/cherry flavours. Matured in all-new French oak barriques, the powerful Reserve Pinot Noir is mouthfilling and savoury, with a superb concentration of sweet-tasting, plummy fruit, a light tannin grip and lovely harmony. Launched from the 1995 vintage, this reserve label is the emerging star of the Gibbston Valley range.

The unwooded Otago Greenstone Chardonnay is fresh and flavoursome, its sliver of sweetness and balanced acidity offering very easy drinking. The French oak-fermented Otago Chardonnay is rich-flavoured, peachy, savoury, complex and long.

The Marlborough Sauvignon Blanc, only produced in favourable vintages, is a classy wine with a delicious depth of passionfruit and melon-evoking flavours, ripe and buoyant. The winery's selection of Central Otago-grown white wines also features a vibrant, appley and zesty Riesling; an oak-aged, briskly herbaceous Sauvignon Blanc; and a very crisp, fractionally sweet, peachy, earthy Pinot Gris.

(*****) **Reserve Pinot Noir**
****½ **Marlborough Sauvignon Blanc**
**** **Pinot Noir**
***½ **Chardonnay**
*** **Pinot Gris, Riesling**
(***) **Greenstone Chardonnay**
½ **Sauvignon Blanc, Ryecroft Red, Waitiri White

KAWARAU ESTATE

Cromwell-Wanaka Highway. Est 1992. Owners: Charles Finny, Wendy and Geoff Hinton, Nicola Sharp. Production: 600 cases.
Its rare but classy debut 1995 Morven Hill Gewürztraminer served notice that this fledgling company will be worth following.

Kawarau Estate is owned by Charles Finny, Wendy and Geoff

Hinton, and Nicola Sharp. Two vineyards have been planted: the 5.5-hectare Dunstan Vineyard at Lowburn, north of Cromwell (where a tasting and sales facility is being established); and the 2.5-hectare, steeply sloping Morven Hill Vineyard at Lake Hayes, near Queenstown.

Operated organically, both vineyards have been awarded full Bio-Gro status. Chardonnay, Pinot Noir, Sauvignon Blanc, Gewürztraminer and Merlot are the principal varieties.

The initial releases have included a fresh, medium-bodied, smooth Chardonnay, made from Marlborough grapes; a deliciously fresh and lively, Pinot Noir-based Rosé; a gently oaked, nettley, flinty, satisfyingly full-flavoured Sauvignon Blanc; and a mouthfilling, richly fragrant Gewürztraminer with deep, peppery flavours.

(***) Gewürztraminer, Rosé, Sauvignon Blanc
(**½) Chardonnay

OMARAMA VINEYARD

Omarama Avenue, Omarama. Est 1994. Owners: Rob and Joan Watson. Production: 150 cases.
With 140 bottles of Pinot Gris, sold only by the glass, in 1994 Rob Watson launched North Otago's first 'commercial' wine.

Watson, a sheep farmer and musterer, planted his first vines in a north-facing basin at Omarama, half-way between Mount Cook and Cromwell, in the mid-1980s. Today three hectares of irrigated Pinot Gris, Morio-Muskat, GM 312-53 (a Geisenheim crossing) and Müller-Thurgau are established in silty, gravelly soils.

The wines, made at Black Ridge, include an 'easy-drinking' White Muscat and the pink-tinged, appetisingly crisp, clearly varietal Pinot Gris.

(**½) Pinot Gris

RIPPON VINEYARD

Mt Aspiring Road, Wanaka. Est 1984. Owners: Rolfe and Lois Mills. Production: 4,500 cases.
If medals are ever handed out for the beauty of New Zealand winery settings, the gold will surely go to Rippon Vineyard. Rolfe and Lois Mills' glorious site in the Southern Alps, on the shores of Lake Wanaka, has graced the covers of several wine books, magazines and calendars.

Mills, in his seventies, is a grandson of Sir Percy Sargood, who once owned Wanaka Station. After planting his first vines – Seibel hybrids and Albany Surprise – in 1976, his first wine was bottled in 1984. His twin motives for pioneering viticulture at Wanaka, Mills recalls, were that he enjoys drinking wine and was advised he would not succeed in his venture.

At over 300 metres above sea level, the vineyard is New Zealand's highest. In a glacial moraine, 13 hectares of Pinot Noir, Chardonnay, Riesling, Gewürztraminer, Sauvignon Blanc, Müller-Thurgau, Osteiner and Syrah have been planted. Axel Rothermel, who gathered his initial winemaking experience in the Rheingau, processed his first Rippon vintage in 1996.

Above all, Rippon is known for its rich, intensely varietal Pinot Noirs. The 'standard' wine is scented and crisp, with excellent depth of plummy, slightly peppery flavour. Alluring in its youth, yet retaining its freshness for several years, the floral, rich-flavoured Selection Pinot Noir (matured in half-new French oak barriques) is the region's first wine to win general recognition as a classic.

The white wines are mouth-wateringly crisp, with fresh, clear flavours. Both the Osteiner and blended Hotere White are typically pale, light, slightly sweet and crisp quaffers. The Chardonnay is appley, lively and steely, with distinct overtones of Chablis.

The Riesling is fresh, limey and frisky; the Gewürztraminer pale and delicately spicy; the barrel-fermented Sauvignon Blanc grassy and freshly acidic. Bright pink, the light, buoyant and slightly sweet Gamay Rosé is full of raspberryish charm.

***** **Selection Pinot Noir**
**** **Pinot Noir**
***½ **Chardonnay**
*** **Gamay Rosé, Gewürztraminer, Riesling, Sauvignon Blanc**
½ **Hotere White, Osteiner

WILLIAM HILL VINEYARD

Dunstan Road, Alexandra. Est 1988. Owners: Bill and Gillian Grant. Production: Nil (1996); 1,500 cases (1995).

One of Central Otago's oldest vineyards lies on a sandy terrace of the Clutha River on the outskirts of Alexandra. Bill Grant, owner of a stone quarrying and building firm, planted his first vines in 1973, but only after a fifteen-year battle with frosts, birds and wasps did he bottle his first 'commercial' wine.

After several years of producing only a few thousand bottles, William Hill is now raising its output. Seven hectares of vines are established – principally Chardonnay and Pinot Noir, with a smaller plot of Gewürztraminer. A winery was built in 1995 and Bill's son, David, has recently assumed control of the company. The winemaker is Dhana Pillai, owner of the nearby Leaning Rock vineyard.

The oak-matured Pinot Noir is ruby-hued, fresh, floral and raspberryish. The Chardonnay, also oak-aged, is tart and appley. The Riesling is tangy and green-edged, and the Gewürztraminer is slightly sweet and gently spicy. In the past these have been very light wines, but David Grant is planning significant quality advances.

** Chardonnay, Gewürztraminer, Pinot Noir, Riesling

INDEX